AN UNANCHORED HEART

An Unanchored Heart

Rory Knight Bruce

Anthony Eyre

MOUNT ORLEANS PRESS

Published in Great Britain in 2022
by Anthony Eyre, Mount Orleans Press
23 High Street, Cricklade SN6 6AP
https://anthonyeyre.com

ISBN 978-1-912945-39-9

A CIP record for this book is available
from the British Library

Printed in the U.K. by
Short Run Press

To R C M : None better ever was

'Droll thing life is—that mysterious arrangement
of merciless logic for a futile purpose. The most you
can hope from it is some knowledge of yourself—that
comes too late—a crop of inextinguishable regrets.'

Joseph Conrad, *Heart of Darkness*

Contents

There are plenty who have been abandoned. They live a life with
occasional smiles, but always with ice and uncertainty
in their hearts. Misgivings are nothing to mistrust.
For those who have done this to them, by leaving them
in a hedgerow or on the steps of a Court of Law,
they have signed a casual certificate of doom.
They have handed us their mistakes—
and we have made them.

"The artist cannot remain a neutral observer in the
battle between justice and injustice. He must
dedicate himself to the search to establish
and proclaim the truth."

Turgenev to Belinsky

Back To The Start

'You stand there with your fixed expression,
Casting doubt on all I have to say,
Why don't you touch me, touch me,
Touch me now.'

Genesis: *The Musical Box*

THAT DAY THE taxi brought me from the station to the farm, my heart was heavy with the sorrow of my father's recent death, and dread of what the future would now hold for me. I had never wanted to come home and, like all good children, hoped he'd live forever. We had lunched together two days before, and he told me he was dying but, callow and selfish, I thought no more about it. I drove back to London in my open-topped vintage Lancia, a pretty Indian girlfriend next to me. Then I got the call. A heart attack in his sleep (spare me the details, no I don't want to see him laid out at the undertakers). Seventy-six.

I wish my dad had told me what he wanted me to do. I wish he had sat me down just once and spelt things out. He never even said he wanted me to have the farm, not even how he wanted to be buried or lessons to be read. He had been a prisoner of war in Italy (having knocked out seven tanks in North Africa) and walked the long walk home, five hundred miles from south of Milan to the toe of Italy, occupied by Germans, September to December, 1943. He did for three of them.

I went back to the camp after he died when I found a yellow crayoned line he had drawn in a map of his walk, urged to do this by the travel writer Eric Newby who had been in prison with him. "Your father was the CAMP barman," Newby told me, with all the inflection that made him such a successful frock salesman after the war before he became a writer. The camp at Fontanellato was a fortress, the countryside outside open, with very little cover, divided by water-filled dykes. I walked five miles, and went out to lunch, leaving behind the Apennines and the wooded mountain tracts covered with snow and bitter cold. I wrote about it, and raised some money for those families that had sheltered escaped prisoners like my father and Newby. Of six hundred liberated from Fontanellato when the Italians capitulated, those who took the 'Long Walk' survived the best, two hundred only. Those who, on the instructions of the Foreign Office, were told to stay put were shot or re-interned by the advancing Germans.

So I did the funeral service as if it had been my own, which will save me time one day. A bit of Sassoon and Shelley, coffin at the altar, *in medias res*. A hunting horn played 'Gone to Ground' at the graveside. I don't want that. Ninety in the parish church, mostly from the local pub that he frequented, and I buried him in the family plot above his parents. One of my mates got hit at the pub drunken wake (which was quite something given that the pugilist had a withered arm). My Indian girlfriend stood at the bar. She had insisted on front-row treatment to smart my wife, soon to be divorced.

My dad's girlfriend lost the house keys (they were in her handbag) so we had to break into my home. MY HOME now. But it wasn't my home. I still had the 'Wailing Finn', the Finnish girlfriend, au pair, cook or call her what you will, to contend with. She had come at fifteen and was only forty-six now. Was I to endure years of this? She was almost permanently drunk, wilful, cunning, clever. Another mate came round a few days later and took out ninety-four bottles she had hidden under beds. Everything. The full top shelf. Christ she had some thirst. She also had two Pekingeses, Freddie and Rollman. One had scurf and the other an eye complaint, each with their own ointments that she applied confusedly. They both ended up with eye complaints and scurf.

The funeral was just the start. Dealing with death has its own protocols, in law and observation, and they don't come cheap. Six grand I reckon, and all those bank accounts to freeze, and me still in a sorry daze. Where was the Will? It was drawn up in 1981, but the London law firm had gone bust. I soon realised why the Finn knew where it was. She had been left half of the farm for her lifetime, my little drunken albatross.

My dad had never been to a lawyer in his life, except to divorce my mum and then to have her maintenance reduced. Here began my first mistake. Sparks, a porcine local lawyer who sweated dishonesty, came recommended by 'a friend.' Oily and solicitous, he told me he would act for the Finn *pro bono* and uphold what he called, with an exhalation of breath, 'The Mother Law.' He would also act for me to save costs. I should have spotted the alarm bells. He was a divorced Catholic whose wife had run off with a foxhunter. He tried to get her back by riding hopelessly, and failed.

Before I sacked him, and he knew the crimes of cost to me he had committed (sixty grand overcharged by my reckoning), I would have regular miasmic meetings with him in his cramped little town office. Tea or coffee? No, let's get on with it I am paying by the hour. His cunning skill was always to be acting fairly for the Finn. He charged me for apportioning all the rents and sent an underling to look after her, and charged me for that too because it wasn't him. Nothing *pro bono* about that. It took two years to get probate, which could not have been more simple.

Even by the strained atmosphere of my childhood upbringing on the farm, nothing had prepared me for this. I got the Finn into The Priory in Roehampton, chosen as it had been my own legal forbear Sir James Knight Bruce's London home (the family coat of arms, I was idiotically proud, still displayed off the reception area). "The worst case of alcoholic denial we have ever seen," came their verdict after a fortnight. Had she been drinking, I asked her on one of my visits, when they let her out into the grounds for an hour or two? "Only wine," came the hesitant reply. Fifteen grand that cost me, and she was back on the sauce within a month.

Part of the reason I took her there was to have some peace and quiet at home to sort things out. Freddie and Rollman got better and I was grateful of their company. On one occasion I took Freddie to a countryside rally in Brighton and left him in the car in a multistorey car park. Someone reported me and the march came to a halt as the number plate of the old farm Citroën Dyane came sharply across the public address system. He was none the worse for wear and I continued the march with him on a lead along the Brighton seafront, his mane blowing in the wind, prancing like a lion, which he also did when we used to get him to round up the sheep on the farm.

"I want to go home," the Finn said to me on one of my Priory visits and I had visions of wafting her off to her family in Turku, to sot herself to the tune of *Finlandia* watching the Northern Lights. "No, OUR home," she said, patting the hospital coverlet, slightly opening her surgical gown and offering two rather firm orbs, her Abydos and Sestos, which took me by surprise. Had it come to this?

It seemed so empty in the house not tip-toeing around with my dad in the drawing room chair, changing TV channels to forget the war or watching porn and drinking whisky. "Better drunk than dreary," he would say, and shoot back another peg, punctuating every short, laconic sentence with an expletive and the silences that drained my nerves. One night he excelled himself when I had a Berkshire beauty to stay who arrived late for dinner. "What do you want to drink cunt, red piss or white piss?" Half of me was the child of the wife who had deserted him. Half of me was everything that caused him hurt. I became immune to being thought useless.

It falls today to few people to inherit the house where they were brought up and they should be thankful for it. They hold memories that, unlike the advertisements of rural sunshine, are not always pleasant. I think my house, Georgian in part, Victorian additions, thick cob walls, outdoor pump, was a meagre post-war cocoon, warmed by a small drawing room fire and drink. If it had been a photograph it would be faded black and white.

Even after twenty years in residence, so many of those memories remain. There is my wooden toy box in which I would nightly pee as I was scared of the long dark passage and waking my dad. Outside the stable is still the same where his old hunter Paddy and I would play and I learned to ride on him. One day I found him dead in the low bog field and didn't cry. In the back orchard was a Gloucester Old Spot, complete with copper nose ring, who was ferocious with me. When the day came for him to be killed, I held the knife, whilst the workmen held him down, and slit his throat. I was five. Janet the Jersey house cow once tossed me with her stubbed horns onto the muck heap. I never learned to milk her.

Two of the early attachments I formed were blind. One was a Friesian cow who would let me ride upon her back and curl up in the crook of her shoulder when she lay down, warm, comforting, maternal. Another was a blind kid goat, my nemesis with the workmen who mocked the attachment I had formed. The day came when she too had to be killed and I was tearful, silent. They mocked me in the meal shed for my softness. I left them and shot her myself. They did not mock me again.

For some the allure of country life is the charming village school with a rosy-cheeked teacher and milk for tea, but not for me. Out of my bedroom window I can still see the old school building two miles away. I walked there and back most days on my own, over the pack-horse bridge and River Creedy, past the pub and up a steep hill. One day I went past the pub and it was on fire, fire engines, thatch ablaze, excitement.

The other children were mostly those of farm workers, brutish and bullying. Having one's head dunked in water in the toilet sink was a favourite. One nine-year-old called Diana offered sex in an old hen coop ("No not you, you're not one of us.") They were bigger than me but I was brighter than them. More bullying. I won the county debating competition, then a national writing competition about cocoa growing in Africa, sponsored by a major chocolate firm. Smears, the head, (left wing, on £20 a week) called me up in front of the school to collect my prize, ten different bars of chocolate. A silence fell. Specks of classroom chalkdust were picked out by the summer sun. "Aren't you going to share your winnings with the class?" he asked. "They are not winnings, they are wages," I replied. From then on he always picked me out as surly and different. "Oh, there's Rory 'The Tiger,'" he would say, sarcastically. He knew I was better than him, and hated it. With the local children he could parade his knowledge and feel superior but he never tried that with me. I took those bars of chocolate home. One I fed to my terrier. The mouse that lived in my bedroom half ate the rest.

Home life for me was all outdoors alone. I would, according to the seasons, collect tadpoles in a jar, or crusader spiders and once took an adder, which my dog had killed, to school. I was briefly more popular for that. There was always farmwork going on and I would join in sometimes. At harvest-time I would slide off the combine chute on two-hundred-weight sacks, called pigs, full of barley, husks in my ears and eyes. I would watch the men making small oat stooks for thatch, little changed since Hardy's time. The swede pullers were mainly gypsy women, bent knee deep in mud.

Later, of course, I would be put to work and I have cultivated every inch of our land. My dad would only appear when something was going wrong, a breached sheep birth at night, a bent buck rake fork on the tractor. He only saw the mother half in me. I wish he had been more kind. Odd then, that when I come in from the farm today, I still hope that he would be sitting in his drawing room chair, saying something nice to me.

It wasn't always like this. There were better days before the Finn, the Ice-Woman, cometh. Foremost of them was time spent with my infirm granny in the mansion on the hill, tended as she was by her once-married lesbian daughter and her female French lover. I would stay with her, reading, playing chess, her giving me a radio and a type-writer for two separate young birthdays. She kept a jar of sixpences in a Dimple whisky bottle bound, by the makers, with a tress of silver netting. I would marvel at it, adding the odd sixpence of my own, when I had mown the lawn at home, her wages for reading me both *Emma* and *Mansfield Park*.

She had grey hair beautifully combed and smelled of Yardley talc and lack of movement. Her family, the Avelings, made steam rollers and traction engines, being half of the Grantham engineering firm Aveling-Barford, and they lived in some splendour at St German's Hall, King's Lynn. Thomas 'Tram' Aveling was her 19th-century forbear, whose innovations are still widely acknowledged by steam enthusiasts. It has been said of him: "Aveling's innovations must rank as some of the most important ever made in the history of the modern world."

A more distant relative was Edward Aveling who lived openly with Eleanor Marx, Karl Marx's youngest daughter. Together they had written, in 1888, *The Woman Question*. A decade later Eleanor discovered that Aveling had secretly married a young actress and became deeply depressed by the faithlessness of the man she loved. On 31 March 1898, Eleanor sent her maid to the local chemist with a note in which she asked for chloroform and a small quantity of prussic acid for her dog. Eleanor retired to her room, wrote two brief suicide notes, undressed, got into bed, and swallowed the poison, dead at forty-three.

My grandmother bore her early onset of arthritis without a murmur, and always mentioned my grandfather as 'Dear Bob'. He had, rising to the rank of major, served in the Trenches and Gallipoli, then flew in reconnaissance planes off ships in the Far East. He would sit in the back taking photographs whilst the pilot had the unenviable task of landing the plane back on deck. Sometimes the biplane bounced, missed its brake wire, and fell off the ship's prow. My grandfather had to be winched uncomplaining from the choppy waters. It gave him a lasting love of taking photos, and there they all are in my home, album after album, his children playing tricks on ponies or bicycles under the great cedar called by them 'The Wireless Tree', like Ford Madox Ford's 'Groby Tree' in *Parade's End*. It was called this because it had the antenna at its top from which electricity, then a novelty, was brought into the house.

I stayed there quite a bit, in the mansion on the hill, put to bed in a folded linen double sheet. When my aunt turned out the light she would call me 'Fauntleroy' to make me less afraid of the dark. For some years I had my terrier Cibboli for conversation. We would curl up in bed like two question marks. He died of mange, contracted from a fox and suffered a slow and bitter death, then untreatable by veterinary medicine. I cry to think of him now and the tears that I wept then, mocked by my father for unmanliness.

At breakfast, I would be put at the head of the table, on my own. I looked around at portraits of my relations on the wall, not important really, now cobwebbed by neglect, and the odd fox mask with amber eyes and mothy fur. I knew the contents of the cereal packet by heart. "They're grrrrrreat!" says Tony the Tiger on the Frosties. In the grate, the Christmas Yule log still sat, charred, garlanded by bits of tinsel and discarded cracker strings, in full June, woebegone.

One Christmas, during a vigorous game of 'Go Down Golly' (this involved me under the table pushing paper cutouts from Robertson's jam jars between the dining table leaves, the grown-ups trying to whack them with crackers) I trod on Clownie my aunt's terrier. He all but took my eye out and I was taken to hospital, my father itching for a brandy in the waiting room. I have the scar to show for it to this day.

"Why don't you spend more time outside?" my father asked on his occasional visits to my grandmother. Why could I do nothing right? And the truth was quite the opposite. My aunt had six milking cows and I would ride one, Daisy, from the park field to the milking shed. "She always does better with *Mrs Dale's Diary* on the radio," my aunt would say and she was right. I lugged the foaming milk in metal pails and watched my aunt make butter. As a reward I got a donkey jacket and she would take me sometimes to the golf course where she had met her girlfriend; they became doubles ladies' champions several times. One day I won a countless haul of threepences on the fruit machine and lay amongst the gorse and breeze of the coastal links and looked up as the odd aeroplane cut a distant vapour in the azure sky, a feeling of freedom, youth and money, and salt-tang in my nostrils.

This is the sky that, twenty years before, had been black with German bombers offloading their destruction upon Exeter, once a jewel like Bath or Edinburgh. How did the cathedral survive and the tablet of my relative on the chancel wall? I am named after him: George Wyndham Hamilton Knight Bruce, Eton, Oxford, first Bishop of Mashonaland, dead at forty-four, "Driven by fever from the mission fields." He had translated the Lord's Prayer into Seshona, and given the Last Rites to many a colonial soldier in the Matabele War.

My nanny, who had been my father's nanny before, told me about the blackouts and rationing, food coupons and little stolen luxuries, which might have been some extra lard. I never tired of her stories, and when she left my home I would visit her in her little terraced house in the market town nearby. It was always dark inside, her mother couldn't stand the light, doilies, a tasselled lamp, her own photo albums of when she had taken a bus trip to the Italian Lakes, and one other to the Austrian Alps. What I liked most was the comforting smell of real tealeaves being brewed in a brown, bone-china pot, and the calm and rhythmic ritual with which it was so obviously daily done.

I had no fear of something worse, for I did not know what was now to come, a succession of au pairs, barely themselves no more than children. The first was earthy out of Normandy. She thought nothing of keeping me in the back of her Austin Seven whilst she embraced her electrician boyfriend in the front, and I thought nothing of it either. But it was the Parisian taxi driver's daughter who won my heart. She was seventeen, angular cheeks, raven hair, tempersome, slender, and pretty.

Into this, my mother one time came, swooping down from her London life on television. She engulfed me in my cot (still bedwetting at an embarrassing eight), with the scent of gin and fags and a stranger's embrace. When I had washed her car, a Ford Zephyr Six, black, with a square bonnet, I rushed back into the house. She was in bed with my dad on the French girl's day off. I got two sixpences for the Dimple pot by way of silence, an outcast me, bewildered and depressed. From me she got a lower rung on the Inferno. I seldom heard her short of words or explanations. "I left him because he was a monster," she once told a lunch guest in my hearing. "So you left two young children with a monster?" came the reply and my mother's silence. "Would you say then that your younger son was a bit of an inconvenience in all this?" continued the guest. My ear cocked for her reply, me beneath the salt, further down the table. "Yeah, baby," she answered, leaning back on her chair and extinguishing her cigarette in the butter dish, which was a favourite tic.

So I thought nothing of it when the French one came for me. It started with bathtime, games with flannels and, taking my wrist, a hand put on her breast. She taught me things I did not know and took me to Paris for a month.

The Farm

'It needed years for anything to seem to happen,
in this dreary life of never-ending toil.'

Emile Zola, *The Earth*

BUT FIRST THE farm itself, red soil, oak woods, bushy hedges full of elms and birdsong. In summer it had the firefly warmth of a Dymock poem, in winter the clod of desolation. Outside were cob barns, great caverns made of mud and straw, where the swedes and bullocks were kept, hocked in standing straw and water. The fields all had names, which I don't remember now. They are on a map somewhere and Cromwell's army, it is said, camped in one before they decided against the sacking of Exeter.

Up a dark lane, aisled by overhanging larches, there once stood a hamlet made of baked mud. Images of it were sent to me a few years ago by a trespassing aerial photographer with a thermal camera. Deep valleys and tussocked bogs formed the upper part of the farm, where the buzzards lived, their scream out of shooting range enough to send you mad. Catkins and buttercups were easy on the touch. You could trace them on your face and make a wish.

Work started at seven without fail. The two old tractors (and a grey 'Fergie', which went to India in the end to help with famine relief; I was sad to see it go with its heat starter and grinding gear stick that stuck in third) would start up and this was my clarion to go outside. I was irrelevant to the working men, but followed them around, riding in the link box in all weathers. To drive the tractor one day was my dream, never dared expressed.

In the meal shed was a vast machine for rolling oats, still there, and a safe, its key long lost, that has not been opened to this day. What millions are in there, all or none? Or, more likely, some long-forgotten pesticide or lethal potion for the sheep that, years later, was banned as it was found to shorten the men's lives. I have not had the heart to carve it open.

One day the largest cob barn fell down. It had enormous wooden doors where once the carters would have reversed the horses with their hayrick-laden trailers. It was left as rubble, under the shroud of a great tarpaulin, where I would play, once hitting my elder brother with a brick so he went to hospital. I mention him just lightly for we were very different people and he seldom went outdoors. And a writer must be an only child.

Amongst the crannies of the cob, hornets lived. I miss them now, but then they were a fearsome foe. One time, I found one in my gumboot as I was getting dressed. To this day, I always tap my boots upside down, just in case. When they became abundant, the men at night brought torches, poles with diesel rags, like priests in those old festivals in Seville at Easter time, and burned them out. I see them in my mind flying still, half alight, doomed bombers with their venom still intact, and took no triumph from their death.

When the snow came in 1963, all schooling was abandoned. At home the pipes froze and food was what we had stored up in tins. For six weeks we sat that blizzard out, the sheep making little nests in the snow like carelessly scattered toffee wrappers, and us abluting in the drifts. I kept my terrier in bed for warmth, and do so to this day, my little comrade of the cold.

In the drawing room was a meagre fire that took an age to start, then burned too hot for any level comfort. To get it to draw, I was made to stand over it with a newspaper held out till my arms ached. Then, bedtime, into the freeze and dark of night, candle power leading in the muffled silence, a womb of nasty weather, the thaw a welcome mercy.

My bedroom was well away from the others, above the larder where the line-caught eels were dried for eating, tasting of cotton wool and garlic, and pheasants shot were left on ceiling hooks to bleed. It had once been an indoor chicken place, to keep them from the fox and there, with the door firmly shut, I had my own imaginary farm. All my sixpences went on Dinky Toys, tractors, a working buck rake (safe from my father's admonitions) with yellow spindles for turning my well-rowed hay, a bailer, a pony with little jumps on which other imaginary children rode and played with me. This was my farm, unobserved.

One summer's day, I took my farm outside, under another cob barn, where all the toys were let go on real grass. The plastic sheep and cows were as alive to me as spring bullocks on new pasture. I shook their manes for them, and checked their hooves and made a wattle corral for their safety. It was a day my father was being painted, an almost life-size mural, him on his grey horse asleep, thirteen foxes sitting round him in a reverie, *The Huntsman's Dream*. Called in, I left my farm to look at it. From outside the back kitchen door, a rumble came, and the suddenness of a small thunder clap. This barn too had now collapsed, worn down by time and weather, the toys consumed like those children in that Welsh mining disaster, petrified. Each one I rescued over days, the mud on them still visible today.

The shearing of the sheep was springtime wonder, and weighing lambs (90 pounds, then off to market) something of a struggle for a child. The routine for each was to put them through a noxious foot bath, trim their feet and then into the weighing cage, a red mark on their neck. I would catch them with a rugby hug, or by one back foot that twitched to be let free. The shearing was done by a winding mechanism, which I would turn for hours, the wool then put in bales with the scent of lanolin. The wool mill was eight miles away, and I would ride there on top of the trailer on a bed of fleece.

One day a workman left a paper in the meal shed, perhaps the *Daily Mirror*, and a pack of ten Park Drive. In it I read an article about a famous actor's son who had turned his back on trappings and gone to live on a hill farm in Wales, outside Machynlleth. There, it said, he occupied his splendid isolation with a four-hundred watt stereo for company. This, like wanting to earn more than my schoolmaster's £20 a week, became one of my early ambitions.

What about the house itself? It has been in my family since the early 17th century. It has seen murders and death (what house of any age has not?) and appears almost drunk on its history and survival. The walls are not straight, and the ceilings dip like spavined jades. Swallows have pecked out the plaster from the Georgian windows and, in the back kitchen, above which a maid once lived when I was small, the door no longer fits. Spiders weave their tresses everywhere, and dust is an invasion understood. Small nodes of mushrooms pock-mark my now bedroom wall, once my father's room where he died in the night, a glass of Ricard untouched on his bedside table. I can still smell his body there and have his same pictures on the wall: a map of the old estate, a photo of a wartime girlfriend and four nudes of which he was fond. I never went into that room before he died, except that one time when I found him with my mother.

The farm had been a wedding present from his parents in the 1950s, when the tenants left. It was basic then and, when I knew it first, had an outside pump for water and a small coal stove in the kitchen. It had and has a dining room little used, where family por-traits are hung, a photo of my granny 'Coming Out' as a Debutante, a full-length portrait of Charles II (it is either by Lely or it isn't; if so, I would have to sell it, so I have never bothered to find out). His eyes follow you round the room. The bishop and the lawyer forbears are there, too, and a man someone in my family married who was rich.

When she was dying, my mother asked if she could have the side-board back. "Are the curtains that I made for the windows still there?" she asked. I kept them both. Other little objects were clearly on their nuptial list: a china cup marked 'God Speed the Plough', bits of silver, and photograph frames that never did get used. On the ceiling, wine stains from some night of revelry, moth in the vermillion carpet and a dining table that, when polished, which it hasn't been for years, told of post-war socialising. A magnificent ram's-head mirror occupies the blocked-up fireside mantle, but even this does not dispel the feeling the room has just been vacated by Miss Havisham.

The single family bathroom was something to behold. Once it had been covered with a Formica floor, but my father, meeting an architect in the pub, had turned it into a French boudoir: there was a bidet, a wooden Moroccan lattice arch halfway down and brown cork tiles. Latterly, the bath had a pneumatic chair, and for six months after he died I kept it, lowering and raising myself into the tepid water. I then sold it locally for £500.

In went a second bathroom, then some basic central heating to stamp my mark. I imported real steel baths from London in which I could soak in warmth. But, like all those ignorant of old houses, I soon found cracks appearing in the walls, brought on by steam and heat. Out went the old kitchen stove and in its place a reconditioned Aga. In the bricked-up alcove, I found a newspaper cutting from 1926, when it had last been filled in.

In the larder I discovered an old range, and an ancient local Posbury stone surround fireplace unknown about in my father's time as it too had been blocked up. The larder has walls perhaps eight feet thick. On the fire I put nightly logs that I have chopped myself, each one in summer piled up lovingly in the barn by me, stacked like children at assembly in a play school yard. Sometimes I add a little peat, which burns too fast, for its aroma. Oddly, it only smells outside the house, so I stand out there some nights and think of when I was in Ireland as a boy, talking to old crofters with all my life before me.

The challenge was the roof of Delabole slate, a thousand metres square. "You'll have to have a new one," a builder friend who came to stay advised, taking an intake of breath as if he was sucking on an imaginary briar pipe. When the wind comes down the valley, those slates chatter but, even with one or two missing, it is amazing how little water drips into the threadbare attic. I replace the odd miscreant with old vinyl records, which has done the trick; albums by Elton John and Mink DeVille.

At the front drive entrance, a broken down, immovable, white wooden gate, which I would paint as a child, lies forlorn. On it hangs a makeshift 'Private' sign, ignored at your peril. At the back lane, an abundance of primroses and primulas in the spring, where the cattle lorries would come to take the sheep away. When we had bullocks, you could see them jump in a frenzy trying not to be herded in, desperate to live a little longer, grazing on the green grass they called home.

An ancient cart wash is outside the back door, where the swallows come for water and build their nests under the tallot eaves. People say when they come to the farm that it has not changed since time began. I am going to keep it like this, My Lost Estate. My Leopard.

The Ripening Seed

'I once had a girl
Or should I say she once had me
She showed me her room
Isn't it good Norwegian Wood?'

The Beatles,
Norwegian Wood from *Rubber Soul* (1965)

IN THE SPRING of 1966, I went to Paris for a month with the taxi driver's daughter. I was ten years old. We took the plane from Exeter to Orly. It was a little airport then and my dad had on occasions taken me there to stand on the viewing platform, when flight was still a novelty.

Combed hair, new grey suit, long trousers, floral tie (which I still wear sometimes), polished shoes, Air France, seatbelt, away. It was a day of sunshine, the plane outside silver like a cigar case. Clouds and more sunshine and a stewardess coming round. "Juice?" she asked in French, and then it all went wrong.

Whether it was a buffet from the clouds or just an unfortunate mistake, but the orange when it arrived was shot into my crotch. Humiliation and tears (thank God I wasn't wearing shorts), then remonstrations from the taxi girl in French and a little cheeky mopping up. Sangfroid from the stewardess, but they paid for the suit to be cleaned and brought it some days later to our door.

I can't remember if I completed the journey in sodden silence or if they put me in a kimono kept for such misfortunes. Once we landed it was into the metro, a smell of rubber from its tyres and occupants with berets and briefcases. Into the open air we passed *pissoirs* on the street, on pavements that my feet had never trod before and which made them bruised and sore.

She lived in a small flat in the suburbs, off a roundabout in a leafy street, not wide like Haussmann, but with room to move and breathe. The front room, which doubled up for dining, had a floor-to-ceiling window that opened onto a tiny balcony. Next to it was a small, portable Dansette record player in cream and red, and a small shelf where the records lived: Johnny Hallyday and The Beatles' *Rubber Soul*. There was her widowed mother and a sister who was not quite right. The toilet was outside in the hallway, shared by a couple of other flats and a residue of inaccurate aiming.

This was not the Paris of gaiety or gaslight, or the haunts of Hemingway, just a humdrum place, the sort you would read about in French language text books: a baker, butcher, onion seller on a bike, Solex, boules, a stationer for the local college, plane trees and silver birch, and people going to work. It fascinated me.

On the roundabout there was a *boucher chevalin*, the horse carcasses strung up not like a Degas painting but *degolas*, all the gore of Zola's *The Belly of Paris*. We would eat horse on a Sunday for a treat. Hot chocolate in a bowl into which I dipped my baguette was my favourite, as I looked up from the simple print tablecloth to the pale blue walls and the wooden Catholic cross, which had not spared the taxi driver's life. There were other horses on the roundabout, painted red and yellow, their nostrils flaring and their pose like Whistlejacket. This was the carousel with its jaunty gypsy music, where I would lurk around and get free rides out of pity from the lady owner. It made me homesick for my animals when the music stopped.

I do not know what the family did by day, and I don't think we ever went to church, but Sunday lunch was their big thing. It was over horse and haricot that the mother said something to her daughters that I didn't understand. "What was she saying?" I asked the au pair daughter for I saw a worried face upon the mother. She didn't want to tell me, no tell me, tell me. And she came right out with it. "She said that you have small white spots under your eyes, which means you will not have a long life." Of course I cried, as would any child confronted for the first time with their own mortality. The not-quite-right one came and held me tight. "*Sale bête,*" breathed the mother.

With the au pair there were expeditions: an empty Louvre where artists with great easels copied the works of the Old Masters, Napoleon's Tomb, the galleries and gardens of the Tuileries, the Eiffel

Tower (I got vertigo on the second stage and we had to come down), a bateaux mouche (no dining) past Notre Dame, and the zoo, which I didn't like, with its unkempt animals and brown bears in chains. There were no Japanese or Nikons then, or American student girls with figures like hanging pears. In many squares, there were ghost-eyed Frenchmen playing boules and smoking Caporals, drinking corkless Beaujolais from the bottle, still trying not to think about the German Occupation.

Then there was the ordinary life itself, just as interesting: we took rides on buses and trams open at the back where I would lean on the copper rail and pretend that I was grown up with a girlfriend. Back home, she would bathe my feet tenderly with a mustard bath. "*C'est si bon?*" she would ask. They were so good, those little thrills.

Then my father came and stayed at the Georges V, and I was relegated. I never got to see his room, but relieved myself once in the towering urinals, tipping the concierge one franc. Hold on, hadn't he taken my mother there pregnant before they married with an as yet unborn elder brother who died of cot death at six months? "Took her to Paris with a bellyful of white mice," he said to me once, but I didn't understand what he meant. My mother never mentioned it either, the Catholic shame. But when my father died, I found a silver christening cup marked: 'ANCKB'. Adam, the first born. Adam Nigel... Nigel was my father's name. The C is for Cleave, which I bear myself, the surname of that rich man in the dining room.

When my mother was suing me years later for some minor error I had written about her in print, she got a right of reply and did now mention the earlier child, citing this as a reason why she had deserted my dad and me. I was sympathetic to that. How many marriages survive the death of a child? Another excuse she made in that tawdry article for her desertion was that my father had told her, early on in their marriage, that "Women are for business, boys are for pleasure," which I really don't think even he believed. And what was my error? When she had been a daytime television quiz show hostess, I wrote that she drove a pink Thunderbird. "It was a pink Cadillac," she screamed down the phone. "I am not Lady Penelope."

It was not so much fun being the three of us in Paris with our different ages. I obviously wasn't the child of my dad and the au pair, our ages being fifty, seventeen and ten. What would people think I was, a stolen child or an intrusive cousin? Certainly not the imaginary boyfriend anymore. My father hired a car and crashed it with me in the back, something about a right of way on a roundabout. The au pair was brilliant, springing out with guttural French, charm, excitement, and the Frenchman backing down. This was all done with a backdrop of the mighty river flowing slowly by, buoying up barges with bicycles, dogs and hangings baskets in their *mise-en-Seine*.

Finally, we made it to a restaurant in the Bois de Boulogne, a red squirrel dancing on the frond branch leaves outside. In a tank were fresh trout swimming and a memorable lunch. I chose my own and back it came, dressed in toasted almonds. Before that a trolley with twenty starters had appeared. My father was formal in public with the taxi driver's daughter, so here we became siblings whilst the odd diner winked at my old man.

"*Assis, assis,*" he shouted after lunch as we drove out of the city down to Burgundy. He thought it was a place name, stopping and scouring the map in the Ford Taunus. Eventually, a helpful man pointed out he should be looking for the A6 autoroute. It was nothing much in those days as the houses petered out, giving way to flat open fields with horizoned tree clumps and great berths of forestry where an army might have hid one time in waiting. In Dijon, I had my first kir, that wonderful mixture of white wine and cassis, which means 'pig's trotters' for its colour. We stayed in a roadside inn and I walked alone into the gardens, where there was a trout stream with sluice gates. It was as chalk-blue clear as the shallow rivers of Hampshire. In the green lush meadows, Charolais cows fluffed white, statues of stillness as the clouds passed by above. *Profonde.*

In my room there was a bath in which you could only sit up. There were sounds of sex next door. Then we drove on to a farm owned by the au pair's relations, everything deeply rural and dogs for me to play with in the yard. Then it was back to Paris where, with my father gone, things took a different turn.

First it was the woman at the carousel who took me under the tarpaulin at night and pressed her kisses. She was ancient to my eyes, perhaps forty, but I can't say I resisted. Then she sent me home to tea and silence. But the musk of my despoil must have reached the not-quite-right one. She, too, began stealing into my room; I may well have shared it with her anyway, divided in the bed by a hard bolster. That was it, those not so scary nights of warmth and wrong. She paid me like a child, with little key rings from a corner shop: 'Fina', '4L', 'Fiat', 'Une C'Est Du Soleil'. I have them now before me as I write, little trophies of my exploits. "Zanc Evan." At night, she whispered to me in German.

It was over lunch with John Osborne one day years later that he turned and said to me: "I can never go out to lunch in Brighton without wanting to take a woman to bed in the afternoon." Bugger Brighton. Many would feel the same way about Paris. It was after hunting in the forests of the Brisee in the 1990s, with that unrivalled combination of good friendship, a château, fine wine, ratafia, the scent of crushed ferns, saddle soap and sweat, some night-time dancing and a plunge at midnight naked with the others in the fountain, that I found myself in Paris waiting for my train to England, early. I set my bib at the 'Terminus Nord', for a bottle of Sancerre and a dozen oysters. I could not believe that she had followed me, a fellow guest, silk shirt open, dark hair, like the taxi driver's daughter. She was nineteen and had just begun at Oxford her brother told me (I was forty and married with a girlfriend.) She just sat down, and lit the slimmest white filtered cigarette, set in the middle of her mouth. "I thought I'd get the earlier train as well," she said, as a waiter guided in her chair, her knee touching mine.

What would I not give now to have that lunch again? Gone were my nervous days of tearing up my napkin (they were linen, anyway) or asking about horoscope star signs. And these too were the days before I would drink too much, fearing I would fail, and talk about myself so stupidly. I was now the hunter hunted, and here this dancing doe before me. "I've lived in Paris. We could take a flat for six months in Montmartre," she said. I wish we could, *Norwegian Wood*.' I wish too I'd done it now and we had lived in some absurd eyrie, reading books and me pretending to be a *littérateur* or *écrivain*. I wish I'd had the guts and money, not pressed down like some Gulliver by an uncertain but assumed future set in stone, the mule's burden of inheritance. For she was a beauty. Why, even some of the waiters winked at the old man.

A few weeks later, things got a little out of hand. We were sitting in her Oxford rooms having banished (with some difficulty, I might add, as he thought I was her uncle) some moon-calved undergrad, and went to share a bath. Steam, vodka, lemon, one of us at each end, she at the taps good girl. Had she told me she was partly Russian and her family were high up in espionage? "So, if you don't marry me I can have you killed." We slept together before a small coal fire in her sitting room. As I looked up, there in the flickering light was a photograph of her Russian grandfather, murdered by the NKVD. She did not murder me, but did just what she said she would and went to live in Paris with another.

That château in Burgundy became something of a destination for me. My host was ever hospitable and had a pack of hounds, which always made for merriment and a broader view of conduct. One time he took me in his Bentley to meet an old farmer, Monsieur Thavenot, as we were about to come hunting on his land. Here was a real farmer with a beret and a rheumy eye and, so he told me, not long to live. Underneath his chair, he kept a sleeping goose, which he stroked with great affection, to be turned to foie gras later on.

My host, too, had been at Oxford and his friends were bright, some borderline camp, highly amusing and delighted to take part in his somewhat chaotic but generous hospitality. Other guests might include a smattering of European royalty and aristocrats, politicians or diplomats. Ever brilliant company was former Australian prime minister Bob Hawke, with whom I shared some very merry evenings. At a dinner at a nearby château he asked to speak to me under the table. We faced each other on all fours. "There is something I want you to know. That Condoleezza Rice is third rate," he said, testing my journalistic ability to keep my mouth shut. Learning he had come to live nearby with a library and little money, we had Oscar Wilde's grandson, Merlin Holland, over for dinner. Showing him the hounds next morning, given that his grandfather had described hunting as the "unspeakable in pursuit of the uneatable," it was a picture to see the uncomfortable bemusement on his face. "Interesting", was his wan and non-committal observation.

The château was freezing cold, which some took as encouragement for mischief. I learned a lot from my host. "It is important to be Catholic," he said to me one day. "You just confess your sins and start again," adding, with a smile: "You naughty boy." So again one summer I took a girl there from an English farming family, blonde, mid twenties, with a ready blush, tall, a figure like a Somalian runner, shy and unconfident. But she was an exceptional horsewoman, which took our breath away, and she could drink any man into talking nonsense. One day, we had lunch in the local town and driving back in a warm breeze to the château, a deer ran across in front of us. We watched as it jumped some wire and turned towards a wooden cabin with a fine aluminium smoke stack, logs piled up for the winter store. "Let's live there," she said, and that nightmare returned like a ghost haunting me. For I loved her and with her I could perhaps have been a real farmer, too.

Together in Paris, I had to be quite furtive. No drinks at the Crillon or staying at The Louisiane. Dinner at Le Petit Saint Benoit was out. So we cruised Montmartre, ducking in and out of bars and jazz clubs (even there I spotted an English duke of my acquaintance and had to scuttle into a doorway). "Aren't you married to Francoise Hardy?" a woman asked me in one bar, mercifully out of earshot from the girl. Then a frenzy just like John had said took hold. We found a porn shop that had cubicles for two. She chose the film, group as I recall, and we set to. I looked up, and there were four men peering through a hole in the ceiling. We were what these butlers saw.

What happened to the taxi driver's daughter, I do not know. We came back to England, and then I went away to boarding school, and she left. Before she did, she came to see me and took me out to lunch at a Sussex hotel, Gravetye Manor, grand, ancient countryside with goldfish in a pond and well-known gardens. If I knew the day that I would die, I would have that lunch again as my 'Last Supper': snails, duck with orange, then profiteroles. I have lived whole years with people whose names I can't remember but this was not like that. She was leaving to go back to France, and then America I understood.

I have often wondered about that street, the little flat and the not-quite-right sister. I have her dictionary with her address in it: 4, Rue Paul Bert, 94, Saint-Maur. But I do not have the heart to go, rustling around in my own past and imposing it on her. She would be seventy by now. I have one letter from her, and I always cross my sevens like she did. I don't suppose it matters that it was addressed to my dad, not asking after me.

A child in London

'Dirty old river, must you keep rolling,
Flowing into the night?
People so busy, make me feel dizzy,
Taxi light shines so bright.'

The Kinks, *Waterloo Sunset*

THEY SAY IF you can remember London in the Sixties, you weren't there. But I was there, and I can remember it, dressed in grey flannels from Billings & Edmonds and kipper ties from Mr Fish or Blades, a child witnessing grown-ups in their early thirties, barely more than children themselves. It was a time of black and white: black and white cars and television, and the luke grey sky that drifted above my mother's rented house in Chiswick, static above the barge hulks that had died on the Thames Reach, on which I played most days.

My mother was by now a daytime TV quiz show hostess at the BBC in Lime Grove. She was recognised in every corner shop, and on her way to work. This may have also have been partly because she drove an open-topped pink Cadillac, and wore dark glasses and a silk Hermes headscarf while smoking. Later on, following their divorce, her third husband referred to her bitterly as 'Cruella de Vil', and he might have had this image in mind. One year, she turned on the Christmas lights in Newport Pagnell, as she rented a weekend cottage nearby, and I remember craning up at her, my hand holding some makeshift barrier, a security guard asking me what I thought I was doing, the starlit sky behind all bible black.

From my unwelcome presence in her house, shared with husband number two, a film producer, I watched the aeroplanes from my small bedroom window, silver fish with substantial names like BOAC and Pan American. I bit the film producer once when he attempted, and very nearly succeeded, in drowning my elder brother in the bath. People from the film world came and went, peacocks and pansies, a fug of scent and cigarettes and drunken laughter. My mother smoked in bed, and the fire brigade got called one night when she had immolated the sheets. She signed autographs in gratitude. Another time, they filmed a section of the Beatles' *A Hard Day's Night* in the pub next door, which involved Ringo Starr and a lion. My mum got to have lunch with Ringo. I got to stroke the lion. My playmate from there was the publican's son and his Alsatian.

A fellow Irish neighbour was another TV host, Eamonn Andrews, all blarney and bonhomie, with his Irish wife, Gráinne. They were there that fateful December night in 1969, when a man at the party in my mother's house nearly drowned. I was there, too, back inside from the usual rigamarole of being beaten up by local boys, to witness this calamity. It has been told so many times in so many memoirs that you would but wonder that half of London 'Society' had borne witness to it.

It concerned the Guinness heir and amateur champion jockey Gay Kindersley who, for a bet, had volunteered to swim the river, there and back. Fit from his race riding and nights spent in the Jermyn Street steam baths, he made the far bank. On the return journey, the tide was too much for him, and he was carried under a concrete barge. Those in dinner jackets watching did not offer to jump in, but urged him on with ribald banter. Perhaps life meant more and less then, and social cruelty was just commonplace. After all, his cousin, Tara Browne, had just recently died in a Chelsea car crash, neatly embroidered into a song by the Beatles, *A Day In The Life*. Gay came back eventually to shore, to life and two large brandies.

I went back to the house some years ago. It was modern, probably built out of a bomb crater, with a balcony and a small garden which, during my peripatetic occupancy, always smelt of cat piss. It seemed so small and all its gaiety was gone. They had a speedboat, which I remember going on once and, on the riverside steps, wooden boards to stem the rising tide of the Thames. Now, even the barge hulks had disappeared.

Sometimes I would go with my mother to the BBC studios in Lime Grove, and wait for hours whilst they all smoked and laughed and clapped. The studio audiences would come in and be paid in tea and warmth, and, in the backroom, all headphones and wires, my mother's second husband produced the shows *Pit Your Wits* and *Pencil and Paper*. They were a success of their type and time. The marriage didn't last, of course. Their divorce was all over the papers. "Cruelty," my mother cited. "The most slender case of cruelty that has ever come before me," said the divorce judge, granting it.

The next thing I knew I was wallowing in an enormous basement bath off Hyde Park's Rutland Gate, being read T.H. White's *Mistress Masham's Repose* by my mother and being energetically soaped by her with lemon verbena. I did not like that book then, and still can't see the joy in it today. The flat to me was vast, with a grand piano in the drawing room and the actor Peter Finch living as a lodger off some partitioned glass-door corridor. I cannot remember my bedroom but one Christmas I was told to go to the kitchen and turn down the gas on the roasting turkey. This did not end well. Rotating the oven knob, I unlit the gas but, not knowing about flats and gas, simply turned the knob up again. We eventually ate the turkey at five.

Now entered for my mother a period of calm and with her change of address came a change of husband and religion. For she had married a white Russian prince and converted to Russian orthodoxy. This man was charming, slow, untempered, softly spoken, resigned to his loss of status and estates following the Russian Revolution. His family had been important and his grandfather had been the last Tsar's prime minister but now, having come to England with only the shirt on his back, he seemed resigned to a life spared and the simple social joys that London had to offer. He, too, had been married a couple of times before, with one son my age, Gregory, who had a pronounced limp. He had, apparently, been run over by the number 14 bus outside the Natural History Museum. Greg the Peg.

The papers were once again agog and I have pictures of the Prince and Princess from my mother's voluminous scrap albums (mainly of and about herself) at the opening of art exhibitions and racing at Ascot. By now she had ventured into the emerging trade of public relations, which they did together. They went to the Aga Khan's wedding in Paris, and weekended at Blenheim or Woburn or Renishaw, and seemed genuinely happy. They were not, so far as I was aware, part of London's 'Swinging Sixties' but more of an established element of London Society, and that they were, albeit a Russian title, now a 'Prince and Princess,' made them acceptable.

They didn't seem to have much money, and drove around London, at terrifying speed in my mother's case, in a red mini. The Russian was always kind to me and offerings from their clients came my way. These included all the new board games from Waddingtons and an endless supply of Canada Dry ginger ale in small tins, to which I became attached. By day, to make myself scarce and take myself out of the house, I went to Harrods and played with the pets for sale. My mother had a spontaneous generosity, not to make up for any parental absence, which she never acknowledged, but it must have been the Irish in her. When I was back at home in Devon, having had my tonsils out, a Moulton bike arrived to make me better. It would have been pointless to say to her that what might work on the flat streets of Knightsbridge was really not a lot of use on the muddy lanes of the West Country.

I think with the help of my Irish grandfather, who not only had his own estates but had been befriended by the American millionaire Sir Alfred Chester Beatty, they then bought a house in Trevor Place, a short walk again from Harrods. When, after a summer spent with my grandparents farming, swimming, and wandering the fields in Ireland, the small plane touched down at Heathrow, I had a reasonable expectation of going home and being reunited with my dog. But I was met by my mother and a man in a dark suit, a lawyer, hovering, sprung into a hired Bentley and driven into London. I was made a Ward of Court.

"Now, you're going away to school," she told me in her suffocating drawing room. It was there that I saw my natural parents together out of bed for the one and only time in my life, to discuss my future schooling. When, in 2018, my mother died and I laid her to rest in Ireland, in the disturbing circumstances I shall later recall, I pondered again that brief parental hour. I pondered not only the meeting, and how awkward I felt, but the good that came out of it. The short story to follow tells the tale.

ॐ

The Black Watch

Like most people in middle age, I have had my fair share of bad luck; fortune, more often than not, has seemed to go other people's way. I have never found a needle in a haystack or been called 'one in a million.'

One piece of bad luck I had was in 1982, reporting on a job in Kirkcaldy on the East coast of Scotland, where moving cars keep on moving and windscreen wipers should be employed at all hours to scrape away the chip papers that blow around the promenade of this windy city. Taking the precaution of removing my wristwatch and leaving it in the car I had hired, I undertook the interview and drove back to Edinburgh to return the vehicle. Five minutes after leaving the forecourt in Picardy Place, I realised I had left my watch on the passenger seat. Racing back to the counter, I told this to the man in charge. "We have checked the car, and there is no watch in it," he told me firmly, a patent lie. When I remonstrated, he responded with menaces that might well have involved a 'concrete slipper' or a 'Paisley Kiss' if I did not scarper fast. I left the premises with a heavy heart, resigned to the loss of my watch. For the next thirty-six years, I never wore another.

For this had been no ordinary watch. It had been, in 1967, a joint gift from my divorced parents whom, that very day, I had seen together for an hour, for the one and only time, in my mother's London town house in Knightsbridge. Asking me to absent myself—whilst they no doubt wrangled about the burden of school fees and who would be least inconvenienced by my holiday plans—I took myself off, aged eleven, to drift amongst the shops of London. Usually this was to Harrods, where I would sit on a stool with headphones at the 'Way In' café on the fourth floor, enjoying free warmth and music, or to the pet shop and piano department on the first floor, watching the puppies play.

On this occasion, I went again, as I had been doing for the previous three days, to stare in the nearby window of the world famous jewellery shop Kutchinsky. In the display were watches, bracelets, tiaras and all the glamorous perquisites without which a wealthy Londoner was not fully dressed. Entry to this world of fabulous adornments was by way of a buzzer, and a liveried doorman, perhaps a former soldier eking out his pension, stood guard.

He had noticed me, a soon to be small prep school boy, gazing at the window, my eyes focused on a black-faced watch with illuminated green hour marks and a white date box, bearing the name on the front: 'Rotary Aquaplunge'. I do not know what made me, on this third day, loll in the glass alcove of the shop door, with the buzzer probably at my head height. Without pressing it, which I would never have had the courage to do, the concierge opened the door and beckoned me in. He put a hand on my slender shoulder as if to say this was no place for me, an innocent amongst the emblems of the rich. Emboldened, I asked to see the watch and a somewhat disdainful female assistant took it from its place in the window and, with white gloves and a resigned flourish, spread it out on the counter. My heart was beating fast. It had, she explained, various technicalities all of which were lost on me, except one. The watch had a capacity to be comfortably worn to a depth of fifty metres. There and then I imagined being the envy of my prep school friends as I plunged into our unheated outdoor pool, all of eight feet deep at the diving board end and where, until only recently, as I was to find out, naked swimming had been the norm.

Returning to my parents, who seemed to be in a good mood with each other as the afternoon sun streamed through the drawing room windows, I chose my moment and asked them if I could have the watch. My father, not one for gestures of frivolous generosity, looked at my mother, who said, "Oh, go on." And he drew his farm account cheque book out of his inside breast pocket. "Bugger off," he said, and I raced out of the house with a signed cheque for £30.

I thought it might have gone in the hour I had been away as I raced down Trevor Place, past the Harrods Repository and the greasy spoon where I sometimes also lurked, and arrived breathless before the Kutchinsky doorman. Never was a child more proud and grateful than when I slipped the watch under the cuff of my left hand ("Remember, you always wear a watch on your non writing wrist," my mother had told me, as she knew about etiquette and such things).

When I showed it to my parents, it was as if I had achieved something, which I now understand is what psychologists call retail therapy. I could not wait until nightfall to see the green hour marks glow in the dark, which they did like silkworms. Next morning, when the euphoria of my purchase had died down, I started worrying about taking the watch to school. My mother allayed my fears and, taking her gold paperknife from Collingwood (she was, of course, one of the wealthy adults to whom accoutrements meant status), made a small scratch mark on the back of the watchcase. It was 'The Mark of Zorro'. "This will always be your watch now," she said, and for the next fifteen years it was, until that fateful day in Edinburgh when I had left it in the hire car.

I can mark all my moments, not just in minutes but in milestones, from that watch when I owned it. It was on my wrist when I ran school races, addressed the debating society and when, with much anxiety, opened my A level *results in the hushed cloisters of the nearby Brompton Oratory that would take me, and my watch, off to university. Of course, I was far too scared ever to wear it under water.*

I always felt a feeling of sadness and stupidity that I had lost the watch, for we had done so much together. But the dawn of the internet gave me some hope. Often I would scour the web late at night to see if, like the needle in a haystack, it might turn up. Two weeks after my mother died, and, walking from her funeral in the bright sunlight of the Irish village where her family had built the church, I felt a renewed and silly impetus to look again.

There, in a shop in Cyprus, was a watch: 'Rotary Aquaplunge: Late 1960s,' it said. I rang the owner, Andreas Gregoriades of Timeline in Nicosia, and he told me that it had come from a Scottish collector of many watches, who seldom wore them and had emigrated to Cyprus. He was slightly puzzled by my request to be sent a photograph of the back casing. The watch now sits upon my wrist, an extravagant purchase for £750. I look at it in wonder and I think of my parents and how, in the only hour I ever saw them together, they seemed happy and not displeased with me. And when I take it off at night I look at the back. And there is the small scratch, like 'The Mark of Zorro'.

I wish my mother had been alive for me to tell her this tale, for she had a remarkable memory and intelligence until almost the very end. When I last saw her in Kilkenny hospital, just alive, silent under a single white sheet, her face was masked like Mick Jagger on the cover of *Goats Head Soup*. Another person who would have appreciated it is that great storyteller of both London and the countryside, Ray Davies of the Kinks. In 1995, I was sitting having lunch with him in Dunblane in Scotland, when I happened to mention I had seen him play in a farmer's field outside Exeter when I was the age about which this chapter is written. "It wasn't outside Exeter," he told me. "It was in Pinhoe the night that England won the World Cup. I never forget a gig where I have played."

Sussex and the Downs

'If you've been bad—oh, Lord, I bet you have
And you've not been hit by flying lead
You'd better close your eyes, bow your head
Wait for the ricochet.'

Deep Purple, *Child in Time*

NOT FAR FROM the Hog's Back near Guildford, where Leonard Bast went night-time missing in Forster's *Howards End*, is Box Hill and the then emerging Gatwick airport of the 1960s. Beyond them is a small, semi-suburban village. It is surrounded by gorse and bracken heathland, a profusion of garden centres and houses with their names on the fronts of their short drives. The smell of leylandii hedges and creosote from the wooden painted fences that partition these small-gardened homes of toil and little merit fills the air.

Down a long, straight lane, a Victorian mansion without wings, a grassed turning circle and outside metal fire escapes, took its place by an open heathy common. This was Copthorne School, which was, from a sunny September afternoon in 1967, to be my seat of learning (school number 107) until the snow melted and Common Entrance was passed three years later in the spring of my fourteenth year and the new decade.

We were no brocade of innocents. There was a pecking order and on arrival I was on the lowest rung, bullied, homesick and alone. But I could sing and kick a football, which stood me well. I rose in time to play the Lord Chancellor in *Iolanthe*, garlanded with praise, embraced in furs by other mothers, and scored a solo goal against the hated foe of Holmwood House. My mentor and my English master was in a wheelchair from polio. He smoked cheroots and drank a little freely. "Nothing trivial I hope," he would say when a boy shied off games with a lame chit. "You could grow cabbages in there," was another cry as he tugged at an errant ear on nightly roll call as we traipsed up the wooden staircase to our dormitories of depravity.

There is a strange *omertà* amongst small boys. Parents like to believe they are making Airfix models or art collages, puzzling over Latin and writing happy letters home. There was a garden patch I shared with the later famous satirist and talk show panellist Francis Wheen, but my thing was dramatics. I began as a weasel or a stoat in *Wind In the Willows,* greasepaint and whiskers, before graduating to Dick Deadeye in *H.M.S. Pinafore* and then my starring legal role. Our music master was 'Fingers' Gill, bald, tall but stooped, almost blind, glasses with inch-thick lenses, and a sweaty hand he made us hold as we guided him in darkness back to his lodgings. He was a maestro on the organ and piano. How lustily we sang *D'ye ken John Peel* on Saturday mornings, tittering with emphasis about his 'coat so GAY'. Across the face of 'Fingers' a knowing smile would creep, for he was a kind man and meant the boys no harm.

So much has been written about the sexual predations of teachers at prep schools in the 1960s. It seems that any adding to it is simply met with resignation and ennui or, as was so often the case at the time, disbelief. But it is the harsh injustice of it that still haunts the victim boys in adulthood, when their hopes and lives are less and shorter, and they fear for children of their own. Before my own addition, I can say I loved my time in Sussex.

Firstly, there were the exciting and occasional days out, to Gravetye Manor, once again a special destination and those iridescent goldfish, and to the homes of other boys who always welcomed me as I lived so far away. Oast houses, leaning like grandparents with walking sticks, nestled in meadows and at the end of deep tree-arched lanes, or stood out like nipples on The Downs. In these homes were normal parents, farmers, people who had jobs that might involve commuting. Oates taught me to eat sausages with marmalade (which I still do) and took me down to Brighton and the skating rink. With the Wheens, I first tasted peanut butter. Myles had a Great Dane and lived in a large, modern bungalow. He wrote to me some years later when that dog died. The Chiltons lunched me at the Cooden Beach Hotel in Bexhill-on-Sea, the town so churlishly disliked by playwright David

Hare from his surburban childhood there. I like to think I once saw the author Simon Raven dining alone, napkin tucked into his shirt collar, musing on his masterpiece, *The Rich Pay Late*, and picking up a waiter with his bill.

'D.G.L.S.', Mr Sale, wheel-chair bound from polio without complaint, ran the football team. For a year, I was his wheel-chair pusher, wages ten shillings a term. This was an 'honour' accorded to the naughtier boys. On match days I would accompany him in his black Morris 1000, with red seats and adapted pedals. The first eleven would be clapped out of assembly on a Saturday by the whole school with cheers of "Good Luck", and we would bottle down the Sussex lanes to whichever opponent we were playing. At Mowden near the Brighton coast, I was afterwards brought before the host headmaster, Mr Snell. He had taught my father there in the early 1930s, and asked me how he was. What intrigued me most about that place was that the school swimming pool was housed under the wooden floorboards of the gym.

The journeys back to Copthorne took a more meandering turn. Hoarse from shouting at us pitch-side, Mr Sale would slake his thirst in various taverns to which he was well known. Then, I would crane him, small cheroot in hand, back into the car as we made our roll call return to school in the tail-lit evening. He nurtured in me a love of language. Only once did we disagree. I had written in an essay about a sylvan glade being 'grotesque', thinking it meant a place where a grotto might stand. I was wrong, of course. Never again did I trust a thesaurus.

My mother came sporadically to take me out, my father only twice. She was all furs and fancy cars, he full of inconvenienced defensiveness. I would have been just as happy if neither of them had bothered. Once, as I was getting into another parent's car, to be given Sunday lunch amongst their animals and normality, I spotted a mulberry-coloured Bentley speeding, braking, stopping in front of the school lozenge turning circle. It was owned and being driven by a bachelor member of the Sainsbury family. "How could you be so disloyal?" my mother was screeching to me when she got me in the back, slipping on a fat super-eight cartridge of Neil Diamond's *Love on the Rocks*. "You knew I was coming to take you out." Despite softening and shipping me a couple of flutes of champagne at the Chequers in Forest Row, I would rather have spent the day in a normal household.

"Have you had a salubrious stay?" the headmaster asked my father, who told him he had spent the night in Angmering-on-Sea. "Salubrious, salubrious," was all my father muttered all day long as we went around the Sussex countryside looking for Partridge Green, a small village where he had once had a girlfriend and, later, named his spaniel after it. He turned up the drive of Gravetye, took one look, and left. Instead, he took me to stay and swim at the Felbridge hotel, where I was eyed up by travelling salesmen as my father slept on a sun lounger. "That is a great crested grebe," he said as we drove by another village duckpond, failing, for long, to break the agonising silence. "Why don't you ever look out of the window?" was another unhelpful sleight. It was a relief to get back to my Latin Primer.

It would be madness to deny that young boys, coddled up together in dormitories and shared ordeals, did not form 'attachments'. One I knew carved another's name on his forearm with a pair of mathematical dividers, a laceration of love and a scar that would not heal. I was always the girl part in ballroom dancing and never got the hang of it. Communal baths were all done naked. Those masters who indulged in the odd stroke of a boy's back thought of it as perks. We thought of none of this as queer. We were too busy being young and knew no different. One day, in broad daylight, Mortmain, who was just thirteen and pretty good with bat and ball, was talking to me as we sat on the rose garden steps, by the chapel tower clock that chimed incessantly each quarter. Other boys were walking by but this did not stop him whipping out his escutcheon and within thirty seconds had 'scored a turbid six'. Then there was matron, perhaps twenty-two, who tried to make me walk up straight by balancing books upon my head and held me close in front of her, pretty, blonde and wrong. Often I went to her after games to have my limbs stroked with witch hazel. Once we had a bath together, awkwardly.

I had an 'attachment' of my own, with whom I would trade soccer cards and gave a postal order of ten shillings, my whole term's wheel-chair pushing allowance. I told him about Mortmain. "Can you score a six?" he asked me suddenly. I blushed for he had called my bluff and I lied and I said "Yes," which was not true. Therein lay my doom, putting paid to his romantic propositions. All I got was one burning embrace by my coat peg after dark. This was not enough for him. A master came to the school whose sole intention was to ravish pupils. It was not long before my attachment was seduced by him in the decorous purlieus of the Art Room, on a well-stained mattress. He told me this, and that teachers brought in from other schools had clambered on him also, passing him round like a bowl of peanuts. But far worse was to follow.

Francis Wheen, my partner in the failed garden patch adventure, had, by the mid 1980s, made a name for himself as a biographer, diarist and writer for *The Independent* and *Private Eye*. But, beneath his gilded talent lurked a strong desire to bring that teacher to justice. He had tracked him down abroad and amassed evidence of sexual misdemeanours with young boys over several continents. Now he was closing in on him and he got in touch to ask if I would like to have my say. We had lunch together, always a joy, bright, mischievous and not a little camp. "I'm wearing the old school tie," he said, pulling up his jersey, "and the snake belt."

He told me the police had been in touch with all the boys at school and they would like to talk to me and for me to make a statement. I did nothing. Then the police came calling. What followed was a farce. I agreed to meet one police officer in London in the gardens at the Holland Park café. Arriving early, I saw a second officer hiding in the bushes. Once rumbled, they set about their questioning. Given that they had got testimonies of wrong-doing from plenty of my school contemporaries, I reasoned to them that I had little to add. Things straight away turned nasty. "But we have been informed that you were one of the ring leaders," one of them said. That could not be right and I was not going to fall for the 'carrot and stick' treatment. I declined to offer further help.

Why had the police been so determined to get my testimony? Quite by chance some years later I found out. To relive the happiness of my Sussex schooldays, I would for many years go to the Ardingly Show, that wonderful event of Sussex splendour where pennants fly and horse flesh pounds the turf. One year, it was to be graced by royalty, so I had to be vetted for security as I was one of the guests at the lunch to welcome the Duchess of Cornwall. The face that came back on my letter of approval was older now, grey about the temples, but unmistakable. The officer in charge had been my old attachment, the peanut bowl. He had also been in charge of the teacher's investigation. In the end, Wheen and my 'attachment' got what they wanted as the teacher got twelve years.

Each year, when I go back to Ardingly, staying with just the sort of family who fifty years before looked after me, farming, fun and friendly, I wonder if I could live in Sussex, home of my youth for three years. It was so empty then, with all the villages beautiful and quiet. Now those pretty streets are crammed with cars commuting. Ditchling, Brightling, Charleston, Firle each have had their beauty dimmed by traffic noise. Yet they have their beauty still. Once I went back to Gravetye, and took a girl to lunch, snails, duck à l'orange and profiteroles. Afterwards we slept together standing up in a nearby meadow byre, me thinking about someone else.

Buckinghamshire and Beyond

'And so it was that later
As the miller told his tale
That her face, at first just ghostly
Turned a whiter shade of pale.'

Procol Harum, *A Whiter Shade of Pale*

THE BOYS' PUBLIC SCHOOL, that great British institution, is often portrayed with envy as a seat of depravity, depravation and decadence. It involves the suppression and expression of feelings; the requirement to be an individual yet also part of a team; to face sometimes cruel competition but also to show and enjoy compassion, in short, a paradox of passions. But for those to whom it is a refuge from an unsettled home, it can be a lifelong blessing.

Beyond the small, red-brick Midland town of Buckingham, there stands an idyll so complete, so perfect in its valleys and its buildings, that no one should be in any doubt of the power of wealth, God, refinement, architecture, landscape and taste to create an earthly heaven. Spread over seven hundred acres, this man-made Elysium is announced in one direction by a great Corinthian Arch, in another by a classically arched bridge that floats above an artificial lake, and further on, two 'pepper pots' or pavilions complete this splendid scene.

Once on the broad level of the mansion house itself, two crescent pillared colonnades, an equestrian statue and a marble hall, a Pantheon in homage, may be found. At its southern end, a large wooden door opens onto a flagstone portico. It was here, for the very first time, I held this view and took in the salty spring air, the distant humbling of the villages beyond, and dreamt of being something. Here was the vista, the landscape of my youth, of which Alexander Pope had written in *An Epistle to Several Persons*:

'Nature shall join you; time shall make it grow.
A work to wonder at—perhaps a Stowe.'

When I entered the school in March of 1970, Stowe stood, as
had been the intention of its founding headmaster, J.F. Roxburgh, in
the top six of the great English public schools. That was straightway
fostered on us, as were weekly classes on the history of the house
and aristocratic families to whom it had been home, and ethos fell
upon us like the Midland rain. For my first term, I huddled in a new
boys' house, waiting for my place in the main school building in the
autumn. There were no predations then from the older boys, about
which the twenty or so of us had separately been warned in leaving
words from our prep school headmasters.

Madly, I had brought three letters with me from my 'attachment',
which I kept under my pillow. These I soon burned, not without
sorrow, in the woods one day, mercifully without being found out.
And what woods they were, dotted with glorious temples and
eye-catchers, 'grotesques' if you will, to which one day a fellow pupil
took me to reveal his hidden treasure. English was a Nairobi boy and,
since childhood, had a Kenyan nanny, a *baboe*, devoted to him. Each
month she would write him a letter, and each month he would devour
its contents with well-practised relish.

So it was we walked in dew-drop May over grassland verdant as the
Veld, to rest our limbs under a monument to Queen Caroline in sunshine. After some initial rustling, he produced '*La Bombe Surprise*'. It was
a marijuana joint, rolled with three cigarette papers and a cardboard
roach. Inexpertly, I filled my virgin lungs, with all the splutter of a young
kitten drinking milk. Dizziness came over me and a nauseous feeling.
Sky became earth, and earth unsafe beneath my feet. I could not move.
For English this was everyday, and his hard head thought nothing of it.

I was going to be sick but there was no time for that. From
nowhere came a shouting voice. It was an under-gardener from the
school, who recognised our herbal waft. "Run," said English and, in
my delirium, I obeyed. This was hardly *Kubla Khan* as we burst ourselves, stumbling and falling, now up again, two miles onwards to the
safety of the school. English jettisoned the envelope's contents. Back
in my dormitory, I hid, head spinning, under the covers.

Three weeks later, I was caught smoking in a simulated grouse butt at Gallyons Shooting School in Cambridge, on an educational day out. My partner in crime became a lifelong friend. We were not punished. Then there were idle walks to the 'greasy spoon' three miles away in town, The Baron's Grill. There I would attempt fruitlessly to attract the eye of local girls but, not being equipped with a leather jacket and Triumph Norton Commando, failed miserably. Christ that countryside was cold. The sky was an endless grey and when the summer came, the shrieks of cricket on the South Front lawn were nothing but annoying. I preferred the Gothic library and there would work and read and dream in silence.

My final acting, aged fifteen, was as Carol Melkett in Peter Shaffer's *Black Comedy*, a part that Lynn Redgrave had made her own on Broadway, as had my friend Anna Chancellor in a London revival in the 1990s. My mother had given me a turquoise mini-dress with feather trimmings. One manoeuvre involved jumping over the back of a sofa as the stage turned from dark to light. The dress came open at the front. Six hundred wolf-whistles made my shame complete. But I got good notices and quite a lot of unwanted attention. 'Pansy' Pete, a slightly older boy, even tried it on whilst playing football, sliding into me and, when I was down, brazenly making a grab.

I sunk back into the adolescent shadows. I may have daringly worn dabs of Patchouli oil and bell-bottom flares from the King's Road, and even had a Kensington Market Afghan coat for weekends, but this was nothing out of the ordinary for the time. We were allowed to grow our hair and try to look like Brian Jones. The one who did it best was Part, a cynical London boy whose father had a general store in Chelsea and whose mother had married second time a gentleman farmer in the Cotswolds. He was spot on with his music, underground, and also rolled a lethal reefer. Above the shop in Sloane Street we would sit on the flat roof, inhaling, and I would pretend to be asleep when he was snogging girls. In the country, he had a den, where we plumed up daily. How his family did not spot that we were off our faces, I will never know. He took me to a villa on Gozo off Malta and, each night, we stole the family car and went drinking Bacardi and Coke in horrid tourist bars. One night he slept with the family nanny of his two young stepsisters whilst I was in the room, her protesting moans rising above a Bill Haley record on permanent repeat. She had a boyfriend back at home she kept telling him, but he persisted. The last thing that I heard her say as she gave in was: "Oh well, what the eye don't see, the heart don't grieve over."

But it was not all high tide and green grass. That friendship, too, went wrong, another theft by him, this time his brother's driving licence. We hired two mopeds, both underage, and drove to a Rolling Stones concert at Wembley Arena. On the way back, we were picked up by the police outside Peter Jones and told to report the next week to the Chelsea police station. I thought no more about it and went to a teenage party near Oxford, pretty villages but flat, monotonous countryside. I got stalked at the Oxford Bus Station by a trench-coated pervert. I escaped by running to my bus and sitting next to a woman, asking her: "Would you mind pretending you are my mother as that man out there is chasing me?" She agreed.

Nor did I think anything of it on the Monday morning when I was given pride of place in my host's helicopter for a ride back to the Battersea Heliport. Opening the door of my mother's now enormous house in Thurloe Square, she was waiting in the drawing room. "You have brought disgrace upon the family," she seethed. The police, in my absence, had been round to see her. What followed was four days of interrogation at the police station. My mother pulled out all her charms to stop me going to Court. "What would the papers say?" she argued. She was presenting a television programme called *Police Five* at the time. I was let off and afterwards she forgave me over a four-course rooftop lunch at the Meridiana restaurant in South Kensington. Part was punished with a Community Order and never spoke to me again.

There were few top bands that I had not seen by 1973. The radio had been my farmyard escape in childhood. The concerts were the escape of my teenage years. In February of 1971, there was to be a double bill of Genesis and Supertramp in the school music hall. Early in the afternoon, I squeezed through an open window and hid in the footlights to watch and hear Supertramp rehearse, alone. After some hours, I was caught by Burdon, the prefect in charge of the music hall, and told to leave. We were stopped, however, by that fine Old Stoic Roger Hodgson, bassist of Supertramp, who told him I could stay. I don't think Supertramp have ever played, before or since, to an audience comprising just a fourteen-year-old schoolboy, now seated in the front row.

Oddly, two less famous musical moments from my schooldays remain with me. One was that prodigy Howard Goodall, whose turns on the chapel organ as we left the service would begin with some serious choral music and then break into, amongst other ditties, *I'm Popeye the Sailor Man*. Then there was my study-mate Jeremy (he later changed his name to Jess), who adored Donny Osmond and was a fine pianist. At one end-of-term concert he sang, and got away with it because he was a North Londoner: "I used to be an Auschwitz hero, now I'm stuck in Rio de Janeiro, Oh, Those good old, bad old days."

One day in the Baron's Grill I heard from the bikers, for they were frequenters of Friars, Aylesbury, a famous pop dive, about David Bowie. I got tickets, but they were for Taunton. I rustled up three friends, one of whom helped out doing Community Service in the school mini-bus, which was stolen for the journey. It was only afterwards with it safely back in its shed that we realised none of us had driving licences. But we had caught the matinee performance, one of two that day when Ziggy played guitar. I also went to the concert at the Hammersmith Odeon on the 3rd of July, 1973, which he announced on stage was to be his last. It was widely filmed and reported as a shock. But the bikers had tipped me off. I got there just in time as, that afternoon, I had to cut short my Biology O level to get the train from Bletchley, leaving behind a locust half dissected in formaldehyde. I passed.

Brian Stephan was the master we most admired, with a poodle called Muffin on his lap and a briar-pipe, he was as old as Father Time to us. He taught me English. Slightly to the Left as I look back, he carried his wisdom in the burlap of his prodigious memory. Had he really been a racing driver in the Twenties and played piano in the jazz clubs of Chicago? Now he lived in a village near the school, married to another master's widow and to life at school. In the two years he taught me, he always gave me B+, nothing more or less, for my eager English essay efforts. I repaid him badly with a C at A level. In his later years, he wrote his own reminiscences, *Hearsay and Memory*, where we learned so little about a man of such sagacity. Perhaps he was just too kind to be a writer. His only dislike was for T.H. White. Whether or not this was because White had made something of himself as a writer and gone to Hollywood, or because he was a homosexual, I cannot say.

The Headmaster was in thrall of my mother and was always popping up at picnics in the grounds, just as I was smoking or drinking champagne out of the back of her Bentley. He reluctantly made me Head Boy. "Against my better judgement, I am going to make you Head Boy," he told me in his ornate Grinling Gibbons study, to which I, slightly stunned, slowly replied: "Against my better judgement, I am going to accept." Years later, I got the secret records of my school career, in support of the Oxford place I would turn down, and read what the Headmaster had written in his submission: 'Probably the best if most unorthodox Head Boy in the twelve years that I have been Headmaster.' In these notes my history tutor just wrote: 'Dilettante.'

I did not visit many farms in the Buckinghamshire countryside, but cycled to plenty of churches and villages: Marsh Gibbon, Dadford, Syresham, Stratton Audley, Yardley Gobion, Grendon Underwood. It was flat going on a bicycle and, in the summer, the lanes were full of wild plants and bees. Once or twice I went again to Oxford, to the Randolph. I never took to Oxford and it never took to me; too suburban, with men wearing college scarves beyond a seemly age, or clinging on to youth in their heraldic track suits, like ageing football managers. Even at my Oxbridge interview I was jinxed. Walking with an interviewing don through a quad, there was a young man working a cement mixer whom I knew from school. He squirted us both with water. Later, when I was a guest speaker at the Oxford Union I lost both times. I got my rejection in earlier, not taking up my deferred place at St John's.

Towards the end of my school days, the White Russian Prince was replaced by another man, another religion, East End this time, something of a Peter Sellers lookalike. My mother took to Zionism with alacrity, another little orphaning for me. I should have spotted the menorah candle on the mantelpiece at home, and the Chelsea boots outside my mother's bedroom door. I felt the bitterness of Baudelaire when his father died and his mother hastily remarried. So it is we learn to live our lives as we dream—alone.

Neville did his best. He was my mother's fashionable bit of rough. That he adored her I have no doubt. That it turned out bad, after a Register Office wedding and a forty-year run, could be traced to these earlier years. My mother was a spendthrift, and Neville was bad with the accounts. Was he a mensch or a jerk? They dined out all the time under the light of an unrealistic silvery moon. An open-topped Rolls-Royce joined the Bentley and then a Porsche, all three at the same time. I got to drive the Porsche a bit, when they had too much to drink, and I would take them home, myself not entirely sober. Nor can I say that I was not a beneficiary of their 'client lunches', fine three-hour affairs for which the client paid, Chez Victor, The White Tower, The Mirabelle, The Ritz, Les Trois Canards on Knightsbridge Green. Occasionally Neville called me his son when talking to the waiters, which I rather liked, as he had no children of his own.

But we both soon realised he would have more fun with my mother if I was out the way. I could not face Devon. It was fine for the first three days and then my father tired of the very small talk he made anyway, and I was still too young to chuck back whisky with him. My aunt and her girlfriend moved to Portugal, to a small lemon farm outside Faro, a life of scratch golf and a meagre living. When I went to stay with them, years later, sleeping on a sofa surrounded by ten rescue dogs, they were reduced to riding an old motorbike. But in the cafés and taverns where I went with them, they were loved.

So I drifted down the alleyways of London, into Rupert and Dean in Soho, hanging out in music shops in Denmark's Tin Pan Alley. My hairdresser was in Pimlico, a salon with oak wooden floors, wicker chairs and a caged parrot in the corner. It could have been the setting for a Cockney Rebel cover. I bought a drum kit that I couldn't play and stuck up records sleeves in my tiny attic bedroom. I sold it soon afterwards at a profit.

Girls were still a breath away and dates were rather hit and miss affairs. One I took to see *Easy Rider* at the Paris Pullman (full kaftan and patchouli rig for this) but didn't get a load off Annie. Another, after a few fumbled exchanges of letters to our schools ('Hang loose', she wrote in one; I wondered was this a reference to my having reached puberty), I took to the King's Road Odeon to see *Borsalino*. "The girl can come in but you're too young," said the man behind the booth. I had to slip him a fiver to give in. Was it worth it? Some kissing, which I started too early and longed for it and the film to end, walking out into the evening daylight, embarrassed both. I had mumbled on the game I dare not bite.

But there was still an England to be explored. It was Neville who came up with the idea, me just back from Reading Festival where I'd seen Genesis, the Faces with Rod Stewart, Status Quo and that other Old Stoic of sauce, avant garde and erudition, George Melly, fronting John Chilton's Feetwarmers, belt out *Your Feet's Too Big*. I camped with my friend Tadge, a daring local boy who came to school then disappeared. He could have pulled the birds in The Baron's Grill. We swam across the Thames to get early morning milk from a float, the current worryingly strong. To make those standing in the field at the front of the stage sit down, those at the back urinated into their empty beer cans and hurled them forward.

Neville had a fourth car in the fleet, a three-litre silver Ford Capri, with an all-important speed bump on the bonnet. He handed me the keys. "Get lost for a few weeks," he said, me just seventeen, and I did. Not just rural England, but Wales and Scotland, too. I took three schoolfriends with me, one of whom had actually passed a driving test. We set off for three weeks of freedom and camping, sponging a bed, sleeping rough, petrol at fifty pence a gallon. First I took it for a spin to Lavender Hill, with the 'Old Dear,' as my starlet mother was known for some reason to my school friends out of hearing. I managed to 'do a ton' under the bridge at Queenstown Road and me just with L plates.

Our exodus from the capital was more sedate, to Wells and the scrumpy fields of Somerset, Glastonbury Tor, Bath and Bristol, those lazy semi-cities, bathed in light and darkness behind closed doors. That first night we camped in a meadow of chickens, an ox-bow stream for washing. My tent-mate threw up at dawn, the grateful chickens devouring their regurgitated brethren that, only hours before, had been nestled in a pub bar basket. On to Wales and Merthyr, Crick-howell, Brecon, the chain library of Hereford Cathedral, Tintern Abbey, Ludlow.

At Bridgnorth, we got to stay indoors, a run-down farmhouse where its one-time fighter pilot owner lived as a recluse, an old sheepdog (still called 'Puppy') in the kitchen by his feet. Like all people who live alone, it was not always possible to separate his facts from flights of fancy. By day we knocked down an old pigsty and trailed him with a bull to market, and sat about, drinking cups of tea and smoking. It soon became apparent, however, we were in the company of an exceptional man, a bachelor who understood the young. We all kept in touch with him separately throughout our grown-up lives.

One night he opened his hand and on his palm were four neatly rolled joints. "Wages," he said, and we consumed them. He lived under Wenlock Edge, that long escarpment so admired by A.E. Housman, who never went there. But it was a good few days of soil and sunshine, where the slow movement and burr of Shropshire was perhaps unchanged since the poet's made-up days. Grass divided the middle of the smaller roads, chickens crossed the village streets without looking, and the pubs were full of farmhand swains. Our host made his living scanning pregnant ewes and kept a shire horse in a barn. He was not a 'countryman' but a man who had made his life in the country, for privacy and peace of mind. There are few places more suited to this than the Borderlands of England and Wales, where mist and mysticism intertwine and tall stories tower to be believed. I rather envied him his life, a life of giving up, without dependents and all his time his own.

Years later, when I had got a proper job in journalism, I was having lunch with a literary editor who told me, without a shred of blush, that he had never been to the Lake District. Even as a teenager, I could not wait to go there, with all those daffodils, opium, Wordsworth, 'Dry Bob' Southey, Coleridge and John Peel. On the way we stopped at Blackpool, one night in a B&B, shared room, as miserable as *Death in Leamington*. I walked alone along the promenade, futile, overcome, the gaudy glare, the forced laughter, the brief respite from hellish jobs, factories, mills and mines, shrieks from the Ghost Train, parents counting money, wondering if they could afford the trip, rows of desolation.

At Wigton, just north of Penrith, a real farm, and a 'Hound Dog' for fell racing, was our next abode. In Cumbria you "don't get owt for nowt", and we were put to work by farmer Gilbert Baird, another barn to be demolished from seven every morning. It was not the work that was the marathon, but the feeding times: sandwich at seven, full breakfast at nine, elevenses, cooked lunch, tea at four. On our last night of the week, the family took us out, to a ribald show at the Wheeltappers and Shunters Social Club or equivalent, three-course meal included. Even when we got home, they insisted on a sandwich and a glass of milk.

Another night we went to the dogs, 'hound trailing' high on Cleator Moor amongst the ferns and fells, a quick pint in the Odd-fellows Arms at Caldbeck on the way and a visit to John Peel's grave. "What's your dog called?" I asked Mr Baird, as we sheltered behind makeshift bookmakers' stands, the panorama of the fells before us. "The Hound Dog," he replied. "Just Gilbert's Hound Dog." I felt a warm comfort from Gilbert's few words, self-contained, like a blunt instrument chipping rocks. But these dogs are a sporting lifeblood here, a canine identity for Cumbria. Many are kept in small kennels in the villages, treated like royalty or one of the family, coats brushed daily and nails clipped on their hare-feet. I once rang Melvyn Bragg, and apologised for disturbing him which he said I was. When I explained I was writing about hound trailing, he kept *me* on the telephone for twenty minutes. He had been brought up hound trailing as a boy, his uncle had won the trailing Grand National, and it was an important connection to the county that made him, and the play he wrote about Cumberland, *The Hired Man*.

From Cumberland, the Solway Firth wide divides England from its Celtic neighbour Caledonia. Gretna was our first stop, and a stay loch fishing on a lowland estate, then to Lochmaben Castle, birthplace of King Robert the Bruce, whose crest and coat of arms I bear, *Fuimus*, 'We were', short for *Fuimus rex*, 'We were kings.' But it was his saying, watching a spider in a cave sheltering from his English pursuers, that we learned at birth: "If at first you don't succeed, try, try and try again."

My family is not particularly important in the chain of clanship, and really is known, if at all, as 'The Aberdare Bruces'. A descendant of the chief and forbear of mine came down to Wales from Scotland in the 17th century, settling in Aberdare. Longing for his homeland, he insisted that his workmen wore Highland dress. One day, a geologist came to his lands, and told him that, unlike his neighbours, he had got no coal. He pondered that the kilts would have to go. He pondered that his status as a gentleman was under threat. "You have got not coal," the geologist repeated. "You have got iron." And so the kilts and family fortunes were assured, a peerage for one son, a knighthood for another, the third promoted to a bishopric. He made a steelworks employing thousands, and became an MP for Maidstone. When he died early, Disraeli, the other Kent MP, married his widow and her fortune. A final vestige of his wealth is my farm, all that remains of the kilts and millions.

There had been two boys at school who talked romantically of Scotland, and it appealed to me. Now I was driving for the first time into Edinburgh, down Queensferry Road, and then to park outside the castle. I went to a pub, ate a stovie, heard the 'One O'Clock Gun'. Outside the pub, there was a chalkboard menu sign that should have read 'salads'. Someone had altered it to read: 'Come inside for a wide variety of LADS'. I made a pact with those boys that we would all go to Edinburgh University. I was the only one who did, but that was still two years away.

From Edinburgh we crossed the Highland Line, to stay in a vast mansion north of Inverness. Although there must have been thirty bedrooms, we were all piled into one. I slept on the floor in my sleeping bag, not quite *Brigadoon* or the Highland welcome of those romantic stories, more a case of "Ye'll have had your tea." But something about the Scottish character and landscape got into me then, and has never left.

There is a common and proud heritage to Scotland. No one ever rushed to claim their Englishness, but, given a drop of Scottish blood or a Scottish surname and you are on the way to being an accepted native. For the true Scot, which I do not claim to be, their longest journey is a lifelong voyage to assert their Scottishness. Years later, I asked my oldest Scottish friend if, given that I had just been dining with my Clan Chief, did he think I could call myself Scottish, given that I am called Bruce? "So are lots of Australians," he replied.

So ended our adolescent journey, a rainy drive south with only one windscreen wiper keeping time. "We only came on this journey to see if we liked you," the vomiting one said as we neared London. There was a resounding silence. Once back, I thought it only right to polish Neville's car, which I did with a bucket of water and a Brillo pad. It began to gleam. Only when the water had dried did I realise I had scoured off the silver paintwork and it had to be resprayed.

❧

It is not 'Better to travel than to Arrive'

On the way home, I thought about Robert Louis Stevenson's saying: "Little do ye know your own blessedness; for to travel hopefully is a better thing than to arrive." In my relief, I am not sure I agreed with him.

Writing about travel is a hallowed art, and those who do it, and I am not one, carry about them a desert boot world-weariness as if they are something special. It is a fallacious halo, tinged with not a little snobbery. I once directed Mary Miers, who writes about her travels in the Highlands, to my friend Tom Helme, the artistic co-founder of the company that changed all our homes, Farrow & Ball, a man of immense refinement and taste. On the West Coast of Scotland he has rescued an Edwardian estate and brought it to a standard of modern European civilisation. On my assurances, he agreed to see her, opened his house with a stay and hospitality. In return, she wrote about him as a 'paint manufacturer'.

In the mid 1980s, when I was flogging space at the Spectator, there was an effete, Oxford-educated Old Harrovian, Philip Marsden-Smedley (we called him 'Mars Bar' in the office, his family had made money making darning wool) who worked in something called 'Direct Marketing', basically getting people to put those loose leaflets into the magazine. He was annoyingly good looking, and had an affected way of speaking, and a manicured lisp. His sense of grandeur morphed him into the award-winning travel writer Philip Marsden, and from his prestigious eerie he could look down on us, mere journalists or salesmen in the printed trade. I noticed, however, some years later, he was not slow to trill like a bird to some weekend supplement when he was trying to sell his family home in Cornwall.

Sent to interview Jan Morris in Wales (who, she told me, wrote by speaking into a dictaphone), I spent a lapidary day with her at the Welsh cottage shared with her ex-wife. I may not have been on tip-top form as I had spent the night before reunited with the Indian girlfriend in a downtown Porthmadog hotel. Jan was not an easy subject, bossing, correcting and polishing my questions and her answers. But it was after lunch that her true colours emerged. Standing up and offering to clear the plates, she told me: "Sit down, that's woman's work." It was certainly embarrassing for me, and also, I suspect, for the ex-wife sitting opposite, who duly did the honours.

Then there was that dandy of the diaspora, Paddy Leigh Fermor, with whom I spent several happy days—more accurately, long and drunken lunches and dinners, over many years in Karadamyli. Even in 1986, when I told the Spectator's Literary Editor, Mark Amory, that I was going to see him, he remarked that he was "out of date". You would arrive to three ouzos and a swim. At dinner, beer mats were placed on top of full glasses of wine, frequently topped up. The perfect host. Only once did I make the mistake of saying on leaving I had enjoyed his book, Mani. "Joan wrote it you know," he said, refer-ring to his wife. She certainly undertook all the arduous mountain walks with him, making notes, and, no doubt, making things up.

One weekend staying in Cornwall, a fellow guest was the literary agent Gillon Aitken, who represented Bruce Chatwin, Salman Rushdie and other big names. He asked me to come and see him with a book idea. It was the only time I thought about travel writing, and he soon disabused me. Arriving in his smoke-filled office (smoking in the workplace had been comprehensively banned by then) we had a chat. From his laden bookshelf of his own published authors, he got down two books, one by Sebald, the other by Theroux. "I want you to write like them," he told me, his sapphire eyes giving me full beam. Having read them, I thought they just made things up. All writing has to have an anchor of fact to be believed. You cannot just meet random strangers on a journey and ascribe your thoughts to them, or patronise grotty places, eulogise your own sense of beauty, belittle suburbs and talk to old folks on the bus. With Gillon, I realised I could never, like Sebald, turn Felixstowe into some snowy mountain top with a blue flat lake, a Bavarian Konigssee.

If in later life there seems unheralded to appear a litany of woes, so sometimes in youth there are occasional surprises of happiness. I returned to school, no more worldly wise, a prefect, Head of House, Head Boy, Oxbridge, rugby, and editing the school magazine, mainly so I could squeeze in my adolescent poems in the blank spaces we had to fill between sports reports and old articles about the main house in its private splendour. Five girls arrived and one day I fell in love.

Nicola was a day girl, one of four daughters, the mother at home, the father had pissed off. They lived in a stone-built bungalow not far away and there, for the next year, I would spend some very happy days and nights, fussed over by five women. This was not a tale told by the Miller, but by the Merchant:

> 'Ladyes, I prey yow that ye be nat wrooth;
> I kan nat glose, I am a rude man—
> And sodeynly anon this Damyan
> Gan pullen up the smok, and in he throng.'

What I would not give for that one summer now, when we did nothing much, swim, walk the dog, baby-sit for teachers, ride the pony Kelpie and one other whose name I can't remember, my little Stainsby girl, a Galadriel of wantoness. We did it all, we broken every code. Some nights we talked till dawn entwined on the sofa, all the silly things that later life still longs for but looks foolish. Some might think *She Said* by Barclay James Harvest is not much, but it was just one soundtrack to our love.

Nicola had friends. There was Charlie Ross, the auctioneer and later *Flog It!* frontman, never short of laughs and words, and Stephen Yardley, famous to us then as the lead in the television series *The XYY Man*. He was hilarious and had an actor's way of speaking, long and low-voiced, that got all our attention. She drove a red Fiat 500, and gave me more than I gave back. With her I saw the Buckinghamshire countryside, happy. I was a family for a while.

Some nights we would go and drink at the Fox pub in Juniper Hill with her elder sister, Amanda, where Flora Thompson wrote *Lark Rise to Candleford*. By day, our love lay in the romantic ruins of Shelswell Park, a picnic and a spliff. Ringo the great dane was our companion, but then he went missing without us one day, never found.

"I was wondering if you were queer?" my mother asked me as we sneaked a lunchtime pint in the Queen's Elm pub off the Fulham Road. The Irish landlord, Sean Treacy, was a friend of hers and wrote *A Smell of Broken Glass*, depressing fragments about his time behind the pumps and barrels. Under the eye-height pint glass shelf, I could see Laurie Lee and the veteran *Evening Standard* cartoonist JAK in the next door bar, chatting up two girls, one black one white. I told her about Nicola, and I think she was relieved. We split up in an Italian restaurant, Dino's in South Kensington, she to go to model in Japan, me to go to university. We had planned to go to see the Rolling Stones at Knebworth, but that didn't work out. I sold my ticket to an eager student who came to the door of Thurloe Square: "Could you tell me which seat I will be in?" he asked as he handed over fifty quid.

The last night I spent at Stowe, I was alone as all the school had gone. I wanted to walk one last time down its labyrinthine ways, and hear the final silent cacophony of shouts and laughter for myself. I went to see 'Ma' Craig, head chef, chin-whiskered, built like Colette's French bulldog, Toby-Chien. She had leant me her van to take my trunk and things away next morning. She didn't soften in my thanking her, but that was just her way. As I crossed a back courtyard where the food bins got left out, I met John the servitor, whose job it was to empty them. "Come upstairs and we'll slosh some gin in a glass," he said. So, I sat with him with his pigeon toes and glance that wouldn't meet mine, face taught and white from drinking, like a lampshade where the bulb is never off, a dingy little room with an unmade bed in the corner. The navy at fourteen, parents from the Midlands, terraced, from then on always on his own in company. He liked people and solitude, and didn't question things. "Funny to say," he said as I was leaving, "this job keeps me busy and I think of it as family." I shed a tear for that and him, for Stowe had been my family, too.

I saw Nicola one last time, in the early 2000s at the literary festival at Port Eliot in Cornwall. We didn't recognise each other and had to be introduced. By then she was widowed, three children, and a husband never found, lost at sea off the West Coast of Scotland. She wore a headscarf, to hide the cancer that would claim her young life. But the elder sister I did see quite by chance, a little later on, before she too succumbed. I was in a borrowed kaftan (having wrongly been told it was a surfers' 'fancy dress' party) drinking in a village hall bar on the North Cornish coast. "Your mother always kept in touch with me and gave me her cast-off dresses," she recalled, rattling off designer names such as Gina Fratini and Piero di Monzi. That made me like my mum. Then I met a pretty Penlee lifeboat widow who fed me simultaneously Viagra and half a tab of acid. This was my night off from being a parliamentary candidate. "'Twas a mercy that he drowned," the doe-eyed Demelza told me. "I didn't love him," she added as my advances warmed her to her theme. She got paid out a million from the disaster fund and then the ruddy Kernows started coming round for courting, and she with two calves at foot. She led me out through the ladies' toilet window, into a car bound at speed for her council house in Wadebridge. Later that night she dumped me on waste ground to find my own way home. As my mother might have remarked: "What would the papers say?"

Ireland: By the time I got to Woodstock

'Being drunk and weary
I went to Molly's chamber
Takin' my money with me
But I never knew the danger
For about six or maybe seven
In walked Captain Farrell
I jumped up, fired off my pistols
And I shot him with both barrels.'

Thin Lizzy, *Whiskey in the Jar* (Traditional)

IT IS NOT easy to place Ireland in my life but, since I am half Irish on my mother's side, it has always been with me. My mother when she left Devon may have bequeathed me little, but she did bequeath me her remarkable parents, one a Group Captain with an OBE, DFC (and bar), the other one of the most courageous Catholic Christians you could wish to meet. "God is good," she wrote to me in my last month at Stowe, and died a week later. She never made a thing of her Catholicism, but never missed a service on a Sunday. I had often from childhood been to stay with them at the paradise that was my grandfather's historic Wicklow fruit farm and estate. It was a life made mellow by money; settled, active, breakfast, lunch and supper all on time, porridge, carrot soup and, best of all, boiled ham with parsley sauce, fluffy potatoes grown at home.

Charles Herbert Tighc, after Malvern and Trinity College, Dublin, a brave war in Palestine and France, returned to his native Ireland and Ballina Park. He was once caricatured in *Tatler* as 'Tight Lieutenant Fly'. Although the estate had been in his family for two hundred years, it was the generous gift of a bachelor uncle that allowed him to live there in considerable style, swimming pool, butler, twenty outdoor men who universally looked up to him and called him, 'The Group'.

Then there was the main family estate, Woodstock, at Inistioge, Kilkenny, a shell since 1922, when it fell victim to 'The Troubles' and was burned down. Of the long history of my grandfather's family, there were many MPs, judicious marriages (my mother was proud to be related to many of the Irish peerage *and* the Earl of Darnley), and, in 1905, more than 20,000 acres, now all but gone. The poetess Mary 'Psyche' Tighe was a friend of Byron, Keats and the Shelleys. A marble headstone of her by Flaxman marks her life at Woodstock and nearby grave. John Wesley had been to stay and preach. One or other of the 'Two Ladies of Llangollen' was a cousin, or perhaps it was both. Their intimate Welsh soirées in their cottage orne (preserved and open to this day) included Lord Byron and The Duke of Wellington, who brought odd bits of furniture to embellish the intriguing architecture of this low-ceilinged dwelling. Another family member had been murdered in the Russell Square hotel in London during the First World War in suspicious circumstances. T.E. Lawrence's father, Thomas Robert Tighe Chapman, Baronet, was another relative, which a genealogist once told me makes 'Lawrence of Arabia' my seventh cousin. Oddly, none of Lawrence's biographers have made this Tighe connection, which might have gone some way to explain the illegitimate Lawrence's confusion about his social status, his high intelligence and aristocratic mien.

There was literary prominence on my grandmother's side as well, but this was less talked about. Her grandfather had been the poet, essayist and friend of Tennyson, William Allingham, over whom there also hung some question of legitimacy. But there is no question about his legacy. In Irish schools even today his poem, *The Fairies*, is still learned and read:

'Up the airy mountain,
Down the rushy glen,
We daren't go a-hunting
For fear of little men:
Wee folk, good folk,

Trooping all together
Green Jacket, red cap,
And white owl's feather.'

When, on the centenary of his death in 1989, I was asked to go and speak about Allingham on Sean Rafferty's BBC radio programme, I did it with a local woman from 'The Allingham Society' in Ireland who was speaking from a radio booth somewhere in Donegal. She was adamant and vociferous on air in her attempts to discredit me. "He can't be a descendent of William Allingham, he's got an English accent," she rasped at one point. It would seem churlish to point out that Allingham's father was himself English.

But the greatest family heroine of them all was Lady Louisa Gordon-Lennox, who, as a young child, had tied her godfather the Duke of Wellington's sword buckle at the famous Duchess of Richmond's ball the night before the Battle of Waterloo. He gave her his watch for safe keeping. Later, much to the dismay of her father, the Duke of Richmond, she married into Woodstock, the Tighes and the Emerald Isle. This did not, however, prevent him, on one occasion, coming to stay for four months. All this has been recorded with the felicity that only the Irish can have for their own history, in *The Story of Woodstock*, by local historian Thomas J. Whyte. Above my fireplace is a portrait of William Tighe of Woodstock, MP, painted by Batoni when William was on his two-year Grand Tour. It may well be a copy, as it was known in the family as 'The Phoney Batoni'.

What Louisa Tighe achieved in more than fifty years as chatelaine of Woodstock was to build churches, both Protestant and Catholic, houses, schools and workshops making lace, employment for the locals all around. Then there were the acres of terraced and formal gardens, which no rebel torch could destroy. With the wide salmon river Nore running through, Inistioge has a claim to be the prettiest village in Ireland. The Circle of Friends café recalls the film made there in 1995, starring Minnie Driver.

Nothing in my Irish childhood could rival the happiness of working for my grandfather. We would drive down to Woodstock in his black capacious Jaguar and spend the day clearing rides or felling scrub, the smell of pine and wet ferns underfoot, for Nature's hand did not stand still. Where once forty gardeners had kept it up, we were now a handful of willing volunteers, the farm workers from Wicklow and me, and Cody the old gardener who stayed on from loyalty and the days of splendour he remembered as a child. Now the gardens are run by the Irish State, which has spent millions on their restoration. I still sit amongst the ruins of the old house (having paid my four euros parking fee) and wonder, in that *Kind Hearts and Coronets* sort of way, what might have been in it for me if they hadn't 'shot Captain Farrell.'

These were my Irish teenage years of summer sun and endless skies. There were Irish cousins in the house at Ballina Park, but none were particularly friendly to me, and my mother's elder sister, a loud and lumpen figure, took out her dislike of my mother on me. One of her favourite rules was, at teenage parties, that those under fifteen had to go home an hour early at eleven o'clock. I was the only fourteen-year-old. "The thing about Ireland is you have got to knock on the door from the inside from an early age," Tom Somerville, descendent of Edith Somerville, told me one evening some years later over cheese and whiskey, at Drishane, his Castletownshend home. I understand that now.

But for a farm-mad teenager such deep-seated nuances of social difference meant nothing to me. Nor, I think, did they mean much to the farmworkers with whom I daily toiled. When a new combine harvester came, it was as if a ship had been launched, and the potato harvester was another modern miracle. But, by and large, life on the farm was done by many hands, perhaps even then fifty years behind our own farm life in Devon.

The swineherd was a seldom sober man. The hogs he castrated with a rusty razor. When I travelled with him with a lorryload of fruit to Dublin market, gypsies or gurriers would be mending pots and pans by the side of the road, their ponies tethered grazing on some meagre verge, and wisps of smoke plumed up from an ever-tended fire, the children like the boy in El Greco's *La Fábula*. When they came to the farm at fruit-picking time, I never saw figures more forlorn, families of ten or more, working in cowed and desperate silence. There was no wassail for them. They knew their place, and it was ever to be dispossessed, without security or rights, no vote or home even in the New

Republic. My grandfather gave them work and a lay-by off the farm to pitch their wooden caravans. Pay day was a revelation. I would sit with him behind a makeshift table and they would queue up, a record having been kept of how many baskets of fruit (plums, raspberries, tomatoes, strawberries, apples) they had collected. Some would have tried to weigh down their baskets with stones, unsuccessfully. Nine hundred pounds we paid out one week. I never held so much money in my hand before.

Visits to the ironmonger and the smithy, travelling the cows to be served by a hill farm bull, were all part of this farming life. Occasionally we went to another small farm my grandfather owned, a bothy on Wicklow's Sugarloaf Mountain, where the old couple still spoke only Gaelic and their peat fire never went out.

The men on the farm at Ballina Park worked without complaint, happy, perhaps, in the simple garth of being drunk and weary. Certainly they had no inkling of life within the house, and, even if they did, they did not begrudge the gulf and thought no more about it. The steward's son, Matt Law, was my friend. I never went into his house but, after work, he being still at school or not in evidence upon the farm, I would knock on his side door and we might go into the grain barns ratting just to frighten ourselves silly. His father's sheepdog was a hand in this. By the timber yard, an old car had been left abandoned. We would play in this for hours. The gear-stick still worked, and the steering wheel had some movement in it. We must have travelled miles in that stationary car, never into adulthood or far horizons. For some reason, he always let me drive and my insistence would not persuade him to have it otherwise. Where we were equals was on our night-time ramblings. A favourite was the night-time three-mile walk to sit in the garden of Hunter's Hotel and listen to the grown-ups laugh within and wonder at their folly. We were happy to spot trout in the Vartry, under the shadow of the old stone bridge. There was a green sign in the garden that read: 'Gentlemen may not, and others will not, pick the flowers.' I never showed that to Matt.

At five o'clock each evening when I was in the house, my whole world changed. Into the bath and some crushed velvet loon pants, then driven to a pub (one might even have been called The Dewdrop Inn) to meet others of our teenage gang and sometimes go to a party.

My Irish cousins did not have to explain themselves to anyone. They were all friends from school holidays. For me it was a battle to get a word in, often to be met with bemusement as to what I was actually doing there. My downfall was at Powerscourt, under the waterfall of that great Wicklow mansion. Heady with beer, I made a pass at a cousin. What I next remember was being fed coffee in the kitchen, itself the size of any self-respecting rectory, waiting with rising horror for my grandparents to pick me up on their way back from dinner in Dublin. Into the back of the Jag, smell of scent, two dinner guests of theirs, sweeping nausea. The car stopped by the side of the road, close by the dim glow of a gurrier fire, where I attempted unsuccessfully to be sick. "We have a long history of car sickness in our family," I heard my grandmother say. Next morning, she had a quiet word with me, protecting me from a grandfatherly lecture, and I loved her for it. God is good.

Over the years, I have returned many times to Ireland, always with a feeling of optimism and naive love for the sport, friendship and confused pub conversations. Ballina Park was sold in the late 1970s, and my grandfather died in 1995. I paid to fly my mother over from the Holy Land, where she and Neville had started up a pottery. "I've left him behind," she told me as I carried her suitcase into Hunter's Hotel, for the funeral and the wake. "No... I've left him." Apparently he had been jailed for once again trying to give the tax man the slip. "It's called 'Flight into Egypt', not 'Flight from Israel,'" I replied, and paid for her to go and fetch him back. From then on, and the reason for several of my visits, my mother and Neville went to live in Ireland in circumstances far removed from their days as 'Bentley Boys'; rented cottages, a living making fruit preserves and marmalade in family crested jars.

Of the houses that have shown the greatest kindness to me, none has surpassed Garech Browne at the fairytale Luggala, or his cousin Kieran Guinness in Westmeath, Richard Filgate in Louth, Giles and Alexandra FitzHerbert in Wexford, or their good neighbours, the Durdin Robertson's at Huntington Castle in Carlow. I have had some very happy stays with Sir Jack Leslie and his niece Sammy at Glaslough. All have been kind enough to consider me as Irish when in their homes, an insider for a little while, however made up that might be.

My mother never liked me staying long. Even when she had a rented cottage at Altamont in Carlow, those magical and exotic gardens made famous by their owner Corona North, there was another nearby cottage to plonk me in. Two days was enough. When Corona died, they moved again, to another smaller cottage. I did not stay there. In her eighties, my mother started failing and I would send her money for her heating bills, much of which I think was spent on screw-top wine. The end, when it came, was fairly swift, but held for me another twist and turn.

With her White Russian prince, my mother had another son, now fifty, and I had not seen him for more than twenty years. "Get your skates on, she is not long to live," he rang me one day, and so I went to the Carlow nursing home where, with typical finesse, she had commandeered the best room in the place, private bathroom, garden view. My mother rarely mentioned this other son, except to say he would turn up and ask her for money. Now, oddly, he was sleeping in her nursing home bedroom; she had been transferred to Kilkenny hospital.

"You can't see her without His Highness's permission," a kindly nurse at the hospital told me. There in the darkness loomed this tall, Slavic figure in a black overcoat, black hair, black mood, a gatekeeper to the 'Old Dear's' final hours. Neville was at the bedside stroking her arm, something of a change from the occasions on which, she had told me, he had tried to strangle her.

"How many religions have we got here?" he said at length. "How much faith?" I replied, as the princeling urged me: "Touch her, go on touch her." My mother, thanks be to God and morphine, was oblivious to all this. I did not want to touch her. The princeling had the measure of the nurses. Two brought in some drink and food and he, taking them to one side, muttered: "Go out and treat yourselves," wafting some of my mother's notes—they were *my* notes—from under his cape. I almost think they curtsied. She died next morning, for which relief much thanks.

I took the Russian out to breakfast, him being grand and otiose with the waitress, me paying the bill, as we sat outside the Lord Bagenal hotel near the nursing home, me looking at the water of the River Barrow running by. I was struck by the almost violent anger of his words, his lack of comprehension of himself. He told me that all his school year at Bedales had signed a petition to have him removed (Minnie Driver was one of them). He left. He had a poor relationship with his father, had followed Neville and Mum to Israel before he over-heard them say: "We only came here to get away from him." He had married briefly and young and now lived in a rented flat in Margate, quite a successful film prop maker I should say to give him credit. He had clearly stoked Neville against me, not that much encouragement was needed.

But Neville loved my mum, called her 'Princess', and treated her as if she were a gilt-edged client, a trophy public relations account. Yes, there may have been a few throttlings towards the end, but by then his mind and eyesight were failing. These were only the throws of infirmity and age.

The princeling said he'd organise the funeral and, on the way, emptied my mum's bank account of ten grand. Is that what she intended? I will never know. A silence fell on these proceedings. My request to see a Will or ask if this is what she wanted were refused by everyone, the undertaker, the nursing home, and the unhappy princeling. But he did the funeral well, a Catholic Communion in the family church in Inistioge, a burial in the Protestant family church-yard next door. I left him to it, turning up to read a small passage she had written aged fifteen in her school book, Rye St Antony, Oxford, about the Dublin Horse Show, black ink, cursive script. As I read in church before a congregation of fifty, most unknown to me (it was a communion service open to all), Neville late, the priest giddy, three choristers, one of whom I could not help thinking resembled the 7th Marquess of Salisbury, an autumn sun played on the white marble altar, given by Louisa Tighe. I opened my mum's black schoolbook and read:

ॐ

A day at the Dublin Horse Show

We arrived there at about eleven. It was a glorious summer day; the Dublin Horse Show was at its best. The jumps were glistening white against a pure green background.

The noise and hubbub of the show had started early. Some people could be seen mingling with the crowd, the usual horsey sort of people, with long legs and felt hats tapping their boots with riding crops.

All the fashions of Dublin were there, too: Ladies with flimsy silk frocks and white hats perched on their heads, most of them stilting along on very high-heeled shoes.

We came to the 'Big Clock' where we found loose boxes stretching down the line. Intelligent heads surveyed the world from the top hatch of their loose boxes, or made conversations with their next-door neighbours. Walking down the line, we came upon a little enclosure where smart-looking Hackney ponies were moving about.

When we had admired these we walked back to the clock, where we turned left. We continued down this lane until we came to the 'Big Hall.' We left the blazing sun and walked into the cool interior.

In this hall were many little stalls where all the best equipment stores like Callaghans, the Irish Industries, and Schweppes were represented. The soda water manufacturers have a stall with a soda water bottle overflowing into a fountain; this bottle is over four feet high! Kia-Ora fruit juice had a large stand, so had Player's the cigarette makers. Miss Wynne had a lovely little stall where all her arts and crafts were exhibited. There were a great number of stalls, all attractively attired.

The jumping started in the afternoon. It was interesting for a while but it palled a bit when you had to watch forty children's ponies jumping.

So the day went on, countless numbers of people from all the countries of the world passed through the main turnstiles. There was many a meeting of old friends; people who had not seen each other for years talked of old times. Some people laughed, some clapped, horses neighed, the band played, and the flag of the Royal Dublin Society, and all the nations, flew overhead.

What to me was wholly unexpected was that as I went to resume my seat in an empty pew towards the back of the church, the congregation clapped. I did not know a lot of them, but the FitzHerberts and Alexander and Moira Durdin Robertson came to hold my hand. Many, who had just come for confession, did not know my mum. At the graveside, the princeling started smoking, firing up a cheroot for Neville—why shouldn't he have one, blind and now bereaved, before he moved on to a balloon of brandy at the wake in the nearby pub? My heart wasn't in that bit. I sensed my presence was accessory. Don't stand up gentlemen, I'm only passing through. Two ginger ales, a chicken sandwich, thank the priest. "Oh," he said, "I thought in your reading you mentioned 'THE BIG COCK.'" I went into Thomastown and lunched alone. As I passed the pub in Inistioge, two hours later, there was the princeling outside in his long frock Kursaal coat, waving his arms about and talking to the mourners as if he owned the place. I took the boat back to England, earlier than planned.

Ballrooms and a building site

'He looked without seeing anything—
thinking of himself... Then, after a time,
he murmured with conviction—speaking
half aloud to himself in the shock of the
penetrating thought: "I am a lost man."'

Joseph Conrad, *An Outcast of the Islands*

O F ALL THE fatuities in the Ages of Man, few can rival that Seventies osmosis of the Gap Year. It came out of nowhere and allowed ordinary, callow, indulged youths to think that, if they went to another country, made passing friendships or slept with foreign barmen, somehow they would return to go to university more worldly wise and interesting. Later on, I knew of several who did not come back (one swallowed by a crocodile in Tanzania, another rescued drug-insensate from a house boat in Ladakh). I only have to hear the names of Angkor Wat or Alice Springs to raise a wearied eyebrow.

Perhaps some of this feeling may have been jealousy on my part. Although I had parents who were as keen as any to get rid of me, they were not going to pay for the privilege or indeed to subsidise what might be my enjoyment. My mother had done 'The Season' at the age when she might have done a Gap Year and, as my father pointed out, as he slipped me half a pint in the local on my eighteenth, at my age he was eating 'Desert Turkey' on a tank turret off Tobruk. I think 'Desert Turkey' was another name for spam or Bully beef. Not for me the overland to India in a magic bus or working as a ski bum in Gstaad. I had some excuse to 'Gap' as I had taken Oxbridge in the seventh term, so still had nine months to fill till university.

I had a short-term job on Chelsea Green at Andre Villon's Chelsea

Pantry, starting each day at seven. My first task each morning, which I did with Philip Lowe from Stowe, was to roast some chickens and open up at eight. The clientele were not just the well to do but also from the Peabody Estate housing tenement opposite; they would shuffle in with little money, so we cut the prices for them. By eleven I was rather on my own as Lowe kept a bottle of vodka behind the fizzy drinks in the chill cabinet and would gradually get more and more drunk. I had to stop him giving things away.

Andre Villon had a column on the *Express*. Each week, I would go down to Fleet Street with his recipes, my first experience of the 'Black Lubyanka' that would later, for a year from 1987-88, become my first home with the *Evening Standard*. I am not sure what the readers made of his suggestions, but the little back kitchen where he worked, living above the shop with a succession of young men, crawled with maggots. The last hour of every day was spent trying to wash them away, fruitlessly. Once I was sent to deliver a roast chicken to Glebe Place and the door was answered in person by Lady Jacqueline Rufus-Isaacs, one of the great beauties of her day, then the lover of Lord Snowdon. Others would sometimes bring their chickens back as undercooked.

All this was going well for fifty pence an hour, and Nicola and I would sometimes picnic on the food I scavenged. After a month, I asked Andre for a rise to sixty pence, and he said he would think about it. He didn't have to think twice. One day an open-topped white Bentley with red interiors pulled up, driven by my mother and with my grandfather in the passenger seat. They had bought it after lunch and brandies for fourteen grand from H.R. Owen. My rise was not forthcoming. Lowe died in a car crash in the South of France a year later, and not yet twenty-one.

Broadening my employment horizons, I took the 52 bus from Knightsbridge to Victoria and the Labour Exchange, something of a dead-end street for employment prospects, thinly peopled by white men with roll-ups and a sprinkling of Natty Dreads. There were two reasons for this. Firstly, I needed a rugby-caused knee operation in London and, secondly, Neville, ever helpful, had convinced my mother that I should be paying rent in my own home.

So it was that bitter January of 1976, I fingered through the playing cards of job opportunity. One was for washing sports cars in Brompton Cross, the other to work as a general labourer on a house conversion off the Gloucester Road. There was no question that Mum or Neville might give me a leg up into their heady world of public relations. "If you help out a young person with a reference they always let you down," my mother had told me firmly, an odd remark given that her whole trade was about making shallow connections. I chose the building job.

My building site was 4-6, Southwell Gardens, a mansion house complete with a drawing room on the *piano nobile*, rosewood banisters, basement, cornicing and bedrooms for a family and servants. It was to be turned into flats. There were also, when I arrived for my interview, quite a few breeze blocks and cement bags in the hall. The foreman was a sparrow, wiry man, Frank Booth, something like Sam Weller in *The Pickwick Papers*. It is easy for me to remember his name as in the street opposite was a blue plaque to the social pioneer Charles Booth. "I don't think I'll get my name up there somehow," was one of the first things Frank Booth said to me, and hired me for £50 a week, £5 extra for Saturday mornings. My Neville Tax was £9, weekly.

Booth was unably assisted by his large stepson, Roger, who lived in Coulsdon and always arrived late, exhausted, often because he said his ancient Enfield motorbike had broken down again. He was a man, perhaps thirty, of slow speech and movement. As we demolished walls or mixed cement, he would impart to me the last night's episode of *Coronation Street*, a harmless enough diversion, made better in that he never asked me anything.

"I expect she's tight as a mouse's ear," Frank said to me one day when asking about Nicola. I did not pass this remark on to her. The daily routine was also crude and primitive: no toilet paper (nor any chance of sneaking it in), packed lunch, two ten-minute tea breaks, and a useless fire burning in what had been the ground floor sitting room, round which we huddled on broken furniture or upturned packing cases. It was then that I could snatch a quick read of my book. That is the only time I remember Roger asking me anything. "What's that book you're reading?" It was the Conrad book, *An Outcast of the Islands*. "No, what's it about?" he continued. I think I may have explained it in a patronising way, for which, later, I was inwardly ashamed. I tried to make it sound like an adventure story, or a travel article from a tabloid paper. "I'd like to read it after you," he said, and I warmed to him for that.

I also warmed to Frank Booth. When the rag-and-bone man and his pony and flat cart came round on a Thursday, you could hear him streets away shouting "Any old iron," which he elided into "Rion... rion". We gave him lead pipes or a boiler casing, the jade grateful of the rest. Frank always gave me a share of the takings, two quid, and afterwards sang out the ending of *Strawberry Fair* ('Shan't be round tomorrer, the donkey's pissed on the strawberries.') Sometimes he would send me on errands, all the way to Lavender Hill on my bike to collect some screws. I think he was just giving me time off.

When it came for me to go to the London Clinic for my knee operation, I got more time off. In my final consultation with the surgeon, Mr Churchill-Davidson, he passed me a Silk Cut from the silver cigarette box on his broad desk. Nicola came to visit me and somehow got into bed. I walked out on crutches a week later. When I got home, there were two small brown envelopes from Frank. He had found out where I lived and paid my wages.

As spring turned to summer, a great heatwave came upon the capital. We toiled half naked even in the shade of indoor rooms. The great respite was a tea break at eleven and three. One time, a plasterer, hired by the day, a Scotsman as it happened, did the tea, which was my job. I drank it back eagerly only to find, halfway through, he had put a rind of soap in the bottom. Frank did not have him back. Some days the owner and developer would turn up in a Rolls-Royce, and we would heave out more cement and sand. I never spoke to him, thirty, greased-back hair, public school. Later on in the day I would be asked to put a bag or two into Frank's car, and never questioned why. Once, towards the end of my time with him, he asked me to get a bradawl from a box. In it I found a glass of cider, and was shocked. I gave him the tool, kept quiet and did not admire him less.

"I know, you're an eccentric millionaire," the bank till girl said to me one day as I was lodging my earnings in Williams & Glyn's bank in South Kensington. It must have been the incongruity of my attire: an old school RAF boiler suit, red spotted neckerchief and dusty visage. After four months, I had saved enough money, even with the Neville

Tax, to think of going abroad. So it was, I missed most of the hottest summer ever on record in London for the only slightly cooler climes of Greece.

Before that, like my Irish stays, there was the double life of manual work by day and social parties in the evening. Following in her stilting footsteps as a debutante, my mother had made me a 'Deb's Delight' to 'Do The Season'. This was a pretty good passport to hell where at cocktail parties or gatherings in inexpensive restaurants I would once again meet people who knew each other and try to get along. Some stood out: the magnificent Lady 'Bubbles' Rothermere, the ghastly Tessa Dahl, whom my mother had round endlessly, both ignoring me, or the young men, just names of pity to me now: François Richli or Jeremy Graham Browne, Rufus-Isaacs or Siddeley, coiffed and cocksure, who hung out in a small basement club off Sloane Square, Frankie's, where Brandy Alexanders were the thing.

Sometimes I was included in the dinner parties at Thurloe Square, butler, cook and a pre-dinner male hairdresser for my mum, who came to put in a mane extension, popular in the Seventies. Guests might include the furniture designer and sculptor George Ciancimino (he did stuff for the pop band 10cc), David Hicks, who made her dining room carpet, or her interior decorator Ronnie Oak, camp as Mr Inman in *Are You Being Served?*; Clement Freud was creepy. "My son was Head Boy of Stowe," she told him, introducing me. "How much did they pay you to do that?" asked the satirist, famous for flogging dog food on the telly and later on accused of raping girls. "Nothing," I replied. The best was Jilly Cooper, no bra, tits hovering above the vichyssoise, a halo around her golden hair, white summer dress. When she wrote *Emily* she named the main character, 'impossible, irresistible RORY Balniel'. I later became a good university friend of the surname.

Then there was The Season's organiser, Peter Townend, who knew who everybody was and had a weakness for the company of young gentlemen and the *Almanach de Gotha*. "Sly Cat," he would say, sidling up to me and pointing at some girl. "Sly Puss," was another grade of caution. He knew all their faces and foibles and dined out for free nightly on champagne and nibbles. He was a figure of his own creation, and 'The Season' was his life. The charity balls in the Dorchester, Park Lane or Berkeley were the very worst. We all put on our black tie and a front for him that we were enjoying ourselves, at least I did. I don't think I made a single lasting friend from them.

Townend had done 'The Season' for ever, knew all the mothers when they were coming out, had been to most of their weddings. For years after he would persuade me to take him to lunch, the Westbury Hotel, Rules, Launceston Place, he was no cheap date. Once, over lunch in Rules, we both ordered a pudding of fruit compote that contained whole grapes amongst the cream. He bit into a pip and a fragment of his front tooth shot into my cranachan. I continued eating manfully, somehow swallowing the dental fuss, unnoticed.

Why did I do The Season? Graded by class, social expectation, heredity and simple circumstance, I did it until, like so many things (following your father into the City or the Regiment) it became a tolerated norm. I shudder now to think of those early evening beer nights at The Australian on Milner Street, which was the starting point, a mixture of brickies and braying Berties. Other nights it might be to meet up at The Gasworks, off that kinky bend between Chelsea and Fulham. The food was memorably vile (especially the duck à l'orange), the wine almost undrinkable to anything but a young and thirsty palate. This was made up for by a roaring fire with a priapic homosexual chess set in the drawing room and a low-ceilinged dining room upstairs where you could sit at a long, candle-lit table and press close to a girl and apologise if she didn't like it, muttering about cramped conditions. It was there one night that a rosy-cheeked 'Mayfair Merc' snogged me on the stairs as I was going to the gents.

Perhaps they are forgotten now, but in the 1970s the 'Mayfair Mercenary'—female, aged between school leaver and twenty-five—were only on the hunt for social advancement, a good time and someone to pay for it. So, I was quite surprised, being on the younger side of her requirements, and certainly not well off. Perhaps she had been told of my smart London address (perhaps by me) or was just practising for a bigger fishing expedition. I said that I was going to Greece and she said "Could I come?" Fifty quid for the ticket from a 'bucket shop' on the Edgware Road, and fifty quid to spend on two months in Attica, and all because I got an 'A' in Ancient History and fancied seeing some ruins.

❧

Having said that I think most travel writing is no good, and that I do not pretend to be any good at it myself, some things about that Greek trip are worth recalling. The first is that my travelling companion was stoical about my lack of money and austerity. We slept separately in graveyards, on tavern flat roofs, in public parks in Athens with dogs barking all night, and in the homes of kindly Greeks, sometimes on a bed or mattress in their gardens, sometimes in a room itself.

On Paxos, she had a young Scottish lord who was looking after a yacht, whose eye I think she wished to catch. I later heard that he died young. Otherwise it was catch-as-catch-can, living off large, round baker's loaves, small strips of lamb *souvlaki*, and, on a good night, a few ouzos. Each day was an endeavour about how we should travel, mainly hitch-hiking, the bus a last resort, and where to spend the night. The Mani was our main terrain, long before I had heard of Paddy Leigh Fermor but only a decade after he made his home with his wife, Joan, in Karadamyli.

The modes of transport were of a variety. Outside Delphi after a swim, we got a ride on the top of a water melon lorry. Another time by Mistras, it was in a trailer pulled by a motorised cultivator; it would have been quicker walking. Then there were the lorries where the drivers thought that we were German. I could not help but fall asleep in their hot cabins. Nowhere did we not find somewhere to sleep, even on the beach. If we were taken into a home, it would be to eat figs and honey, meagre homes with widows wearing black, kind, trusting and hospitable, perhaps a little backgammon with the son.

Outside Kalamata, an open-topped yellow sports car (playing Pink Floyd's *Shine On You Crazy Diamond*) took us to Karadamyli itself, when a thunderstorm broke. I spent three nights sleeping inside an upturned wooden boat. Here a widow took me in and, in return for washing up in her small taverna by the sea, would feed me and be cheerful. This was Lela, great friend (as I would years later find out) of the Leigh Fermor's. Lela's then was just a small room and minute terrace.

When I next went back to Lela's in 1988, she was just the same, and didn't really remember me, one of the many young travellers to whom she had shown friendship. But it was just these simple acts of kindness that allowed me to get to know the Greeks, albeit superficially. There could be no better country as a traveller to be really poor. When, many times and years later, I would stay and have those lunches and dinners at Lela's, I would spend more freely than I should. Part of this was no doubt because I had been so cared for in my poverty. Once I was overcome with a girl on the best outside table when the lights and customers were gone, the battered sea behind and the mournful cobb in silhouette, where there is a tablet to three soldiers drowned.

Another time I took the Indian girlfriend, after she had found me *in flagrante* with a schoolgirl, and, over lunch told me of three men she'd slept with whilst we were going out. There was further punishment at the beach as she stripped half-naked, sunbathing to the sound of straining and snapping German trunks, trimmed dark frond barely concealed. Her breasts, however, saag aloo, were hardly 'Gerty, Greekly perfect.' On the walk back to another village house, perhaps five miles and gorges, I monstered her in groves of olives, on rocks and dusty grass with proprietorial revenge, donkeys and widows watching and some passing hikers outside a church we did it in, a prayer and ten drachmas, *flores para los muertos,* thrice. This was not lovemaking, but Jacob and the Angel. As Somerset Maugham said to John Osborne when he told him about his first wife's adultery with a local Midland dentist. "And you trusted a woman?"

Often I dined alone at Lela's, sometimes with the Leigh Fermors and later still with the Italian writer Roberto Calasso who took Paddy's house each summer after he died. It was over dinner one night at Lela's with Roberto that we talked and ranged widely in our subjects, from Strindberg to Ibsen and Wedekind. "You have got to dig deep with your writing," he said, elegantly dressed in a flowing white muslin shirt, toying with my cuff. I realised, for all the laughter between us, that I was in the company of a great and serious man, and he was right. We summered together for two years, he taking the Leigh Fermor residence, me in a shepherd's village terraced house, where the sheep went by each morning at five and an old woman would walk her billy goat down the small main street, trundling it like a wheel barrow by holding up its back legs. We met up almost daily for some memorable dinners, the amiable spirit of both Leigh Fermor and Bruce Chatwin, both of whom Roberto published, hovering over us.

Scotland, The Knave

'O young Lochinvar is come out of the west,
Through all the wide Border his steed was the best;
And save his good broadsword he weapons had none,
He rode all unarm'd, and he rode all alone.'

Sir Walter Scott, *Lochinvar*

PITY THE BAIRN who first sees his native Scotland through a child's eyes. He will not have the advantage of comparison with other landscapes and nations, more cramped, perhaps, and less noble, a contrast against which to measure the faults and fascination of this great country, home to all who call it so, unless you chance to come from England, when the journey for inclusion and acceptance is a merry lifelong one. When I got on the sleeper that early October night in 1976 at King's Cross, like the bride-to-be in *I Know Where I'm Going!*, taken by taxi by my Scottish nannie (Neville and Mum were out to dinner and a little light Thameside dancing at the Villa dei Cesari), it was to cross a rubicon that would be my home for the next five years. I still have the ticket, First Class, £32, ONE WAY, and £100 in my pocket to last me the first year.

'Hibs, Ya Bass,' was the first scrawled sign I saw at Waverley. Another 'Hearts bite their gonads.' Welcome to this northern tribal land. I lugged my old school trunk to the taxi rank and to the Accommodation Centre of the University of Edinburgh to be allocated my berth. It was to share a room and my landlady had a Cairn terrier, annoyingly called Rory, in a basement flat off the Telford Bridge. I caught the end of Freshers' Week, stole some cider with another student from a reception for the Baha'i Society and sat in George Square drinking. The boy I shared a room with snored and the landlady wanted me to walk her dog before lessons, so I wasn't having that. Back at the Accommodation Centre, I met another student on the steps, Lionel

Halford, Scots, tall, good looking, Scottish public school, embarking on a law degree. He became my first-year best friend. We went on visits to the countryside, bound by youthful enthusiasms and a determination to have fun.

It was with his mother that I was first introduced to The Tilted Wig, one of the great New Town bars. There you might rub shoulders on a Friday night with a top Q.C. or rugby international, advocates and artists in a scene out of a Renoir painting or the native 'Enlightenment'. The bar staff wore green livery and the owners, Paddy and Jean Crossan, had the measure of their clientele. Ladies in fur coats with houses in the country Paddy called 'The mink and sables', a chieftain or two down to see their 'Man of Business' were 'The Woodentops'. In the summer there was a courtyard garden, and we would go there after sport or lectures, for an hour or two. In winter, such was the changing and amusing clientele, aided by the freezing cold outside, that it was often not possible to leave before closing time. It is the only pub that I have ever considered 'my local'. I never did approve of those who called it 'The Wilted Tig'.

After my reappearance at rehousing, I was given a room in Pollock Halls of Residence, that modern 1960s complex where breakfast and supper came all in for £13 a week and the ladies serving always called you 'Hen'. From here each day I went to lectures in my chosen subjects, English Literature & Language and History of Art. Halford had a girlfriend who had a mini car, and with them I went one Saturday to Hopetoun House, which Alexander Pope might have described as 'A Stowe': Palladian, spacious, the wind and haar drifting off the Firth of Forth. Later we went to a pub by the water at The House of the Binns, The Black Bitch tavern, with a Rod Stewart tribute band.

What were those other hell holes we went to back in town? Nights in The Jinglin' Geordie and Nicky Tams, The Southside Bar, or Sandy Bells and half-a-dozen others, beer and chasers racked up and thrown back in the ten minutes given for drinking-up time. There was nothing craft ale or well met about them, desperate places where more drink did nothing to improve the conversation. Cheaper were the Union bars but we never went to them with their cabals of students thinking about socialism and fuelled on bitter envy in any form it took.

At Jim's Inn off the High Street, you could only go in the afternoon with a cleaner or a workman, or if you worked a nightshift. I was taken there by a woman who ran the university library basement coffee bar, ginger hair, perhaps ten years older than me. "Have you ever seen the girls of the Abruzzo mountains?" she said, with unexpected finesse, and I her Tuan Jim. I hadn't and they weren't in Jim's. I should have liked to take things further. She lived on a 'Wimpey' near the racecourse at Musselburgh and was always pleased to see me during my fag breaks in the basement. The male drinking denizens at Jim's I might have also befriended at the bookies in Nicolson Square. Other times I went to the Hill Street Bar in what was still left of the slum Southside. Playing pool one lunchtime, as a girl in the corner with silver tassels on her tits was stripping, a boiler-suited removal man came in (he wore the uniform of the Shore Porters' Society). He plunged a crow bar through the pool table and directed his words to my opponent: "Don't sleep with my wife again." I was winning at the time.

Then there was the Traverse theatre in the Grassmarket. I was never sure if I was supposed to be a member as I befriended a German Steiner student barmaid who always let me in. There you could rub shoulders with the repertory players. Robbie Coltrane was a regular, though I never got to speak to him. The plays were good, audiences of a hundred, no more, as we sat in darkness on spongy square foam seats. I saw a play—with *Gimme Shelter* as the theme tune—about a one-night stand in Lloret de Mar and *The Slab Boys*, gritty Glasgow at its best. In between, I met a girl, left wing and local, smelling of onion crisps and a life of poverty. She asked to come back to my room, and we talked till dawn. "Let's not get too serious," she had said. I wish we had. When I spotted her a week later, I lowered my head, pathetic in my shame and social aspirations.

Was it The Traverse that made me want to try my hand as a playwright? Either way, my first term's English Language essay was 'Write a passage of dialogue in a play and analyse it.' I misread the question, which was for four hundred words, and wrote four thousand. My lady tutor was impressed, if not by my text by my endeavour, and sent it off to the National Theatre who rejected it. Having written so much, my lady tutor encouraged me to keep going, which I did. So was born *The*

Deptford Liver, really a play based on my building-site experiences of a working-class boy who meets a posh girl whose worlds drift together and apart, the usual love and loss. It was performed for three nights in March 1977 at the George Square theatre, where, for want of another actor, I modestly took the lead. It did not help that following a mass distribution of bill stickers, others appeared saying: 'What About the Wapping Kidney?' The idea for *A Deptford Liver* came to me as it was where Charles Marlow, the narrator in several Conrad novels, lived. It is also where the playwright Christopher Marlowe was murdered in a tavern in 1593. But it was from another Conrad novel, *Victory,* from which I took my theme of thwarted love. "Ah, Davidson, woe to the man whose heart has not learned while young to hope, to love—and to put its trust in life." Weren't those words the greatest ever written? It was some years later I read the words elsewhere, in Turgenev, in almost the same order. Had Ford Madox Ford, who often helped out Conrad, had a hand in this? Either way it does not lessen them to me. I have them carved above my mantelpiece. As for Marlowe, it was in *The Jew of Malta* that the conversely bleakest line is offered, no less brilliant in its force: "Thou hast committed fornication?" Barabas interrupts the Jew: "But that was in another country, and besides the wench is dead."

The reviews were appalling. Allen Wright, veteran theatre critic in *The Scotsman*, pronounced it: "Possibly the worst piece of original drama ever to come before me." John Grosser of *The Times* walked out. But we were not disheartened even if we made more money on the interval tea and biscuits than ticket sales. The final night party was the best bit. The play had made a profit of £130, added to which the Nairn Amateur Dramatic Society paid £7 for the rights to stage their own production (they never did). Halford went on to be a very successful student playwright with his own *Metaphysical Bits and Bobs* and I never trod the boards again.

But I did get to breach the leading lady. "I thought you were never going to make a pass. I thought you were queer," she said to me as we eventually rehearsed our lines in her single student bed. Where had I heard that before? This was Sue, and I had eyed her up in the student canteen, managing to get to her after one night with her best friend Shona. It was not just the critics who had not liked the play. Three Scottish students followed me to outside Sue's room one night, 'fuelled on bitter envy', and gave me a good beating, to which I succumbed without resistance. Their strangulated utterances kept me up to date with their hatred of the English as their kicks and fists rained down upon my foetal body. Four nights in the Royal Infirmary with cracked ribs saw me right again.

There was another hospital visit for me not long after as Sue got pregnant. Being the adopted daughter of GPs, hospital was nothing new to her. She was kept overnight in an octagonal ward at the Eastern General hospital in Leith, where I visited her before and after her termination, etherised upon a table, a sad situation for two young people having to make a grown-up decision, and, cruelly, not thinking much of it. That stayed on my conscience, even when Sue told me afterwards (after all the fruit and sympathy) I was one of three who might have been the father.

But out of this and *The Deptford Liver* came a life. My efforts had been noticed by the student publishing house and I was elected to their board. This involved standing outside a room of fifty student politicians, who had to vote for me or not. My proposer was a radical London conservative, whose oratory matched a young Disraeli. "You may not like him, you may even never have heard of him," he began. He then mentioned the play, which several of them had helped on and come to the last night party. Silence gave way to hilarity as my proposer magnified my obnoxious confidence and the room erupted into laughter and the lesser strains of relish to give me 'another good kicking'. I was elected by a vast majority, no doubt so that I could be further quarry for their obloquy. My proposer some months later slept with Sue.

I had forgotten Sue in the forty years that followed until one day, in 2020, I picked up Deborah Orr's posthumous memoir, *Motherwell*. She had of course been married to Will Self, the novelist *éclat*. Getting over the irritation of the first few lines—in which she is 'just *shy* of eighteen' when she first leaves home and then begins by describing this desolate sub-Gorbals or Scotstoun landscape as a 'stunning, *dystopian* panorama' (she mercifully avoided *Kafkaesque*)—Orr leaves behind her *Guardian* journalese to give a heartfelt and harrowing account of life on a council estate under the shadows of endangered steel works, car factories on the brink of collapse, and coal mines more restive than in Zola's *Germinal*.

Orr doesn't really mention anyone except her close family, giving as tight an account of make-do poverty and pride as Orwell does on visiting a couple in Barnsley for *The Road to Wigan Pier*. Then, towards the end, as a student at St Andrew's University (an odd choice, given its high proportion of English and landed students) she meets a young man 'who exuded quiet confidence... and turned out to be the heir apparent to the Earl of Elgin'.

This was my cousin many times removed, Charlie Bruce, with whom I have maintained a long and distant friendship since we shared a flat together in Edinburgh after university. He was the real thing, an hereditary Scottish lord. I wrote to him to ask if he had seen his mention. "I don't remember her," he replied, not out of impoliteness but in truth when there were so many students to meet at university, and this was, according to Orr, but a fleeting encounter. I wrote to him again, as much to remember my own time being taken to Sue's terraced home at Wishaw, very near to Motherwell.

From Wishaw to Motherwell

You have seen your mention in Deborah Orr's Motherwell, which made me think again not just about her book, but also the time I stayed nearby in Wishaw, two miles distant in the spring of 1977. It was in the Old Manse in New Mains Road (I have looked it up on Zoopla, and it is even as we speak for sale, offers over £330,000). I never thought that I would think of it again.

I was, at that time, a would-be playwright, and had just had performed my oeuvre The Deptford Liver over three nights at the George Square Theatre in Edinburgh. I took consolation for the poor notices as the lead actor in the arms of the leading lady, a beautiful orphan whose adopted parents were a GP and his wife from Wishaw. I think I was the first boy that Sue, for it was she, ever took home, by bus as it happens, snaking through those small mining villages beneath the now M8.

The parents had a party, with reeling and dancing and those gathered in the front room were perhaps twenty of their medical friends, a blur of good cheer, not drinking particularly. What followed though, I will never forget. The father was not just a GP but a medical advisor to the Hartwood Psychiatric Hospital in nearby Shotts. On the Sunday morning I went to look at it. Remember, before then, the farthest north that I had been exposed to deprivation was a weekend in Solihull on the outskirts of Birmingham (oddly, with another GP's family, his wife saying "Take us as you find us" as I entered the main road, mock-Tudor semi that was their home).

The hospital surely stood, in all its horror and mournful architecture, as the epitome of: 'Abandon Hope All Ye Who Enter Here'. Sue, although she had been sent to St Margaret's private school in Edinburgh, also had a summer job as a nurse at this Hadean holt. She told me that one of her daily jobs was to put bromide in the patients' tea, as they were forever having sex in the bushes in the grounds.

But, like Deborah Orr's parents, she and her adoptive family loved where they lived, its welded community of shared hardships and endeavours to find work and simply to survive. Like her, too, they would walk in the woods of Chatelherault. Deborah Orr cannot bring herself to say that these now public gardens were once the home of the Dukes of Hamilton. Two years ago, I did a reporting job there as all that remains of Hamilton Palace are the wonderful 18th-century French pavilions, which were once lodges for the ducal foxhounds.

You are right to say that Deborah was born a victim. She was born into a man's world of coal and steel. In bettering herself, she distanced herself from her parents and their values, hard work, their council flats and houses, and eventually, in a glimmer of hope, getting a dog. This is what makes her book a sad song.

Over the past thirty years, I have had several encounters with Will Self. Deborah has been very sparing in her criticism of him, but on marrying him at the age of thirty-five she must have known what she was in for. It may be ironic that one thing that has made her book a bestseller is that it was written by 'Will Self's wife', as not many people outside Farringdon Road had ever heard of Deborah Orr. Last summer, at a wedding in Worcestershire, I talked to Will for half an hour in the garden after the service with his new French girlfriend, a gitaniste. It was hilarious for me. He stood over me bird-like, a crane, wafting a marijuana joint, and used at least ten words I will never remember and had never heard before. I kept thinking he was going to pass the joint to me and sort of waved my right hand in front of him, pretending in the end that I was just brushing something off my shoulder. But he spoke all the time with an un-self-regarding seriousness. A bravura performance just for me. Difficult to live with all the time, I would imagine.

I think Deborah Orr should have gone to the Glasgow School of Art. That would not have been too big a leap for her, and she could have been a Scottish painter, a Joan Eardley or Anne Redpath if you will. She must have known what to expect from St Andrew's before she went there, with its ancient history and colleges. As it turned out, it became, like Motherwell, another source and subject for her blame and fuelled her alienation.

The struggles of Linwood and Ravenscraig seem so far away now, but they were very much alive when I was first a student at Edinburgh. I went to see both plants with Sue. Fraught as they were with industrial disputes, that they were closed down, putting whole generations of men out of work, has never been forgotten. But, and it is another irony, the Orr parents would never have wanted their son to go to the factories, furnaces or mines.

In 1987, I helped host a Spectator lunch at Prestonfield House hotel, to celebrate the magazine's annual Scottish Issue. There were several assembled 'Great and Good': The Earl and Countess of Mansfield and Mansfield (I had asked them because you put me to stay with them for your 21st birthday), writers Roddy Martine and Allan Massie, the unsurpassed vernacular poet Norman MacCaig, National Gallery of Scotland director Tim Clifford (before his knighthood) and his wife, Jane. I was seated with Jane Clifford on my right and MacCaig next to her. "You have a fine set of teeth, Mrs Clifford," I overheard MacCaig saying after about half an hour. "May I suggest you address them to your food."

But the best was the last. The guests drifted off and opposite me now, dram in hand in the gloaming of the tapestries of the private dining room, was Jimmy Reid. I asked that hero of the Clyde and alienation, why was it that Linwood closed down, and his reply was chilling. "The Protestants and the Catholics could not agree upon shared urinals."

Why have I written this to you now? When, in 1994, I wrote about doing 'A Macnab' for the Sunday Telegraph (to catch a salmon, stalk a stag and shoot a brace of grouse in one day), I got a lovely long letter from your father. In it he told me about your family connection with John Buchan's book, John Macnab.

&

I got a final text from Charlie Bruce, a succinct display of lordly wisdom. "Jimmy Reid, what a man." And then, about the urinals: "Sadly, it was ever thus." In 1996, I had lunch alone with his father, Lord Elgin, at the family home, Broomhall, in Fife. Charlie's Canadian wife had just disappeared abroad and to her native home with their three young children, kidnapped, which I knew about, but did not mention. Lord Elgin mentioned it, as we drank a bottle of white wine with our lunch, the windows looking out onto the beautiful lawns and the Firth of Forth beyond. A war hero, Head of the House of Bruce, the proudest of men; in the quietness of the room, Lord Elgin cried at the wrongness of it all and, in the silence, I felt his sorrow.

Things dwindled with Sue over another year or so. I moved into a New Town flat and a better class of person. We never said we loved each other or anything like that and besides, there was a rival for my hand. Conor Quiller Clare was a reader in history, Catholic, Irish, married with three kids, a left-wing Scottish Nationalist. He had a penchant for Guinness, oratory, and emotional flights of fancy. I was to be, for a year or so, his latest one, 'The Boy'. No doubt we made a laughable pair to the more serious academics of the Staff Club when we lunched there in the formal dining room, surrounded by pent-up tutors with their own frustrated peccadilloes, thinking they were firebrands of class struggle or faded pennants of the Spanish Civil War.

They talked of Gramsci and Canetti, of Moravia and Italo Calvino. One of them, with whom I later took the Drama course, was, without a hint of irony, a bachelor called Roger Mee. They were never once ashamed, in their arrested lives, of envy, and, even when tanked on sherry and warm white, useless idiots, still holding by the creeds of their genocidal heroes, more Orville than Orwell.

Each Wednesday we would sit in a smoke-filled publishing office, twelve or so students, a business manager to discuss the next appalling bit of Kailyard trash we were to publish. Often the suggestions, put forward by Leninist medics or cronies of Gordon Brown, were about Scottish struggles, women's rights, miners' rights or the struggles of the working class, which always make academics feel more comfortable. They would have lapped up Deborah Orr. And Conor was a ringleader, black mane of hair and a voice like Michael MacLiammoir, a four-leaf charismatic.

No one dared to tell him that he could not write. Great swathes of his fine pearls came before us, torrents of unpunctuated night-time bashings, heavily annotated with obscure footnotes. But he would take me to the Doric Tavern, a couple of gin and waters and beef mince wrapped in liver (very Dickens, Shaw and Joyce) and afterwards to The Nelson Street hotel in the New Town to drink all afternoon, men only, *I'm Just a Jealous Guy* playing on the jukebox.

But he was good to me. Together we edited *The New Edinburgh Review*, three issues a year, £40 a time for me, pennies from Heaven. He wrote to my parents saying I was starving. They never replied. His literary likes were not mine: Malcolm Muggeridge, C.P. Snow and Kenneth Allsop and his namesake and greatest favourite, Conor Cruise O'Brien. Together we got drunk one night. "You were lachrymose last night," Conor Q remonstrated next day. Then he tried to get me into the BBC, radio, Portman Place, and took me out to lunch with some Brighton dandies. He was jealous of their attention to me, and nothing was going to come of it. Once, he came at me, trousers down, drunk, in the office, broad daylight, emerging from the toilet, Johnson out and flapping. I got him a cab home. Another time he found out where I lived and banged me up one night, pleading to be let in. I heard those plaintive cries dribbled through the letter box, turned over with my girlfriend, and went back to sleep. In the end he found another victim for his unrequited love.

There was a less glamorous side to this world of words, actually repping the books. Even the goaties in their little eyries that I tried to flog them to could see right through the list, dreary, some cobbled together as anthologies on the red future of the smoke-stacked Caledonian motherland. Then we hit three goldmines in a row: a reprint of John Buchan's *Huntingtower* to go with a television show, *Who Owns Scotland?*; a life's labour by some disenchanted forester; and *No Not While The Giro*, by Glasgow's own son Jim Kelman, who later went on to win the Booker Prize with a book mostly composed of swear words. My role was as a sort of editor.

Huntingtower was Conor's little baby. He wrote an introduction for the paperback almost as long as the children's story itself. My colleague

Bruce Young did the honours with the metaphorical machete. *Who Owns Scotland?*, by John McEwen, examined with unchecked bitterness those landowning Scots who have earned and spent millions on their estates. Despite the typesetters spelling the author's name wrong (MacEwen on the spine) the book fared well. I fared less well with McEwen himself. Sent to see him in his Perthshire bungalow, I had the temerity to ask if I could correct some of the titled names he had got wrong? He chased me down his crazy paving front path, shaking one fist at me and holding his socialist red beret on his head with the other.

For Jim Kelman I had nothing but admiration. I met up with him one lunchtime in a west end Glasgow bar, the sort that Alex Harvey might have frequented. After a few pints and whisky chasers, we repaired to a public billiard hall, perhaps twelve full-sized tables in rows, coffins to hope, shrouded in cigarette smoke. He then produced a bottle of Cointreau and we began to play. We weren't playing for the game but for his manuscript. Halfway through I remembered from *The Odyssey* that the way to win over your host is to lose. He took three frames off me, and handed me his Golden Calf in a plastic supermarket bag.

There was a yet lower rung of trade to be endured to support my would-be writer's life. That summer I signed on the dole for a month, and got a job as a fishmonger's driver, Campbell's of Stafford Street, purveyors of fine fish by royal appointment. My day began at seven, and I would drive the mini-van to Leith and Newhaven to pick up the newly trawlered bounty, back to the shop and on my rounds, restaurants, private houses and hotels.

Three boys worked below the shop, gutting and filleting all day on scaly floors and surfaces, all under twenty-five. Ecce hated me. "Don't call me Hector," he screamed, bony fingers, like half snapped langoustines, making a two handed throttling motion on a scrawny neck beneath a head already bald. One day he put me in the lobster boiler, threatening to turn the steamer on. He told me to get some fish from the walk-in cold store, then locked me in for fifteen minutes.

On the Saturday lunchtime when we had our wages to knock off, he stopped me. "I'll have that, we're going to the pub." There followed an inglorious 'session', which I managed to survive till six o'clock, salvaging my bus money. I slept until it all began again on Monday morning, banished to a bunk bed in a cupboard off the sitting room where I was living temporarily.

I got to know my daily rounds, but an incident put paid to me in time. Driving up The Mound, the back of the minivan came open. A crate of haddock fell out of the back. Before I could rescue some of the errant fish, the number 27 ran over a small shoal. Never mind, I thought, and put the gritty ones underneath the others and carried on my way. They were for the kitchens of the Caledonian hotel. Nothing can prepare the innocent civilian for the nautical precision of such places, or the regimented creatures toiling there who seldom saw the light of day. "Four pounds short," said the commis chef, weighing in my finny cargo. "You have cheated me." Returning to the fish shop, he had already rung them up and I was fired. "Clean out the van and go," said my upstairs boss. As I was doing this, I opened the back of the van again and the door handle broke off. "Go now. NOW." I was spared at least another pub-time session.

The job was certainly an eye-opener, never more so than when I made a delivery to The Edinburgh Wine Bar. Here, I saw from the stairs, was an elegant drawing room restaurant and bar, civilisation in peopled form at its nest of tables, and pretty girls as waitresses. The cook took her delivery, and me aback. "Would you like a cup of coffee?" she asked. This was Pilla Birkbeck, a scion of all good Highland things and with that cup I crossed another rubicon. These were the people who really owned Scotland and I was going to get to know them. I did not initially repay her kindness, going back with Sue and Halford to celebrate my birthday. They overlooked my being sick into a champagne ice bucket, and later I got a letter for toilet damages, £6.50, politely asked for and paid.

Before that, Halford had me to stay with his family for a week in Ayrshire, where we had a holiday job selling horse manure, supplied free by his hunting mother and stepfather. We placed an advertisement in the local paper and the calls came flooding in, often just a single bag to a council estate window box. The biggest order was for twenty bags from an Indian in Alloway who had just bought a new build. I think we cleared £100. It was fun and easy money.

In return I asked him and Sue to stay with me in Devon, which was a big mistake. By now my dad and the Finn had installed Exeter

University students in the Big House, and they queued like penguins for his lavish and drunken hospitality. None of them was ever nice to me, seeing me not as one of their friends but as unnecessarily taking up a place at table, which they guarded jealously. I never liked him either in their company, a simple bully with his extravagance, paedo almost, as he was fifty-five. He would take them out on jaunts in his Deux Chevaux, to the pub or to drop in on his friends, showing off, things he never did with me, them gulling my inheritance.

They could not have been less friendly to my guests, going out to dinner leaving us to cook and, when they did come home, intimidating them, the Finn perpetually drunk. Holford wrote to my father afterwards, a sort of tongue-in-cheek 'Thank You' letter, which infuriated him still further. I am glad he wrote, showing himself to be the man of principle that would make him the lawyer he would become. Young people are also young adults and they know unfairness when they see it. It did not matter to them that my father had fought the war or that his wife had run off. What mattered is that they should have been treated as my friends, and that should have been enough. From that moment I knew that in my life, my friends would be my family, and take me as they found me.

Meanwhile, in London, I returned to Thurloe Square with my school trunk and asked the taxi to park by the fire engines. But it was my mum's house that was on fire. As I approached the front steps, she was lugging a large David Tindle painting down them, which she had rescued from the drawing room. I was farmed out to some strange neighbours in the square.

Quite how that fire started was a puzzle, and certainly a puzzle to the insurers (if indeed the house was insured) as they didn't pay up. Had my mum left her curlers on charge in the bedroom? Had Neville left them on on purpose, given his economy with the actualite when it came to paying the taxman, insurance and such like? This did not stop my mum booking into a suite at the Carlton Tower hotel, although I only got as far as the lobby when I visited her there, and spent the summer sofa surfing, unsatisfactorily.

The Graveyard of Nations

'I suppose that in the graveyard of nations
Scotland's epitaph will not be a volume
Like the French, but a single line:
"Ye'll be hearing from us."'

Hugh McMillan, *Anglophobia*

EVERY NEW STUDENT year is a staging post for throwing off friendships from the year before. So, I let Conor go, Halford disappeared from my life, later to become a top QC, and Sue popped up intermittently when I was between girlfriends. But it was a chance conversation in the university library coffee bar with a slow speaking Old Etonian, smoking on a cardboard filtered Russian cigarette, that set me up for my third year and a lifelong friendship.

"Would you like to meet Roddy Martine?" he asked. Roddy was at that time the editor of *Scottish Field* and the author of several books, with many more to come, one of which, *The Swinging Sporran*, about Scottish country dancing, was "for those who think a poussette is some sort of Siamese cat". We first met up in The Antiquary in St Stephen Street on a summer's early evening, 1978, the only time I ever saw him in a pub. He became my landlord for two years and an important influence, worthy of the greatest respect from me and many others. He introduced me to his friends: the writer Douglas Sutherland and his wife, Diana; the acerbic caricaturists Emilio Coia and Hugh Dodd; the eminent banker Angus Grossart; wine man and charity lion Sandy Irvine Robertson; antiquarian Christian Orr Ewing; and clan chief Andrew MacThomas of Finegand. Then there was also Roddy's great friend Brodrick Haldane, the 1930s Society photographer, still taking pictures with his veteran Box Brownie, who lived in a splendid flat with finches flying free in the kitchen in the New Town's India Street.

With my student publishing credentials and Roddy's generosity I got to meet and be accepted by many of the great Edinburgh minds and talents of the day. For this I must also thank my cousin, Allan Maclean, the minister, who found my name on the matriculation role and sought me out. It was he who introduced me to his great friend A.N. Wilson, who would in turn became the greatest friend to me.

Our first meeting was at Allan's small ground-floor flat off St Mary's Cathedral in Palmerston Place. Andrew Wilson was staying with him, at the age of twenty-seven, writing a biography of Sir Walter Scott. Allan greeted me at the door and I came in to his small sitting room, a Poussin tapestry hanging on the wall to my right and A.N. sitting on the sofa. Andrew got up and moved towards the fireplace when I was introduced, typical of his unsurpassed good manners. There were then these two men, higher beings and great friends from Oxford, trussed up like chickens in their respective three-piece suits, equally at ease with learned and quite camp conversation. One or two of their male friends they referred to by the female gender, having names for them like 'Poppy' and 'Sharon'. The evening was as warm as crumpets toasting on an open fire, high church and table. If Darwin or Thackeray or Wattie himself had come upon us, they would not have been out of place.

Nor was Allan without his side of mischief, but always with the reserve of the significant historian, which he was. It was some time later that he was upbraided by his clerical superiors for delivering the burial service of a guinea pig in Rutland Square. Presumably this was some form of 'Rodentine Mass', hidden in plainchant.

Roddy was also the real thing, a writer, editor, photographer, painter, historian, in short an 'Everyman' who, as for many others, became everything to me. He never went to university himself but was, from a young age, interviewing famous people as an equal. Before I knew him, he also ran a travelling discotheque, 'Disco Willy', from which no great house or village hall in Scotland and the north of England was not known to him. He was obviously the backdrop to so many happy memories.

He was also a magnet to a changing band of eccentrics, and took them all in his long, tall stride. Slow to judge and quick to encourage, he overlooked our glaring faults. You never left his company feeling anything but better about yourself. His passion was for Scotland in all its human and historic forms. Yet, he had that most unScottish of traits: fairness. In short, he did for me all the things my own mother could have done for me but never bothered.

He typed me a formal letter of acceptance as his tenant. "When you come we'll go and have dinner at the club," it said, for he had a formal side as well. The flat in Douglas Crescent was in the unfashionable West End, top floor, with attic dormer windows. As I lugged my trunk and books up the polished communal stairs, a brass plaque greeted me at the third floor door. 'Roderick C. Martine, Esq' it announced. Below, in a plate more hastily put up, the name was borne: 'Lord Patrick Conyngham.' This was the first I had heard of the third man, a cuckoo in my nest. I retrieved my key as instructed from under a pot plant in the hall. Both men were out.

It falls to few people to feel such a sense of freedom, my own room, two more years of study and a healthy allowance from my Irish grandfather, my tabula rasa. The drawing room was full of Far East furniture, Dayak table nests with carved oriental boys in saucy poses and loincloths as legs, faded brown leather sofas, leading off to a kitchenette and green bathroom suite. Once there had been a dining room but this was now turned turvey by his lordship's junk, to whit: two or three unmatching suits hung on metal coat hangers by the window, a Dracula cape, some sheaves of poetry written in an angular hand with lots of crossings out, and one or two books on crop circles and mystics.

Roddy's day job was editing his magazine in Glasgow, to which he hurtled anxiously each morning in a company car, just about on time. At weekends he had a rented cottage in the Borders, a Runrig of wrongdoing, skinny-dipping in the Tweed's swire, any drink that came to hand, and the shrill of dipping curlews (or was it maidens?) in the bracken under a concupiscent sky. It was quite basic: single-storey, a poster of Millais' *Autumn Leaves* in the bathroom, another denoting the pennants of Clan Chiefs of Scotland in the front room and a pastel by the Selkirk artist Thomas Scott.

Nearby had lived James Hogg, 'The Ettrick Shepherd', author of that hallucinatory fragment, *The Private Memoirs and Confessions of a Justified Sinner*. When Roddy's great friend, the parliamentary orator Sir Nicholas Fairbairn, had written to him at the cottage, his secretary, by mistake, had written on the envelope 'Near Bugger.' Fairbairn told her to "make Bugger, Biggar." Back came the envelope, 'BUGGER'. Even nearer was the Crook Inn, an ancient coaching howff with colourful art deco interiors, where Hogg had drunk and Robert Burns had written *Willie Wastle,* and the shepherds gathered in the back bar still.

Lord Patrick was not strictly a student, but a sixth form pupil at a finishing school in town, attempting, without success, and by now nineteen, to gain some O levels. He was tall, languid, brave, hilarious, diffident, and bent, pell-mell, on self-destruction. It is said that there is no greater speed than that with which an Irishman will divest himself of his inheritance and Patrick was no exception. He smoked in bed at breakfast, wore silk scarves and dinner jackets during the day, and had a dazzling capacity for drink, friendship and antagonism. I was to become the Charles Ryder to his Sebastian Flyte, and there were rumours that our friendship sometimes took on a nocturnal bent, mystery boys. He kept a photograph of his mother by his bedside, dressed as a wartime nurse, with the Cross of St George on her uniform, which will have witnessed all his goings on. "She's a Wren," he told me soon after we had met. How interesting, I thought that a wartime nurse should marry an Irish marquess. It was years later that I understood she was a descendent of Sir Christopher Wren. Patrick was the first person any of us knew to dye his hair white and sometimes slept out in public gardens, even in the rain.

On my double bed, which did nothing to make smaller the size of my large room, painted mustard, were two notes, one of welcome from my formal landlord and another in the script I had just observed. "Meet me in Kay's Bar at NONE," it read, misspelt. It was signed 'Lord Crispin Flask.' This, he had decided, was to be his *nom de plume* not if but when I wrote about him.

Kay's Bar in the late 1970s was little changed from half a century before, and I imagine not much altered now. Through frosted half doors, there was a long red velvet banquette, copper foot rail at the bar, small oak round tables, casks of real ale, and a back room with a small coal fire sending out the heat of Holofernes. There might well have been a parrot in a gilded cage, stuffed or otherwise. But nothing was going to dim the plumage of the apparition now before me at our noontide rendezvous.

"Flask," intoned the nasal voice, offering a bony handshake and all the hallmarks of superior address. Sun streamed in from a back window, and flecks of dust were caught in its light as other low voices withered into silence. "You look like a nice boy." Seven pints later and Flask the alter ego had been through all the dances: the hesitation tango at first meeting, the fumbling of connections we both had, the exaggerated curriculum of his short time at school in England and his escapades on Ginger Pop, his Irish pony, that took him to the pub and waited outside, for which they had both been banned from Pony Club.

Patrick had made certain to get the upper hand of Roddy, who had rescued him from a grim lodging miles out of town, already. He knew how to please himself, often to excess. "We are going to have a party tonight," he announced, just as I was getting the whiskys in and thinking of calling it a day. "Oysters and Dada." He made a couple of calls from the end of the bar, getting the landlord to dial the numbers on the pub phone, and twenty minutes later a cab appeared with two boxes of oysters, a case of Guinness and another of champagne. There was no question that I had to pay for any of this, and we oozed into the taxi arm in arm, characters in a horse fair painting by Jack B. Yeats.

Out went the table nests, the sofas were thrown back, the pictures taken down and replaced with coat hangers and, by seven o'clock, forty had appeared. There was a prep school blond boy with a long surname, several scions and sprigs of nobility, and some girls from Patrick's typing school. His lordship dressed as Nancy Cunard and, from memory, I was decked in a chef's checked trousers, and anything to hand. Those who were there will have never forgotten it, and several have since claimed to be, a gaudy gallimaufry, a Grand Guignol. In the morning, well mid morning, a young man left the dining room that was Patrick's abode. It was the fishmonger's lad with whom his lordship had done wrong. Roddy had already gone to work, appalled, but happy, humming *Under the Moon of Love*.

This was one of many escapades that Lord Patrick led me on. Roddy was always there, the harbour to the boats of both our broken homes and nights of drink-fuelled revelry. It was not long before an invitation came to take us to some Highlands castle. This was owned by a shipping magnate Patrick had met on his long boat passage back from Australia, where he had been sent to be made a man. We spent the night sleeping where we fell, having watched a full chorus line rehearsing *South Pacific*.

Things did not always run smoothly. Apart from the pilfering of our clothes without concern, Patrick also had a habit of copying out little-known poems and claiming them as his own. 'The devil drives the glockenspiel,' was one of the more original lines he unearthed. His days of wine and roses were not too brief, but often spread with thorns and plonk. When I went to lectures, he would sometimes sleep with the occasional girlfriend I had who stayed the night. This I found out when we were both booked into 'The Clap Clinic' at the Royal Infirmary, and made to stand in line together. His human chaos had no conscience, and soon he took to bringing back all sorts, both men and girls (who loved his toxic charm), including hairdressers and a schoolteacher. He was an antinomian. His favourite song, which he tonelessly repeated, was: *(Sing If You're) Glad to be Gay*.

One time, I found him hiding in the locked bathroom, our eyes meeting either side of the keyhole. "Get rid of him," he seethed. Behind me was a naked South African with a bullet scar on his shoulder. I bundled him out with his clothes, to dress in the hall. The schoolteacher he brought back for quite some time was more circumspect, worrying no doubt about his future career and public image.

We were not always kind to Roddy, who had admirers of his own. One of them, a well-connected Borders lassie of good pedigree, got serious. We saw an ending to our happiness and gravy train. Asking to borrow her car to get some milk, we went missing, pub to pub, for a day and a half. She never came back. Tired of us one time at a Perthshire party, Roddy simply left us there. We hitched back to Edinburgh, crammed into a two seater Fiat X1/9 driven by a junior bank manager from Morningside, and got home before him. Another time he did not leave us as our hostess's behaviour was even worse than ours. She drove her Mercedes sports car into the swimming pool after lunch, dressed in the clothes of her old Spanish lover. Her husband fished her out. The car was recovered later. The Spaniard had drowned himself for love in a nearby river. She took me to the very spot.

This was my Scottish social life, far away from the prying student eyes and the publishing house of which I had by now been elected chairman. Patrick had a friend called Julian Stacey, quite a good artist and quite mad. He had been expelled from Marlborough for stealing a beak's Morgan and going on a joyride. One time he drove my motorbike (bought with the leftover proceeds from the play) fully up two flights of a New Town tenement and into the drawing room of his startled friends. The man downstairs, another of the goatee persuasion, called the police. I hid with Stacey behind a curtain as the girls we had come to visit (Caroline Baxter, later to become a very good painter, and Nicky Hay, from memory) saw off the police with blandishments.

Another time, I took him on it out to Hopetoun House to see the dawn. As we walked alone across the lawns, the house asleep and odd spanner bangings from over the Firth at Rosyth Dockyard, he produced a crumpled photograph from his inside jacket pocket. It was of the ruins of Shelswell Park. Stacey, later, not yet forty, had a death wish. It was granted. He took his own life by jumping off the Telford Bridge.

One man above all straddled these two worlds of 'Town and Gown'. This was Baron Varres, rich, a prophetic gambler with a Mallen streak. He could have been Oscar's double, and often kept a 'Bosie' by his side whom he called 'Peaches'. Patrick and I would dandle him without mercy, for dinners, outings to the cinema and rugby, and just occasionally to play the tables. One time I went with him to the Royale Chimes Casino and, at the door, the owner reminded him in a whisper he was four grand owing. It took some nerve to play that night and he got it back, rewarding me in the taxi with a cigar, and one for the driver, on whom he planted a grateful kiss. I placed £3 on 'eight', and came up £24 better off.

Varres was 'a man o' parts'. His family had once owned a shipping line. He drove a Wolseley car with a walnut fascia, which often came to the attention of the police. He drank champagne and green chartreuse, and there would not have been a better ballroom dancer in the kingdom, quick of mind and toes. He rolled his 'R's and eyes, immaculately dressed and coiffed. He could have risen to the very heights of law or politics, but was really happiest scattering his generosity and wandering hands before our open mouths.

He had a modern flat off Murrayfield, and a housekeeper of

saintly patience, Mrs Flockhart. His soirees were something to behold. He would whisper in his victim's ears and his predation had about it something of the tongue dynasty. I think he locked Patrick in a bedroom one time and beasted him. Leaving sozzled on another night, Patrick got us stuck in the lift for an hour, and later stole a neighbour's pot plant. Varres was called before his housing committee and threatened with eviction. "You behaved like went boys, went boys," he admonished us, and we had to take him out to lunch ourselves for that and feign contrition. We asked him if, for the duration, he would like to call us 'Peaches', and he forgave us.

Another party with Lord Patrick met with even less success. We were summoned to a ball at West Wycombe Park, once home to the licentious 18th-century Hellfire Club. To get me in, Patrick (he had dispensed with his Flask persona in such exalted company) had determined I should impersonate another of his aristocratic friends who could not come, and had given him his invitation instead. At drinks in another house before the ball, the impersonation went to plan, remarkable really as the lord I was impersonating was a cousin of the family. "How you've changed since school," one of the sons said to me, and I moved the conversation quickly on. At West Wycombe I was within reach of the drinks tray in the grand drawing room when the butler announced us. I shook hands with the family in a line. All too quickly I was denounced as an imposter by a foundling adopted into a grand family without the breeding to keep quiet.

Ushered outside onto the lawns, my host came running towards me and I was ejected. Because there were several cabinet ministers present (Mrs Thatcher had just got in to Number Ten) the police presence was strong. Three times I tried to get in under other car blankets or in the boot of friends, each time caught, eventually threatened with imprisonment. I stayed till closing time in a nearby pub, and hatched my plan. West Wycombe is girded by tall walls but, behind a humble cottage, I found a lean-to greenhouse. If I got on it and traversed the brick isosceles, it was only a four-foot jump up onto the estate wall.

At my first attempt I fell into the greenhouse, dinner jacket slashed and blood from a cut above my left eye, the scar still worn. The second go was more successful and I sat, teetering, on the estate wall. What followed was a leap into the dark, about twelve feet into reeds, and then, concussed, I fell into a tributary of the lake. I can still remember the names of those who brought me drinks as I hid in the gardens or behind a parkland tree (Patrick was one of them) and the Dorset beauty who took me home and nursed my wounds.

Years later my host, Sir Francis Dashwood, sent me a novel he had written to review. He was keen on this occasion to point out that I was a cousin of his first wife (my mother would have liked that). "Is it ever too late to send a Thank You letter," I began, and perjured myself by giving it three stars out of five.

One place in Edinburgh that Patrick himself was *persona non grata* (*sine qua non*, *lingua franca* or *Una Paloma Blanca*, as he might have put it) was at Puffin's Club, even though his brother, Lord Simon, ran the Wine Bar where it weekly met for lunch. Varres took me and great delight in pronouncing his name 'Salmon', to which he would, annoyed, utter under his breath, "I'm not a fish." Varres made up for this and drank like one.

Membership was in the gift of a charming and eccentric Highlands baronet (enamoured of my mother, he had once asked if I would help him shoot my Russian stepfather, which I was not keen to do), who invited me to join, £5 a year. This was the legendary lawyer, herald, clan chief and *bon vivant* Sir Iain Moncreiffe of That Ilk. His worthy friends who made it into *Who's Who* would always list amongst their clubs Puffin's (Edinburgh).

Assembled would be a dozen or so friends of the baronet, chieftains, or minor foreign royals. King Zog of Albania was always anticipated, but died. This was made up for by the occasional presence of that dashing politician and writer Sir Fitzroy Maclean, Nicky Fairbairn, and, at least once, the actor Terence Stamp. You arrived, as at the Beefsteak in London, and sat in the next vacant chair. The only rule was you were not allowed to say who you were.

It was Varres who one day in George Square told me with great excitement: "I've met a real lord, come to lunch at Puffin's and you will meet him, too." It was there he introduced me to a fellow student who turned out, through a nod and a wink, to be Lord Norreys of Rycote, a man after the very heart of Sir Iain with his encyclopaedic knowledge of almost everything. The conversation would range from heraldry to land ownership, a bit of all-male social gossip, and much laughter.

This was socialising on an even keel at its very best, and to be young there was an education. When I got to know him, Henry Norreys and I went quite often together, once being locked in after everyone had left. I think it was a measure of our decency and restraint that when the fellow owner of the wine bar, Patrick Heriot-Maitland, came to open up again at seven, we were just sitting in animated conversation. He gave us a large dram apiece for our honesty and Henry and I have remained the best of friends.

"Got married today," one man said to me, taking a vacant seat. A month later when he reappeared: "It didn't last." No one batted an eyelid or talked work, even if they had a job. In the middle of the table was a stuffed puffin in a glass case, which we toasted at the start of lunch and then again on breaking up at four. A couple of old copies of *Burke's Landed Gentry* and *Kelly's* were on the bookshelf. "Once a Puffin, always a Puffin," our host would intone, which brought proceedings to a close, and we would tip out into reality again, blinking in its glare, a glow of happiness that all was right with the world, taking him at his word.

There was another club of a different hue, which was the annual Edinburgh Festival dinner of the Anton Krashny Society. Was this man whom we honoured a dissident Polish artist or poet, no one really knew, and certainly had not met. He was an understandable figment of our collective imaginations, elusive, rarified, tortured, absent. It was typical that Roddy Martine should have been one of those behind his creation and keeper of his flame. The fairly eminent members were drawn from the media. Joan Bakewell, Douglas Rae, Paul Gambaccini were just three I sat down with (again at the Edinburgh Wine Bar) one August evening in 1979. It was the day Mountbatten had been blown up.

Each guest was obliged to say something and be presented with an object, a haggis or old straw sombrero. When it came to my turn, I began by saying perhaps we should first just reflect for a moment upon the awful events of the day in Ireland. "No, I'll have none of it," screamed a fellow guest, rising to his feet and threatening me with menaces. This was Michael Grieve, son of Hugh MacDiarmid and an ardent Scottish Nationalist. An awkward silence fell and neither I nor, I hope, my fellow members can remember what I spoke about afterwards. But I have remained friends with Dame Joan, Douglas and Paul, and we still get together during the festival for dinner when we can. Grieve never would have made a Puffin.

Some years later, the role of guest speaker fell to the BBC's Allan Little, who was asked to address the straw sombrero, which had miraculously survived several peregrinations, this time to a private dining room in a New Town flat. As befits one of Scotland and the BBC's finest foreign correspondents, his enviable, light, brilliant speech was one of the funniest I have ever heard. To this day, Roddy Martine still performs the ritual before dinner by reciting Burns and addressing a steaming haggis.

Sins and Lovers

'Oh who is that young sinner with the handcuffs on his wrists?
And what has he been after that they groan and shake their fists?
And wherefore is he wearing such a conscience-stricken air?
Oh they're taking him to prison for the colour of his hair.'

A.E. Housman, *Oh Who Is That Young Sinner*

IF BARON VARRES had been the human bridge between the town and university, even he could not save me when these two worlds collided. After a wedding reception for Lord Simon Conyngham (at which Guinness XXX, brandy and champagne was consumed at lunchtime in The Tilted Wig), I suddenly remembered I had a meeting to appoint the next editor of the university 'Student' newspaper. Getting onto my motorcycle was my first mistake, the second was running it into a police van at a set of pedestrian traffic lights.

The police, weary at having done their duty at a Saturday football match, swarmed out of the van as I attempted to run away and hide in a basement. It was the time of the Jeremy Thorpe trial. "You can't touch me, I'm a friend of the DPP," I said, as I was manhandled into the back of the van and carted off to jail, underground next to St Giles' Cathedral in the High Street. It was later pointed out by Sheriff Nigel Thomson in the High Court, as I was given a fifteen-month driving ban and my comment was read out, that there is no Director of Public Prosecutions in Scotland.

A young doctor came to examine me in my cell whilst screams from arrested drunken football fans echoed down the corridor of these Hadean chambers. He was a graduate of the medical school and almost apologetic as he passed me fit to spend the night, which I meekly did. In the morning, Roddy came and rescued me, vouching for me and signing me out. I was contrite and remember thinking how was I going to tell my father that I had lost my licence when I was always running errands for him on the farm. I never did tell him and took a little risk ('Send lawyers, guns, and money/Dad, get me out of this.')

Somehow my student chairmanship of the publishing house merged into something of a profile as a student politician. If there was one lasting legacy of my two years in charge it was to change the name of 'Edinburgh University Students' Publications Board' to Polygon. It was, I reasoned, almost impossible to interest a book buyer with such a long and unwieldy name. Polygon, on the other hand, sounded a bit like Penguin or Picador. It is still going today, as an imprint of Birlinn, most closely associated with the runaway successes of Alexander McCall Smith.

'Pubs Board' was always under threat from the university authorities, desperate to quash any unnerving voices in this crucible of learning and Enlightenment. It had some powerful allies, including former student rector Gordon Brown and his brother Andrew who was student chairman before me. As well as the book side of things, it published *Student*, the weekly newspaper, and *Festival Times*, which, it is hard to imagine now, was the only publication then really serving audiences for The Fringe.

Our greatest enemy was Charles Fishburne, the American permanent secretary of the Students' Association, a hard-smoking empire builder. Clever, a stomach churner, he possessed a disarming, slow, way of speaking, as if he was in his own matinee selling snake oil, smoking Marlboro Reds, unsettling. I never trusted him and he barely concealed his dislike of me. He was also knocking off a female Liberal student politician, which students do not like or consider as fair game. He would have liked 'Pubs Board' to move out of its independent offices, into the Students' Association building, and under his watchful eye.

Fed up with this I called, with Tim Willis, then editor of *Student*— who went on to become a well-known figure in print and the *boîtes* of Fleet Street—a General Meeting of the Students' Representative Council. I had first met Tim when we lived on the same New Town street, he in a basement that he shared with David Johnston, a local boy from Fife with a stud earring, a fishtank in a long, darkened room and lots of paraphernalia for smoking 'Puff' and 'Blow.' It was beneath the flat where the painter Anne Redpath once kept her studio and salon, a blue plaque marking this, and pictures we all should like to have.

Johnston was later to become one of Conor's 'Boys', and had undoubted talent as a publisher. My only quibble with him was, some years later, attending a wedding in Northern Ireland, he came back to the cottage where I was staying and slept with my host. This in itself was fine, although there was a lot of growling in the night and a half tumbler of cheap brandy by his bedside in the morning as he nursed his head. I slept in front of a coal fire in the downstairs sitting room, the glow of kelp phosphorescing in the new moon light.

But, next day, at the reception in a Georgian mansion, he asked to see me alone in the moulded ceiling green drawing room and closed the door. "Did I do wrong?" he asked, as we sat together on a high backed Knole sofa. "No, David, you did not do wrong," I assured him. "I said it was my first time," he continued. "David, you did wrong." He died too young. Was it the old sweep of heroin or the new broom of AIDS?

There is nothing a Scot likes better, after beer and brawling, than the notion of a free press. We got eight hundred students to turn up to the McEwan Hall and, with Tim giving the better speech, throwing books we had published around the stage to demonstrate what was under threat, we secured our future as an independent publisher. This allowed me to work with some very talented student writers and publishers, some of whom went on to achieve great things: Bruce Young with the BBC, Lucinda Bredin in arts magazines and, perhaps above us all in a different sphere, Alexander Sherbrooke, who went on to become the influential priest of St Patrick's, Soho Square, where many will have benefitted from his charity and kindness.

From all this came an invitation from the University Conservative Association (Baron Varres was a leading light) for me to stand as their preferred candidate for the sabbatical post of Senior President, one occupied in the recent past by Sir David Steel, Gordon Brown and his brother Andrew. I was not nominally a Conservative, which is perhaps why they asked me, thinking I would fare better as an independent. I accepted.

There is no bear-pit quite like student politics. It did not help my cause that, in the year of my standing, more than a hundred public school students had suddenly arrived at Edinburgh, little 'woodentops' and 'mink and sables' as Paddy Crossan would have called them, all intent on canvassing for me. One, the Old Etonian Edward Baxter, still remembers me begging him not to go on the stump as he was losing me votes and credibility. "Whichever way you vote, a politician gets in," was one of the more depressing slogans I saw daubed on walls along my travels. But on the May morning of the election, I arrived at the McEwan Hall, covered in scaffolding, to find an enormous banner had been put on top of it in the night. 'VOTE RORY' it said. Whoever scaled those heights, no mean feat, I disappointed.

My campaign could not have been fought, and it was a fight, without Louise Simpson, my campaign manager. When I was flagging she would get me up all hours to put up posters and go leafletting. Our catchment was 15,000 students so, in many ways, the size of a small parliamentary constituency. 'VOTE RORY' was the simple message and all over the student halls of residence posters announcing this went up. "Qui Est Rory?" One French student placed in her window in Pollock Halls, which I think added some light relief and won some votes. In the end I came second to Fishburne's Liberal 'Bidie-In Billy'.

But there was still the campaign party to be held. There are perhaps no more than a dozen days, as Philip Larkin observed bleakly, which we can look back upon in our brief lives with the fondest happiness. They are not necessarily weddings, Christmases or births, but often random occasions when the stars align. For me, Sunday 13th May, 1979, at Roddy's Borders cottage, Hopecarton, was one such day. It was never going to be a 'Victory' celebration, but a 'Thank You' to those who had helped on the campaign regardless.

I had sent out printed invitations, but that is where the formalities came to an end. Inspired by the contemporary film about student life on campus in America, *Animal House*, it was decided we should dress in togas. But Moffat in May is not Malibu. From across the fields of the River Tweed and the experimental sheep station that surrounded the cottage they came in wafts and wens, senators and tribunes to the call. Lord Varres was followed by 'Peaches' (wearing a head garland) at a supplicant distance, Lord Michael Cecil by Johnson his fox terrier. From St Andrew's University came Hugo Swire, Michael's best friend from Eton, later to become a leading politician in the David Cameron regime. Bravest of all was Lord Balniel, my university footballing friend (we were in the same team, he in a different league) draped, like me, in just an ironed sheet. To be young was very heaven. "Good Lord!" someone exclaimed as we drank super strength Pimm's out of paper cups. "Which Lord is that?" asked my cousin Allan Maclean, thinking yet another titled student had arrived. It could have been Lord Patrick or Lord Norreys.

By any standards it was not a lavish party but, like all shared endeavours that require comedy and a beating of the elements, it took on a momentum of its own. The girls were just as brave, Pippa Robinson and Fiona de Sales La Terrière spring to mind. There were no sorrows to be drowned but fun to be had. Roddy held the drinks tray and the tiller, his little bothy lit with laughter.

Outside it was a slightly different matter. One couple had decided to make a tryst in an outhouse. A third person, tripping over as he wished to join in, fell on the horizontal couple and the teeth of the horizontal man went through the girl's upper lip. But she was soon patched up.

It was Roddy who responded to the next call to arms. Someone had left a gate open and the black-faced sheep in one field had now got in—rams and all—with the white-faced sheep in the next-door field. This is not what the shepherd had in mind when planning the breeding of experimental sheep. After much herding and penning (the senatorial scions after all probably owned 50,000 acres between them) correct fields and decorum were restored. But the seed had been sown. Somewhere still in the Scottish Borders are an unintentional breed of sheep that might answer to the call of 'Toga.'

A Day at the Races

There was another more regular event that got us students going. This was the Fife point-to-point at the end of each April, better known as Balcormo Races. I was proud that my dad had been a Master of Foxhounds, so went to it willingly, with a sort of cheerful credibility, sometimes with Roddy, at others with the student or Scottish friends I'd made. This really was 'A Day At The Races,' with a harmonious gathering of perhaps 4,000 spectators, all the top sporting families of Scotland and plenty of residents from nearby Kirkaldy, set on a proper day out when we were all 'Jock Tamson's Bairns'.

It often seemed that the horses were not a full part of proceedings. Car-boot hopping was the real sport, so we would come armed with picnics and tins of beer and enter into things fully. For the grandees of the county there would be the Fife Hunt Cub dinner the night before in a private house, but I was never asked to that. After racing we would go to the Ship Inn at Elie, later I think closed down on the day because of unseemly revelry (I remember cars skidding round on the sandy beach, one turning over, which probably did it) and drink our pints looking out over a sun setting harbour. We saw our friends from St Andrew's, close knit, who seem to have made life-long friendships with themselves and for a time with us; Barnaby Rogerson who married Rose Baring (now both travel writers and publishers), James Graham-Stewart (a furniture expert) and Mary Miers, author of books on her beloved Highlands.

Once I got waylaid and stayed the night at Cambo House, where students also lived. Roddy came and got me the next day. Another time I was invited to stay, thanks to their grand-daughter, Virginia Macnab, with Lord and Lady Kilmany. There were hunters and racehorses grazing in the park, a scene so settled that I have always felt a warmth wherever I have seen it: at Galtrim, home in West Meath of Patrick's mother; at Johnnie Greenall's in Derbyshire; Robin Smith-Ryland's Sherbourne Park in Warwickshire; and at my cousin Susan Moore's in Mallow, deeply civilised.

It was at the Fife point-to-point in 1997, staying with Richard Munro Ferguson at Raith, his hidden mansion eyrie near Kirkcaldy, that I last saw Bobby Corbett. Of all the legendary Scots through history, his name must be added to them without reserve. A lifelong hunter and Master of Foxhounds, his generosity to all, and particularly to us the young, was boundless. Funny, erudite, partial to a dram, he was a connoisseur of gardens, art, pop tunes, people and fantastic one-liners. When Princess Margaret came to stay to judge the puppy show, she said to him: "What remarkable scent your roses have," to which he replied: "Would Ma'am care to join the bitch pack?"

No one who ever met him would forget it. He asked me that day to come and stay with him in Ayrshire which I couldn't do to my lasting regret as he died not two years later at only fifty-eight. Many are the stories told of him, and all are kind. He was a great favourite of HM The Queen Mother. He would ring his neighbour Sir Houston Shaw-Stewart nightly to discuss the relative merits of the plot lines in 'Coronation Street'. He is buried in Stair Church, near the castle he bought and restored. On his headstone, which I have visited several times since, the legend is borne: 'Here I lie—prostrate as usual'.

It was Bobby who introduced me to many things (an offer of a Carlsberg Special Brew at breakfast not being one that I took up), including the paintings of that early 'Glasgow Boy', Joseph Crawhall. Some years later I had copied Crawhall's 'The Huntsman' (1908), a huntsman on his black horse in a wooded glade surrounded by his hounds, leaves casting different lights in what the Japanese might call Shibui. It sits within eyesight in my drawing room, where I write, and I look at it quite often and toast his memory.

Several girls I went with to the point-to-point but it was more of an occasion for high spirits than romance. We wrestled, did silly things, sat in the sand dunes at Elie or gave each other piggy backs. One I met there I went out with for a summer. But, studies and student politics again put paid to that, and I had to go to America on publishing work, which didn't help. Nor, I suppose, did the 'Mrs Robinson' relationship I had there with a former child star, Penny, now perhaps thirty-five but still to herself a little girl in a Hollywood bungalow. She picked me up in an L.A. bookstall at the Fair and took me out to dinner and then home to the Heights. There was a dog and proud photos of her youthful glory. We began with blowback and a bath together lit by small candles round the edge. "Make it right," she whispered, slipping on Tim Buckley's 'Greetings From L.A.'. When she slept, eventually, she put two slices of cucumber over her closed eyelids, which I hadn't seen before.

"You were so young and beautiful..." she wrote me some years later. "That night I came to understand the meaning of the words 'Youth is Beauty'. And when I told you you were beautiful you flinched and said no no no. But you were a revelation to me. I wrote about you in my journal at the time and you're still there, on paper in a notebook on a shelf in a house in North Hollywood, California, USA." Poor, Poor Pitiful Me.

My flight to the L.A. Book Fair was barely a week after the toga party, my return journey an eternity. As I stood at LAX waiting for my Laker DC-10 back to Gatwick, it was with trepidation. On 25th May, a DC-10 leaving Chicago for L.A. had crashed on take-off, killing all 277 passengers on board, many of them bound for the L.A. Book Fair. All DC10s were grounded pending investigation, except for mine, the last one out.

Normally a DC-10 will carry up to 380 passengers. We were nine on board, hardly any human ballast for the turbulence that followed. I soon started drinking gin and oranges on the house as we waived around the skies, with only occasional alarming announcements about impending turbulence. The next thing I knew, I was being woken by a Hoover and a cleaner, passed out for the last six hours of my ordeal. There was no admonishment as I was led with my hand luggage to a waiting Mini and driven in the misty Sussex morning to the station, no fuss, no customs, no recriminations. Good for Freddie Laker.

That was not the case in Edinburgh. My absence had been noted and I was hauled before the head of the English department, a kindly, bespectacled don. "Are you an Elgin Bruce or an Aberdare Bruce?" he asked, and handed me a sherry. I wasn't really sure, but opted for Aberdare. This was the Thomas Hardy scholar, Tom Creighton, a charming man quite unlike the curious circle of Conor. It came as no surprise to me that he was a friend of Faith Raven, that great plantswoman, chatelaine of Ardtornish, and mother of the one day to be famous gardener Sarah Raven. He simply asked that I got all my summer essays finished and, after twenty minutes, I left him, a smile on both our faces. That summer there was *Festival Times* to work on with Tim Willis as its editor, and all the free tickets that reviewing involved. I still have a letter from Anthea Turner thanking me for a favourable review, saying sorry she could not come to dinner. In 1996, when she was famous or having a marital split or both, she got in touch with me again, sending me a copy of my gauche missive, which she had kept, and asking to meet up. Sadly, we didn't. Rowan Atkinson was a star turn with my old school contemporary, Howard Goodall, on piano.

But one who did come good was Quentin Crisp, following his one-man show *The Naked Civil Servant*. Roddy and I went to see him in a small community hall off the Ferry Road, not thirty in the audience. There was this rather brave, lonely, small, courageous man, spilling nightly out his life. Afterwards I became a 'Stage-Door Johnny' and asked him if he would like one evening to come to dinner. He accepted and we agreed to pick him up after his early evening show. "I must be back in bed by eleven," he cautioned and we said that would be managed.

How we laughed on the way home seeing we had got a ready victim for our sport. You couldn't keep the guest list short: Lord Varres, Cousin Allan, Patrick, Peaches, the schoolteacher to be, Christian the antiquarian, and, making up for a dozen absent women, Stephanie Lewis, the brilliant *Student* editor who was appointed despite the motorcycle calamity with the police bringing about my absence at her interview. Quentin played the part magnificently, dressed in his trademark black suit and fedora, his fingernails delicately varnished. He would have been seventy at the time.

We laid up the dining-room table in the drawing room of Douglas Crescent, Roddy's pewter wine goblets dusted down and shining, damask napkins, candles lit, even though it was still daylight when we got him there at seven. Lord Varres was in his best velvet suit and element. "Nice cuticles," he said on shaking hands with Quentin, turning the shook hand flat and holding it up for further inspection. What we ate no one will remember, another gallimaufry of laughter at which Quentin was quite the life and soul.

Through drink or for attention, Christian the antiquarian at one stage got out of the drawing-room window and hung on to the window ledge, perilously. We pulled him back in and made him talk to Quentin. Ever the professional, at 10.30 sharp Quentin gathered his cape and cane and we took him home, to the silent, threadbare digs that are no threat to a man so used to audiences, then solitude.

The laughter was on us. Having thought we had captured a butterfly who had, in his early years, spent time as an artists' model and a rent boy, he had captured us with his poise and humour. When he left us, we respected him. I think for all of us who had been there, each of us with degrees of camp about our person, we had met the real thing. And with the respect it was hard not to feel a vestige of sadness, for a life poured in and out of a suitcase for the titilation of others and the colour of his hair.

To The Polls, Ye Sons Of Freedom

'Louis watch the prisons, send the goons around
Is that Paris burning, is the Bastille falling down?
And where are all the mercenaries—paid for by the king?
Have they joined the mob you say, doesn't money mean anything?'

Jefferson Airplane, *Flowers Of The Night*

WHEN HE KNEW that he was dying, bravely in a Cotswold sanatorium, George Orwell was visited by his great friend and *Observer* editor David Astor. Afterwards, he wrote to him about the other Sunday visitors. "I was hearing upper-class English voices. And what voices. A sort of overfedness, a fatuous self-confidence; people who, one instinctively feels, without even being able to see them, are the enemies of anything intelligent or sensitive or beautiful. No wonder everyone hates us so."

If an Old Etonian (albeit a poor one who railed against his wealthy fellow pupils and those he saw as being above him) could feel like this, what chance did I have, with an English accent, to try once again to be elected by the student populous, mainly Scots, many from Labour voting backgrounds, often away from home for the first time? I do not think then there was much appetite for political nationalism amongst the students, they just instinctively hated the English. The English students in turn, those anyway from the public schools, kept to themselves, renting, or in some cases buying, New Town flats, and hosting dinner parties.

But, having been rejected by the voters once (as Mark Twain said: "The people have spoken, the bastards!") I was determined to give it another go, not for the Senior Presidency but as Honorary Secretary, which also carried a year-long sabbatical and wage of £50 a week, an office and a chance to put off going out to work. I also had a first-year student girlfriend, Juliet Crawley, and thought it might be fun to stand and be with her whilst dreaming of one day becoming Home Secretary.

Then a bit of luck came my way, one which would bury the English side of me for once. I joined forces with the Communists. There was going to be an occupation of Old College, that graceful Georgian Square that housed Raeburn portraits of old luminaries, the finance offices, and spacious rooms of the University Court. It was against a proposed steep rent increase for student accommodation and time for me to man the barricades. For a week I produced a daily newsheet of our progress as two hundred students locked themselves into Old College. It was gridlock for the university authorities. I declined an offer from my newfound 'Brothers' to stay in overnight. One of the mink and sables brought a portable television (she was dressed like Nancy Astor in a real fur coat) and I think all the well-off English students saw the injustice of a rent hike, even if it did not affect them in their private flats. One of my winning discoveries was that the university Vice Chancellor was living in an expensive grace-and-favour town house in Heriot Row, the premier New Town street, where Stevenson wrote *Treasure Island*. This had the hardened Left foaming at the mouth and there were chants of "Property is theft". After a week, the university authorities backed down.

I am not saying this gave me an easier time when it came to the elections. There was still a merry band of Marxists and Trotskyites to contend with, as well as dangerous Liberals who believed in absolutely nothing. With Louise Simpson once again at the helm of my campaign, it was a romp. Shortly afterwards I had time to take my Finals and get through. But the day after the election, the cloudy spectre of Dr Charles Fishburne loomed again. He had trumped up a claim that I had exceeded my election expenses. What I had in fact done is to get more leaflets printed elsewhere at the Art College (and not in his controlling Students' Association), all within the £40 allowed. I produced the receipt on his desk, met with a vengeful silence.

My other three sabbaticals were a talented mixture. The Senior President, John Sturrock (narrowly beating Alexander Sherbrooke), was a highly intelligent future lawyer with a decent streak. As Treasurer it was Graham Richardson, I would say independent left and whose family had been great friends with Graham Greene, and who had been at the toga party the year before. But the star turn was the Union President Eleanor Pritchard, Conservative, gutsy, fun, never shy to have a pint in her hand at the right time. I remember her once, mug in hand, dancing on a table, to keep up with and control the rugby boys. It is no wonder that she went on to become a most effective MP and, as Dame Eleanor Laing, deputy speaker in the House of Commons.

Student politics is often about ideology without result. Gordon Brown had tried to stop the university investing in South Africa. The left-wing students wanted to close down the nuclear plant at Torness. I think our objectives were prosaic but more successful. In a play to nationalism we determined to kick out the National Union of Students, to whom an annual levy of £38,000 was due, and replace it with a Scottish Union of Students, joining in with other Scottish universities.

Up from London came the NUS President David Aaronovitch, now a polished commentator with *The Times* and BBC, then a Marxist/Leninist Manchester student (for some reason he left Balliol after six months) to defend their case. I debated with him and he was effective. But London is not Loch Lomond, and all his arguments seemed remote, by geography as well as geopolitics, to the daily concerns of Scottish students. We sent him home to think again. Prior to his arrival, I had also mounted a campaign that, if we were to break away from the NUS and form a Scottish Union of Students with Glasgow, Stirling and St Andrews, the first £10,000 saved would be spent on subsidised beer in the Union bars. It was exhausted within a week.

One of the great supporters of this breakaway was Charles Kennedy, President of the Glasgow University Union at the time. No kinder Scot or worthy orator could you wish to find. When he later became leader of the Liberal Democrats, he always had a word for me as a journalist, our friendship forged from this time. When Charles died in 2015, I wanted to write a note to his young son, Donald. Alastair Campbell, Tony Blair's right-hand man, had written a tribute about Charles, so I emailed him to ask if I could write through him. He responded straight away, good of him given our very different outlooks and beliefs.

Other things, perhaps not so headline grabbing, that we achieved collectively as student politicians, were to ban Scientologist myrmidons and life assurance salesmen from entering university premises, stopping the Students' Representative Council from twinning itself with the IRA, and making it easier for students to do a three-year Batchelor of Arts degree, giving it similar weight to the longer, and more costly, four-year MA course. I also started a weekly news-sheet, *Midweek*, which anyone or any society could put a notice in for free and which is still going forty years later.

Over lunch one day with Conor in the staff room, I saw an advert on the noticeboard for a large, first-floor flat on Regent Terrace to rent. To leave Roddy was the greatest wrench but part of my bourgeois respectability thought that Patrick would not do my image any good. It also had a fine drawing room, with views over to Fife, and two bedrooms, the other of which was occupied by Dermot Keegan, a taciturn Yorkshireman my age, with a great sense of humour. He would need this as, at the time, he was selling sofas to Glaswegians.

My girlfriend—in her first year, eighteen, straight from Marlborough—was Juliet Crawley, the daughter of a clergyman and ten generations of Harrovians, in each of which a family member had played cricket for the school. Soon we got a fox terrier together, Thatcher, from the Edinburgh Dog and Cat Home in Seafield, and I bought a red Mini, Dermot accompanying me and getting £200 knocked off the price to £900. This was the domestic side of my year in student politics. Juliet lived nearby in Great King Street with another student, Catherine Cairns, pretty and highly intelligent who on graduating swept into Warburg Bank, and their landlord was an older, kindly scientist, Leslie Walker, with a fondness for sailing although he had never had any lessons in this art.

Juliet's parents lived in the rectory at Patterdale, near Penrith, not far from Wigton and the 'Hound Dog' of my earlier schoolboy adventures. It was easy to spend weekends there, walking the fells and going to St Patrick's church (where I sometimes read the lesson) on a Sunday. I never so much as had a sherry in all my visits, and Thatcher got the exercise of his heart's content. Sometimes we followed the Ullswater foxhounds, a foot pack, at a distance. I am not sure what age he was when we got him but for the next six years he became a fixture among our friends and us, even after we had split up, a brave little orphan who looked like the dog that appeared on the His Master's Voice record label.

The dinner parties Juliet and Catherine gave were prodigious as Leslie had a dining room that could seat twenty-four and, off it, a drawing room for myriad cocktail parties. The flat was not at all done up, coal fires in the bedrooms, old sofas and carpets and a homely feel. Leslie made a windfall when he invented something for restricting liquid in mechanical operations, but he never changed a thing. Juliet had some lovely Salvesen relations who lived in a vast house in Easter Belmont Road and we would go there sometimes for quite abstinent suppers. They gave her a Triumph Toledo, which we all used, ashtrays brimming.

In it with Henry Norreys, we went to stay with my aunt and uncle in Yorkshire for Crispin Odey's twenty-first. I was an invited 'plus one', me having secured the bedding arrangements. "Could I borrow some shampoo?" I asked my taciturn Yorkshire uncle, married to my father's artist sister, Jean. "Jean goes to the hairdresser and I use macassar," he replied. I had a good chat with Crispin. "All I want to do is earn enough money to buy back my family home," he told me. He certainly did that.

On the way back to Edinburgh, the fan belt broke in Peterlee. With us by now was Kate Faulkner, and both her's and Juliet's silk stockings were brought out to remedy the fault. It did not work. Eventually, at four in the morning, I was compelled to join the AA. At one point, the police stopped and asked if we were ok. As I was speaking to the officer, a call came through saying a man was about to jump off a multistorey car park in Middlesbrough. "Don't you have to respond to that?" I asked him. "If I don't go, it's one less emergency service when he jumps," was his startling reply.

All this was never going to last. In the February of my sabbatical year, it became apparent that, at the age of twenty-four, even I was going to have to get a job. I wrote to the London publishing houses and never got a response. I don't know why I did not think of journalism then, but imagined that it was something other people did. I spent a few days doing public relations work for my mum and Neville, and they both advised against it as a trade.

"Why don't you try an advertising agency?" Anthony Balniel said to me one day over lunch in the Waitress Service Dining Room, where we always (those from English public schools, that is) met up. My letters to them got a better response and they would pay the ticket to the interview, of which I had perhaps five. This was I think what was then known as 'The Milk Round', when firms got graduates in from the top universities. One of them, Benton & Bowles in Knightsbridge, offered me a job as a Junior Account Trainee on five grand a year. I lasted one day before I collapsed.

Before that, I went to America with Juliet, both of us guests of Tinsley Place, an exchange student she had befriended. We were welcomed into both Tinsley's separated families, her father in Connecticut, her mother in Virginia. I think we were both happiest there although I noticed, as we were together on holiday, that Juliet was really happiest doing nothing, reading a not-too-testing book, or the Bible. With Tinsley's mum, I got to work on their Christmas tree farm, mowing all day or riding into town with her stepfather, the former Red Sox baseball star Jackie Jensen. This mild-mannered man was still recognised and welcomed in every shop and store we went to. One night, he took me to an 'Old Timers' game, and signed autographs so patiently, an 'All American Boy.' It was the night I heard that Harry Chapin died.

Admen are not Madmen

'Porky and Best'

Wall's Sausages poster advert, 1970s
(Agency: CDP)

"I THINK WE overworked him," one of the admen was heard to say when I returned six weeks later. What had happened is, during the night of my first day, after an evening drinking in Feelings, the Fulham basement cocktail bar, my appendix had burst. I managed to drive my car from my brother's flat in South Kensington to his office off Marylebone High Street. I know I have said that no writer should have a brother, but that day he saved my life. I dumped the car on a double-yellow line and he called a taxi straight away to take me to A&E at the Middlesex Hospital. A lot of people came to visit me—even my dad—which enraged the matron.

What it did not do is save me from the daily hell of the advertising agency. I dreaded going to work, back at the bottom of the human pile and, amongst two hundred of us, only a handful who might have gone to the Waitress Service Dining Room. My windowless office I shared with three other graduates, one, Melinda Libby, who had been President of the Cambridge Union, another that of Glasgow and one from Warwick, so there was a pattern to their recruitment policy. On about the third day back, I went into an office and saw a photograph on the wall of a car and the writing under it: 'Crashed after a shoot'. Oh, good, I thought, someone here goes shooting. It was a 'photo shoot'.

My client was Henley Cars and showrooms, my boss a car fanatic called Tony Van Tool, North London, he would have worked his way up, with clearly better things to do than nursemaid me. I started work each day at 8.30am, driving my Mini from my rented room in Adam and Eve Mews off Kensington High Street and parking in the grounds of Holy Trinity Brompton church and never caught. (Only once did I get flashed at a lot, realising eventually in the winter darkness that someone had stolen my Mini's headlights.) If I was to look at the reception clock before six in the evening I would be accused of 'having a half day'. In a job that you love, the time whistles by. These hours dragged like a ball and chain, always waiting for the next banal instruction, brusquely delivered. If I look back now, I think from one or two others I worked for, there were elements of bullying. I spent quite a bit of time in the basement disabled toilet, tearful, or on the roof with Joa Thompson (sadly not enough time spent with her) and a planner called Groves-Raines, who would go there to smoke pot.

But Tony gradually softened to me, and I to him. He knew how to work the system and liked fine dining. He introduced me to Poon's in Soho and to a Chinese restaurant up in Camden. When I missed a Monday morning because I had been in Edinburgh, he saw straight through me: "You just wanted another night on the nest," he said. But when I had done good work for him, he would say: "Take your girlfriend out to Wheeler's in Old Compton Street, they let dogs in there, and charge it to the client," which we did. Thatcher sat well behaved under the table.

The problem with the creative process in advertising is that, unlike journalism, it is too cumbersome. There is the client with the big budget, the brand whose integrity must be protected and then, on the advertising side, planners, market researchers, space bookers, the creatives (who showed nothing but contempt for clients) and us, 'The Suits,' barely a species at all. I was fond of my client for Henley, who had been a 'Bevin Boy' and started out as a bouncer at the Locarno Ballroom in Streatham. He had a hutch of an office in Mecklenburg Street, off a multistorey car park, and I would go and present artwork to him through his plumes of Dunhill smoke.

Head of the creative department was Don White, a diminutive fairy, but clearly something of a genius. The children's writer Anthony Horowitz remembers working for him as a junior copywriter (I think at the same time I was there): "He was very flamboyant, witty and intelligent," Horowitz told the *Guardian* in 2005. "But he was also an outrageous homosexual who chased young men all over London and around the world. But he was a very generous, kind man, always full of grand gestures."

The agency's Christmas card for 1981 was a picture of Don astride a champagne bottle with nothing on but a Santa hat, with the tagline: 'I'm dreaming of a *white* Christmas', also an in joke about his widely known use of cocaine. When I left after a year, he gave me a drinks party in the office bar and a leaving card, signed by people who went on to forge important advertising careers (Brian Crook, David Meneer, Julian Walford, Peter Stephenson-Wright, Simon Rhind-Tutt, Vaughan Flood) and the chairman Bruce Reynolds. 'Bruce is leaving,' it said on the outside, and within: 'Sadly, not *that* Bruce,' in reference to the chairman.

"Don represented the dying days of glamour and extravagance in advertising," said Horowitz. "He was one of the fastest writers in the business. You've got to put energy into your work." For Don, as was bound to happen, the energy eventually ran out. Not five years after his straddling the champagne bottle, I was in the *Spectator* office when he was going out. He had been to see Philip Marsden-Smedley, the marketing man, to see if he could get the business to do the magazine's leaflet insert. "It's only small, you won't notice," I'm sure I heard him say, or something equally incorrect. I later heard he'd died of AIDS.

But I often thought of him as I was making up headlines for the twice daily *Londoner's Diary* column I worked on for a decade in the late 1980s and 1990s at the *Evening Standard*. For a jockey called Dobbin who had left his wife for a racing heiress I got: 'Naughty Dobbin gets his oats.' When it was exposed that former England rugby captain Will Carling was having an affair with the Princess of Wales whilst married, it was: 'Caught between a ruck and a hard place'. For a Rastafarian poet at Essex University who had run off with a famous writer's white daughter, 'Essex Mandingo'. The lawyers would not let that one through. When, in March of 1984, I worked for Nigel Dempster for a week, we ran a story about how Lord Cowdray's daughter, Rosie Pearson, had got a job on the *Economist*, which her father owned. Andrew Knight, the editor, denied that he knew who she was when appointing her. Rosie, when I rang her up, didn't know her father owned the weekly. 'For she was only the Boss's Daughter' was the headline, after the Gene Pitney song.

As for Wall's sausage poster 'Porky and Best', I only saw it once, driving back from Essex into London through Walthamstow. As was its intention, I felt a pleasurable glow at getting the pun. But, of course, it should have read 'Porky *is* Best,' which would still have the viewer 'in the know' but would also, as the Suits would say, have re-enforced the leadership of the brand.

When I look back on that year at the advertising agency, it was one of unremitting drudge. I could neither afford to or had the inclination to go out, one of the main reasons for working and living in London. It was a year of paucity and Pot Noodles, but there were the occasional breaks of sunshine. One of them was to be invited by Mum and Neville with Juliet my girlfriend to have Saturday lunch with them at Michel Roux's Waterside Inn at Bray.

It was a sunny spring day as I pulled the Mini up next to Mum's bottle-green Bentley S2 Continental. We drank champagne in the garden and walked on the wooden pontoon to see the pleasure boats, whose wealthy owners waved at us as they passed by. The restaurant had only one other table of diners, an American and his two female companions. All was going well, until the American called over the waiter to make a complaint. The gist of it was that the menu had said a particular vegetable had been twice boiled. The American was adamant it had only been boiled once. Suddenly, from the service door out came Michel Roux, followed by three chefs with chopping knives. I thought it was rather an odd way for a Michelin-starred proprietor to behave.

Later, Juliet and I joined a party for the Beaufort Hunt Ball at Westonbirt School in Gloucestershire. We were surrounded by those voices that so irritated Orwell, so took ourselves off to one of the girls' dormitories for a happy hour. On the Monday morning, I started by conducting a 'store check' on cat food as the agency was pitching for a Kattomeat campaign; I came in at lunchtime. This was considered to be the height of slacking by the campaign leader. I resigned that evening with a month's notice, although the campaign leader did give me the 120 cans of rival cat food I had gathered. I sent them to my dad's three farm cats in Devon.

෫෨

Like many people whose first jobs don't work out after university, I had only vague ideas about what to do next. I was still living in the rented room in Adam and Eve Mews, and Mum and Neville had by now moved to North Oxfordshire, Cherry Court, a small but pretty whitewashed house with ginger pantiles, a cottage annexe, pond for golden orfe and four acres.

Of all the things that are worse than living in London with a job you do not like, living in London without one is top of the list. The days dragged even longer than at the advertising agency. I went to stay with Mum and Neville sometimes, working for them in the garden, and in the summer evenings a Château Talbot and a steak. She insisted on dressing things up in French, a *daube* of beef, *maître d'hôtel* butter, (omelettes were always *aux fines herbes*), just get on with it, it's a barbecue not Boulestin. At her finishing school in Paris they said she had a wonderful French accent, as I am sure did every seventeen-year-old debutante who sashayed through their doors. But she fed us well and herself on remembered compliments, often rambling about how she was descended from Charlemagne and, when soon 'gone with the wine', how she didn't mind where she would be buried.

There was a local pub run by Tracy Reed, stepdaughter of *Third Man* director Sir Carol Reed, and we had some laughs with her, often hoping that her actor cousin Oliver would drop by. Tracy, like my mum (who had been in an episode of *The Saint* with Roger Moore) had a minor part in *Dr Strangelove*. Together nearing closing time, they would duet *Galway Shawl*, and charge their glasses to the Ireland of their childhoods. My mum had a god-daughter to stay for a bit, living in the cottage and being pursued by a nearby marquess. One night he turned up and my mother tackled him in her low-ceilinged drawing room, fire lit, beams, civilised. "You will not be going to the cottage," she said to him. "I thought this was the cottage," he replied. I am afraid my friends and I had a good laugh about that.

The villages round about were hardly pretty, surrounded as they were by flat countryside with the occasional Roman clump near Didcot, the odd church spire with voluntary wardens who wore loden coats. We would sometimes go to Oxford to get the Bentley serviced, having lunch at Raymond Blanc's fledgling Le Manoir aux Quat'Saisons, next door to the garage in Summertown. Back in London it was starvation rations.

One other ray of sunshine in that blank summer of 1982 was an invitation from Patrick to go to a Rolling Stones concert at his family home, Slane Castle in Ireland. I met up with Juliet there and we stayed in a flat empty of furniture in the courtyard. The night before the concert we were invited to the castle for dinner and dancing, and to meet Mick Jagger and Jerry Hall, the latter fresh from a well-publicised affair with racehorse owner Robert Sangster. We were introduced to his Mickship and his Moll in something of a receiving line. On the dance floor, Patrick attempted his own Mick Jagger impersonation, although Mick, who was standing just yards away talking to Patrick's brother, Henry (every inch the Earl of Mount Charles, which he was), didn't seem to notice. We watched the concert from the roof of Slane, the sun going down over the Boyne, with eighty thousand Irishmen below, their Troubles forgotten for a day.

Coming out of the courtyard flat on the morning of the concert, I came across Captain Farrell's nemesis himself, Phil Lynott. He was in full swaggered garb, like a highwayman, one foot raised on a drinking trough, his hands doing something with a needle. I always thought it was cruel when fellow Irishman Bob Geldof was creating his line-up for Live Aid three years later, that he overlooked Thin Lizzy. "I didn't know he was still playing," Geldof was heard to say. (For all the talk of scarcity of tickets for Live Aid, I got one the day before, met my brother by chance when I got in and we sat at the front on a rug).

Nicholas Coleridge was at Slane reporting for *Harpers & Queen*. I made the mistake of telling Patrick that one or two of Nicholas's classmates at Eton had told me they didn't like him, a piece of information that Patrick imparted to him in front of me. As we left the drawing room to go in to dinner, Nicholas took me to one side. "Could I have the names, please?" I said I could not remember. Later, back in London, Nicholas asked Juliet out on a 'date'. When she arrived at his flat, he asked her if she would like to have a bath, which, she told me afterwards, had embarrassed her. I thought it was odd at the time but perhaps it is just one of the strange courtesies extended by people in the fashion world.

Back in London myself, it was time again to think of work. One of the advertising successes of the early 1980s was *London Portrait*, the monthly, free, glossy magazine delivered to the best addresses.

My landlady at Adam and Eve Mews worked for them. So I thought about setting up a version in Scotland. Then I saw a small advert in the *Mail on Sunday* for a three-month, fully-paid business course at the Durham University Business School, and applied. I reasoned that firstly I would get paid and secondly could spend the time perfecting the idea of a free colour magazine for Edinburgh and Glasgow.

I arrived in Durham in September of 1982, escorted there by Patrick Conyngham and the titian-haired beauty Tania Spooner as we had all been at the Edinburgh Festival and they were driving south as well. Patrick insisted on taking me, the condemned man, to the Dun Cow pub, full of wardens from the nearby prison, and then left with the girl on his arm. I came to love the Business School. For others on the course, all older than me, it was a shot in the dark and a roll of the dice. Most had gone bust or been made redundant and wanted nothing more than to set up a tea shop in Darlington, or a small clothing store on Teeside. I think, like me, they were there for the government grant money. But we were well and rigorously taught. I went to the cathedral quite a bit and, one Sunday, to Lindisfarne for the day.

It had not been my intention to spend the whole day on Lindisfarne. As I was driving to the island across the causeway, cars coming the other way were flashing their lights. I wandered round the ruined abbey and the cloistered streets, looked out beyond to Bamburgh Castle, the Farne Islands and the choppy North Sea waters. After a couple of hours, I decided to leave, but the causeway was now fully under water, and would be until nine o'clock.

Resigned to my fate, I walked through stubbled cornfields, curlews grazing on the gleanings. The pub was shut. *Come on Eileen*, on my car radio, was number one. The vicar passed by me so I went to church and supper with him. I wrote 'On Lindisfarne' on the back of a Williams & Glyn cheque, Whitehall Branch, and dated it 19/09/82:

> 'A strange mixture of friend and foe
> Stranded here—most with some thought to go.
> But, why rush to leave this island
> Holier than now?
> Its salt-lapped shores,

Its more than weathered land.
Fate brought me here,
I'll leave by fate's command.

For me, it brought a day of
Simple peace. Cut off, cut in
To movement—and no chance
Of travel. Stillness—and no
Screams of history. So this
Is where St Cuthbert lived—the
Gospel truth. And now is where
The fishermen trawl, under a
Misty roof.

King Oswald, a visitor remembers
You, your priory, castle and extent.
The vicar told me, in his stealth:
"Love thy neighbour as thyself."
And, with his words, I went.'

The metre was to some extent dictated by the width of the cheque and the fading light. But the sentiment was there. I got back late to Durham, missing supper, but would not have missed this memorable visit as it turned out.

Portrait of a Laddie

'Ain't no love in the heart of the city
Ain't no love in the heart of town
Ain't no love, sure 'nuff is a pity,
Ain't no love 'cause you ain't around'

Café Jacques,
Ain't No Love in the Heart of the City (cover)

S HERIFF NIGEL THOMSON had a nephew, an architect by
day, Chris Thomson. By night he was the lead singer of the 1970s
and '80s Edinburgh rock band Café Jacques. They had a ready
following at pubs and parties in the city. They were 'Jock 'n' Soul' and
one of the welcome distractions as I worked alone in a rented West
End office, trying to establish what would, in the summer of 1983,
become *Scottish Portrait* magazine.

Such is the utopia of young dreams, and I was only twenty-six,
that I imagined, as publisher and editor, that we would, with pithy
features and reviews, capture all the upmarket advertising. Free, with
forty thousand copies a month, it was going into Edinburgh and
Glasgow's finest houses, targeted at what they call the ABC1s. It was
soon apparent, however, with only a lukewarm response, that I would
have to become an advertising salesman as well.

London Portrait, which had made millionaires of its founders in
a very short time, was brim full of property advertising. It was, as
journalist Christopher Long wrote at the time, "The dawn-chorus
of a publishing revolution in Britain." But, as I was soon to find out,
property advertising in Scotland was rather a closed shop, guarded by
the solicitors' firms who then mainly made up house sales. They had
their own weekly publication, which served all their needs. *London
Portrait's* publisher, Colin Lansley, who on agreeing to the venture
had picked me up in Chelsea in a Ferrari to take me out to lunch at

Drones, soon came to Scotland to sort things out. In return, I took him to the Doric Tavern and Prestonfield House hotel (with whom I had arranged a free colour page of advertising a month in return for free food). "Too far out of town," was his verdict on this glorious mansion.

I have no doubt that if he had been running the Scottish operation, Colin Lansley would have made a great success of it. He had a powerful aura and advertisers believed in him. We went together to several Edinburgh firms and he always got an order. My youth and inexperience counted against me. I think if we had just stuck to my original idea for an *Edinburgh Portrait*, we might have been smaller, but fared better. I could not caution the London directors enough that Edinburgh and Glasgow are very different places. Remember, at this time there was a car sticker war going on with Glasgow proclaiming 'Glasgow's Miles Better', to which the capital responded: 'Edinburgh—Mildly Superior.'

The London office at first did three good things. They paid off the £8,000 I had invested over six months on time, research, office rent and getting sales material ready. Then they shipped up two Lancia Deltas, one for me and one for the as yet to be appointed advertising executive. This was to be Carina Haddow, the top salesperson at *The Scotsman*. With her, also from London, came Tina Brooks, former head of advertising at *Tatler* (who was often mistakenly called 'Tina Brown', to which she did not demur). If they could not crack Scotland no one could, and Tina would often come back from an advertising lunch having had a shower and, whatever else, I did not ask.

What I failed to do was make inroads in distribution. I tried to get the magazine on the first-class London sleepers and into the top hotels and onto British Caledonian airways. None accepted yet, and within a couple of years they all had their own in-house magazines, so all I had done was awaken them to a sleeping giant for their own success. Meanwhile, the magazine, which was printed in Cornwall, had to be delivered to Scotland and distributed by hand, causing problems of unreliability, worries about home security and, in one case, theft.

Charlie Bruce, he of St Andrew's and the Deborah Orr encounter, was one of the distributors and called me one day from Gilmerton to say the couple on a council estate who had a few thousand magazines to distribute wouldn't hand them over. When I got there the police were trying to separate them and break up a full-blown fight, and Charlie Bruce had had bricks thrown at him. One night I got a call from Barnton from a resident. Barnaby Rogerson had been caught stuffing copies of the magazine into a wheelie bin. All this was of course manna to our rivals. It weakened our advertising strength and we were seen as both amateur and unreliable.

This caused despondency among the advertising team. But it was also unsettling for the editorial side, both of which departments I straddled as I could. This was a great shame as the writers were some of the best around, drawn from the university and a wider pool. Lucinda Bredin and Andrew Billen covered the arts with Geraldine Coates and Frances Fowle, all of whom have gone on to great things. I had a country writer, Humphrey Drummond, who lived in a Perthshire castle and flew falcons. Sandy Irvine Robertson, then still working for J&B in George Street, did the restaurant reviews under a pseudonym, and I got to review cars, which was not altogether a success. It is doubtful if the magazine would have been published at all without the production skills of Fiona de Sales La Terrière in the Edinburgh office.

Our 'staff photographer' was Brodrick Haldane, whose society life Roddy Martine captured so well in his memoirs of him, *Time Exposure*. Now in his seventies, he was a butterfly upon a reel of film. "Never let them know you are going to take their picture," he once said to me. "That's the secret." He was always immaculate, like David Herbert in Tangier, and his flat in the New Town's India Street was like an anteroom of the Wallace Collection. In gratitude years later, when I was on the *Evening Standard*, I would always send him each day a copy of the paper. He, in return, would furnish us with news from the Highlands, a welcome relief for strap-hangers on the tube. Once he rang me with a story about Margaret, Duchess of Argyll, when the phone abruptly went dead. She was staying with him and had just walked into the room. He rang back moments later, breathless with his story and his narrow shave.

Glen Henderson the Porsche dealership leant me a 944 to review. I had to pick up Thatcher from some relations of Gavin Maxwell in

Dumfriesshire so thought I would take it for a spin down there. On my way, I dropped off at Hopetoun House and fell down the stairs. So, with a sprained ankle, I motored on gingerly to the land of 'Unthank'. Thatcher was so pleased to see me, it was impossible to keep him on the back seat. Turning a corner sharply, with his paws on the dashboard, he put a six-inch scratch into its surface. As if this was not enough, I then threw my cigarette out of the window, which, I discovered five minutes later, had instead burned a hole in the back seat. This I tried to cover up with my briefcase when I returned the car. I got away with that. I only did one restaurant review before handing over to Sandy. I had written with approval that the bread-and-butter pudding was as good as at school. The owner threatened to sue.

Then the London office got greedy and impatient. Firstly, they imposed a nominal 'management fee' of £2,000 a month on us, deeply demotivating and, cunning business cynics that they were, came out of nowhere and was not at all in the spirit of our joint enterprise. Then, after six months, they wanted to cut their losses and for me to find a buyer. So, in the cold months of January 1984, I was trying to sell advertising and the magazine.

But there had been social dividends to editing a monthly magazine. I got invited to grand houses, Scone Palace for the weekend, parties with the Bruces at Broomhall or down in the Borders with the Biddulphs at Makerstoun. The Ravens at Ardtornish had many friends amongst their siblings, and often included me in visits to their Argyllshire mansion and estate. There were lunches at Prestonfield with Sandy Irvine Robertson and once when he had members of Status Quo to a charity lunch there, he made me pick them up at Edinburgh airport, by helicopter. I was not throwing lager tins of urine at them then.

Two balls were the highlight of one summer. The first was the regular student gathering at Hopetoun House for about four hundred. This was in part organised by Charlotte Black, Patrick Conyngham's long-suffering girlfriend. To everyone's popular appreciation, the band was Café Jacques. It was there that a pretty girl from the Highlands simply walked me off the dance floor, across the lawns and into a glade, the sun coming up over the Firth of Forth, Full Monty. When we got back to the party, everyone had gone. But there was a solitary black taxi outside the front of the house, which we took back to town.

The other was a 'Blue and Gold' ball held on the Island of Bute, to which I was invited by Caroline Crichton-Stuart. It was hosted by Caroline's father, the Marquess of Bute, and her formidable step-mother, Jennifer. Caroline was working for the National Trust for Scotland in Edinburgh, quiet, vulnerable, lovely, my age, but who had clearly had some late nights out in London in her time. I had met her at a student croquet match, and we got on although I did not know her well. Determined to enter into the spirit of things, I hired a blue and gold Darth Vadar suit from the joke shop in Edinburgh, complete with two-foot long shoulder wings.

We were all put to stay in the Glenburn hotel on Bute, all paid for (I did not know this until I came to pay my bill) by our hosts. As I walked down the promenade to get into the minibus to the party, it became apparent that I was overdressed. Others had opted for a simple gold cummerbund, or a blue velvet bow tie to go with their dinner jackets. I was not the most popular on the dance floor for the set reels later as several people got knocked over by my expansive wings.

But it was the height of my Scottish social acclimatisation. Amongst the guests were the boulevardier Dai Llewellyn, Pickford Sykes, Amber Rudd, Katharine Goodison, Desmond MacCarthy, Michel Cecil, Hugo Swire and Henry Norreys. Hugo de Ferranti flew in and out by helicopter. The Duke of Atholl, known as 'Wee Iain' for his great height, took it all in his immaculate stride. Lord Bute, I noticed, always wore his ties long, something I have done ever since meeting him. His son, Johnnie Dumfries, the racing driver, I spoke to a lot. Caroline had asked me on the family yacht for a week to go round the islands after the party. It is a lasting regret that, because of work, I could not go. Caroline was killed in a car accident a year later, run into as a passenger by a police car.

The Ravens of Ardtornish always had great gatherings of friends for the weekend. My friend was Sarah Raven and she in turn had fas-cinating fellow undergraduates, including the later art impresario Jay Jopling and the novelist to be Guy Kennaway. I stayed there several times with Thatcher and went to Sarah's twenty-first, full of Oxbridge gilded students with their careers already mapped. Most intriguing was her mother, Faith, a powerful intellect, unswervingly and unnervingly direct. No observation was not questioned by her but for its improvement. I loved her for that and used to warm inwardly when she addressed me with what you didn't know was coming next. I never knew her husband John Raven, the Christ's College, Cambridge, don, equally at home with botany and Aristotle, so they said, who had died young in 1980. But there is an alarming footnote in *The Captain: The Life and Times of Simon Raven*, by Michael Barber. John Raven taught Simon Raven Ancient Philosophy, but the novelist had already developed a cavalier penchant for young men. One, in search of Simon was misdirected to John Raven's rooms. Finding no one at home, he stripped off and arranged himself provocatively on the sofa. "Sorry, wrong Raven," John on entering was heard to say.

Such was the constant worry in the office, there was little time to enjoy the fruits of my position. Holidays and weekends were cancelled. Our rivals, with all their financial muscle, did their best to put us out of business. This involved them ringing up those firms that had advertised with us and offering them cheaper rates if they stopped. Then, one financial adviser who did advertise with us, called me in and offered to buy the magazine.

Leslie Ridgers had a small office in Rutland Square. I think he did personal finance or something like that. He produced an investor, and we continued publishing. It was a May Bank Holiday and, relieved, I took the time off to go again to the Isle of Bute. With me was my schoolfriend Vole, with whom I had been round Britain in the Capri as a teenager, and my latest girlfriend, the artist Belinda Eade, and Thatcher.

On a sunlit evening, we sat on the terrace of the Glenburn Hotel, langoustines and Moët & Chandon Imperial, which, Vole had established, was still on offer at post-war prices. We could have been in the South of France, and in our view a quinquereme and yawls cutting calmly though the blue still waters of the bay. Next day we visited some ruins and took Thatcher for a long walk.

On my return to Edinburgh, Leslie Ridgers asked to see me. On his desk were two open letters, both with my name on top. One said that I willingly resigned, the other that I had been fired. He invited me to choose which one to sign. I signed the one with resignation, and walked out into the square, my time as editor and publisher was up. It was a remembered kindness that the office staff took me out to lunch next day, for a thank you and farewell. There was no love in the heart of the city, after all. Although not on the same scale, I thought of the words of Roger Waters when Pink Floyd split up and his fellow bandmates kept the name: "They took my child and sold her in to prostitution."

Where there was, however, great affection was in the Dublin Street flat I shared for two years with the lawyer Tom Murray, now the eminent Queen's Purse Bearer at the Palace of Holyroodhouse. Here was a man with whom I could while away the evenings with always something new to say, perpetual optimism and a truly generous heart. He became and remains one of my greatest friends to whom I have often turned for advice, always given for the better. "To the Wig," he would say if a particular problem was to be solved.

He had a large dining room and this was often filled with my friends. To the girls who came and went he kept the conversation going and a blind eye; a man out of Stevenson or Walter Scott, a Writer to the Signet, member of Muirfield, The New Club and the Royal Company of Archers, everything a Scot should wish to be. It was only as I was leaving that I realised how much time we had spent together, when he said: "Do you think I could have *my* friends back now?"

Nowhere to run to, Baby, there's nowhere to hide

'The times are tough now, just getting tougher
This old world is rough, it's just getting rougher'

Bruce Springsteen, *Cover Me*

THERE COMES A time when a child has to stop blaming their parents for getting divorced, or other people for getting sacked from a first or second job. There comes a time when all these combine, and what others think of you means nothing. It is the moment the child becomes an adult, not hiding behind the class-room corner skeleton of education, the casual and cruel college con-quests. That moment came for me when, aged twenty-seven, I found myself in a dole office in Hammersmith. There were no thoughts of William Morris now, of the Dove pub and Kelmscott Press, no scarf and towpath pint before the Boat Race. It was for a slip of paper, £37.50 a week, to starve and survive.

I had thought about becoming a lawyer and went to see my dad. He took me out in Exeter to the pub. But the words just dried in my mouth when I thought of saying it would be ten grand for the conver-sion course. I was accepted and started on my dole money, to follow in the footsteps of my legal forbear whose name was on the statute books, lectures in Red Lion Square, lunch a sandwich under Fenner Brockway's statue. One Saturday I went to lunch at Lincoln's Inn, where the speakers were Peter Rawlinson and Michael Havers, and sat precociously between them, both charming. I dreamed of going to Ede & Ravenscroft for my gown and horse-hair wig, looking in the window afterwards.

Then I spent a week following a barrister from Baker Street to Brighton. The cases were a meagre diet of speeding offences, soliciting, rent arrears. I would hang around for hours as we waited our turn. It was never like this on television's *Crown Court*, which I used to watch some lunchtimes at university. The lectures that I can remember involved a snail in a ginger beer bottle and a builder who had ravaged a woman—but was it in or outside of her bedroom window and had she been willing? It was tort and torture, airless classrooms and bright foreign students.

I was not well, recovering as I was from some illness I had picked up that summer in India, some of the time spent with Juliet Crawley, who was working as a missionary. This had not helped my concentration in my legal lectures, hampered as they were by worries about health and economy and the long legal road stretching out before me. "You'll make some money by the time you are forty," my kindly pupil master said to me depressingly one day. After a month, I gave up.

Howrah Bridge

It had not been my intention to write about my two-month sojourn mooning about India, but the opportunity will never pass again as I shall not be going back. It made me realise I was an Englishman, and whenever I read the left-leaning lacunae of William Dalrymple it has me reaching for Newbolt and Kipling. Here is a nation that gets things wrong in triplicate. That shaking of the head says it all.

Nothing interesting outweighed the discomfort or the unwanted insistence of Indian travellers to practise their English on me. In Delhi I hired a rickshaw driver for a week to show me various sights. He was an untrustworthy Sikh with whom one day I bought a carpet just to humour him, an additional lugging for my baggage. I have it here on the farm still to remind me of my journey and mistakes.

In the foothills of the Himalayas, Virginia Macnab and Caroline Baxter were working in a Tibetan school at Dehradun. There was no parasol or tiffin for me there. What alcohol was available was made from fermented barley, lethal to any constitution. They remember I arrived with my carpet and bags "and real Gucci shoes." A ritual welcome at every turn was goat's curd tea, undrinkable. Such was the unpleasantness of my journey by train and bus to this sunny upland, I hired a taxi to take me back to Delhi.

In Calcutta, I stayed at the Fairlawn Hotel, a rundown place owned by an English couple who had 'stayed on' after Independence. My room had that day just been repainted so I got a temperature from paint inhalation. Juliet was working for Mother Teresa's Missionaries of Charity, so I thought I should show willing. My job was to dispense medicine to the dying in a hospice. I kept trying to put the pills into the hand with which the patients did their ablutions, so met with some resistance until corrected.

My fellow volunteers were well-meaning messianics from English public schools, joyless and no fun, content to try and save the world and learn a little Urdu. The saddest sight was not the dead bodies of patients strung up by their ankles in the hospice morgue but a lone foxhound walking in the rain down Chowringhee Road. Since that staple sport of the Maharajas and the Empire had been outlawed, the hounds had been left to breed with cur dogs in the streets. This was unmistakably a hound, degraded to scavenging with the limbless poor.

Another snapshot of the way things were was a casual dinner I attended at a Maharajah's town house. However educated, an Indian will not use three words if fifty will do. Often the purpose of the story or observation will get lost on the way. They may have studied Shakespeare at school, but the concept of an actual point to what they are saying seems to have passed them by. So as my bewhiskered host took me outside to the portico, to view the maidan and tank of fetid water just beyond, I had only visual images to stave off the boredom. There, on what must have been a dining-room table to seat forty, now discarded, was a three-legged terrier trying to keep its balance. It said it all to me. I think my host was talking tepid Tagore.

Other sites that failed to impress were the Lake Palace at Udaipur, the Rambagh Palace in Jaipur (a welcome sight was Melinda Libby dining on the verandah on a whistle stop tour) and Jaisalmer in Rajasthan. It was here I rode a camel for four days of discomfort. A local girl one night brought a roast chicken and offered herself for half the price of the fowl, ten rupees. I declined.

Of all the images of India I have, one has remained with me ever since. Making my way by man-pulled rickshaw over the Howrah Bridge in Calcutta, I saw a tall, arian, blond Germanic. He might have been involved in the traffic of humans, guano or gutta-percha. In his left hand he carried a knobkerrie and was brushing away oncoming people as if he was swishing nettles in Bavaria on a Sunday morning. With his right hand, as if to re-enforce his sense of differ-ence and intent, he gave his wrist a brisk 'go away' flicking motion. It reminded me of the Horace ode: 'Odi profanum vulgus et arceo' ('I hate the common people and keep them away.') It is a gesture I have occasionally employed since to good effect. I later observed him in repose, away from a garrulous group of poodle-fakers, in the 'Upper Class' waiting room of the railway station, spread out on a rattan lounger, drinking Seidlitz water.

ک

Instead, I got a job painting and decorating in Chelsea, and was back in my old room off Ken High Street, back to square one. For this I have to thank Virginia Macnab, my friend from Edinburgh, who got me the job, £150 a week. I enjoyed the peace and quiet of it, me on my own all day and the money in my pocket. But it was also Roger Waters who said: "If you become isolated, you decay." So I asked my friends if they could find me work.

I went to a stockbroker's lunch in the City, four hours of claret and Cointreau, and realised I had no head for maths or avarice. I thought about becoming a motorcycle despatch rider, more isolation. Then Mum and Neville took me on again, and I stopped blaming them for anything. Poverty has its own gratitude and forgiveness. They had regular and rather splendid long Sunday lunches, to one of which came Jeremy Thorpe. In the drawing room, there was a photograph of my mum, glamorous, beaming, hair done up. As we were going through to the dining room, Thorpe looked at it and said to me: "Did your mother know Princess Grace well?"

But it was another casual remark by financier Peter Briggs, with whom I briefly lodged in Fulham, that made me realise how bad things were. "You have got to think about what you are good at, and do it," he said. Did this mean I had to go back to advertising? I went to a head hunter off Regent Street. He abused me for wearing a dog-tooth suit. But he also got me three interviews. One was to sell space at the *Observer*, where I was interviewed in pitch darkness in an open-plan office off Blackfriars and offered a position in display advertising at £12,000 a year. Then an agency in Berkeley Square came up with fifteen and Grey Advertising, eighteen. "We really think you'll cut the mustard here," my interviewer said, an expression that I did not understand, and gave me the weekend to consider.

It was a weekend that would change my life forever. My mum was going to Ireland to see her dad and asked me to come too. She was always at her happiest with him, and he adored her. Perhaps, and this is by her own admission, no man really lived up to him, his bravery in the war, his humour, smartness of dress, mischief, quiet authority and generosity. It was a haven to be in their company, to share with them their drinks and laughter.

One evening we were invited to Garech Browne's Luggala for dinner. The house at this time, November 1984, was rented out to the producer of *The Irish RM*, James Mitchell, and his wife, Janie, who had become good friends with my mum. It was more drinks than dinner as the chef came in with barely more than a bowl of potatoes, every bit like a scene in the series starring Peter Bowles as the hapless Resident Magistrate. "That's your lot," he said and stormed out. The conversation somehow turned to the *Spectator* and a suggestion that it was for sale.

My mum was a *Spectator* devotee. She once had a letter published in it about the hazards of using a Magimix, which had resulted in her losing the top of a finger. The letter was framed at Cherry Court, alongside a Nicholas Garland cartoon of a mannequin, which she had bought for £200. Through her I had become a reader, too, familiar with the writers whose names were those of gods. By midnight, I was deputed to ring up the owner, the debonair Old Stoic, Grenadier Guards Officer and oil man Algy Cluff, to see if it was true it was for sale as someone at dinner had a ready buyer.

On the Monday afternoon, in my mother's office, I rang Cluff Oil and asked to speak to him. The conversation that followed with his personal assistant would later become mirthful legend for the archness of its content. "Could I say what it is about?" she asked. "Some things are so important that they can only be spoken of between the two people involved," I replied. There was a silence at the other end. "I will let Mr Cluff know that you have called," she ended.

Not five minutes later, the voice that was the languid intelligence of J.G. Cluff, a voice I would come to revere, was on the phone. My mother first took the call and, true to good, transferred it to me, smoking, surprised and, by now, shaking like a leaf. "Come to my office in St James's tomorrow morning at 9.30," he said when I told him that I had a buyer. I am not sure if I ran around the office but there were shrieks and cries from Mum and me. I was, as a special treat, given the gardener's battered Peugeot van to make the trip to London.

Parking outside the office in St James's, the van looked distinctly out of place, as I brushed dog hair off my suit and straightened my tie in the wing mirror. I think there was a lift to the second floor. I met the PA. I waited. On my left was an open office door with a man making his arrangements for dinner that evening. "So I can expect Winston and Minnie at 7.30," he was saying, referring to Winston Churchill M.P., member of parliament for Manchester Davyhulme, and his wife. This was the socialite David Tang, whom Cluff had taken on as an intern to help with his oil interests in China. At the time, I remember thinking it was a bit early in the morning for 'name dropping.' (On Tang's death aged sixty-three in 2017, bankrupt, it was Cluff who described him, with typical understatement, as "a most unusual person.")

I was then shown into the panelled boardroom. Not three minutes later, Algy Cluff entered, sitting at the far end, as if about to chair a meeting. It was true he told me that the *Spectator* was for sale, but that he had almost finalised its purchase. I was in reach of Parnassus, and I was not going to have the hinterland of hope taken away from me without a fight. Having arrived to offer a buyer, I then got up and took the long journey to his seat to offer my own curriculum vitae. "Do you think, in that case, I could have a job?"

I am not sure what he was thinking in the silence that followed. Was it that I had been to Stowe, his old school, and that he had fond memories? Was it that he was ever the intuitive businessman who could spot something that others could not even spot in themselves. He had, after all, taken on David Tang, whose father, despite his son's social ambitions, owned an upstairs Chinese restaurant in Shaftesbury Avenue. Slowly he raised a nearby telephone receiver to his ear and made a call. I did not know and could not hear what he was saying as fear had deafened me. He rose, moving like one of those giraffes in a nature programme, nonchalantly grazing off a treetop whilst seeing all. "Go to the *Spectator* offices at 4.30 this afternoon. The publisher, James Knox, will be expecting you." I gathered my wits and cv.

It was late October and a mist was swirling around Holborn, almost like a 'pea-souper' from the war, or, in an earlier time, a cloak of misty weather where Verloc in Conrad's *The Secret Agent* might have made his plans and bombs. I arrived at the black front door of 56 Doughty Street, a run-down townhouse a few doors down from the Dickens museum. James Knox, Eton and Cambridge, met me with the professional optimism that made him the brilliant publisher of the *Spectator* that he was to become. His war hero father, Sir Bryce Knox, had also been at Stowe and James had already written *The Trinity Foot Beagles, a History of the Pack*. Did it help that I was an Old Stoic from a hunting family?

What did not help was that I had a double-barrelled surname. When Knox told the newly appointed editor Charles Moore that he was thinking of employing me, Moore objected on the grounds that there were already too many double-barrelled surnames associated with the magazine (Moore has maintained his dislike of double-barrelled names in print ever since). He had a point. There was Mark Heathcoat-Amory as books editor, Mark Stuart-Grumber in advertising and Philip Marden-Smedley in marketing and, of the contributors, Patrick Skene Catling, Stan Gebler Davies, John Martin Robinson, Timothy Garton Ash and Ambrose Evans-Pritchard. I kept quiet that my surname had once been five-barrelled as each Welsh forbear married another estate and a name was added. This was reduced to a manageable two surnames in 1812, when my family got fed up paying an annual hyphen tax. (I have never used the hyphen; it is only used where members of my family have been in the Army, where unhyphenated double-barrelled surnames are not permitted.)

James Knox came to work on a bicycle, and with Moore and A.N. Wilson, this gave rise in 1984 to the political writer Alan Watkin's phrase 'Young Fogeys', which stuck to the *Spectator* at that time. The double-barrels would only seem to re-enforce this image. It is, I suppose, no use arguing to Charles Moore that many American biographers have three names, to which, presumably, he would not object (and, by the time I left the *Spectator* three years later, even the receptionist had a double-barrelled surname).

But this hurdle was jumped by James Knox, who told me that the new owners, the Fairfax family of Australia, would take possession on the 4th of March 1985 and I could start that very day. It may have helped that after my interview, I popped his bicycle into the back of the van and drove him back to his home in Pimlico.

It is true that I became engaged to Juliet Crawley at this time. I went to see her father in the rectory in the Lake District, and he wrote me a short card of acceptance in red biro. It was announced in the paper (well spotted by Joanna Coles at the *Spectator* who, when I went to see James Knox, got me to meet her and Mark Stuart-Grumbar to make sure we'd get on). The truth for both of us was it was the beginning of the end.

I was unemployed and far away from getting married. The rich are different to us. They don't have to worry about money. They may be stupid, entitled, all the things that Orwell so disliked, but theirs is at least a life on easy street. It was Alexander Pope who wrote: 'To err is human, to forgive divine,' but I had erred too far and even Juliet's divinity knew some bounds. We made a wedding date, which came and went. In the end I wrote to her, the coward's way, what we both knew and that was it. We shared Thatcher for the remainder of his short life.

What followed for Juliet was a harder but a better life, a missionary for good in far-flung countries, from Russia to Afghanistan. She had two husbands who were killed on the way, a child by each, and died of cancer at just forty-five. We always kept in touch and the last time I saw her was outside York Minster, her health weak, her courage never failing.

She was a favourite of my mother who always said the two heroines in her life were Juliet and the Princess of Wales. "I suppose you will continue to cut a Byronic swathe through London," my mother said when the engagement was broken off. She had given Juliet a vast gold engagement ring by Stuart Devlin, which she returned.

Ten years after Juliet's death (I had been to the funeral but avoided the recriminations at the wake), her great friends Barnaby Rogerson and Rose Baring, who own the publishing house Eland Books, produced *Juliet: A life In Memories*, 2017. It is edited rather brilliantly by Georgiana Campbell, daughter of Robert Salisbury who had employed Juliet at Afghanaid and with whom she went on several secret missions. I was asked to contribute and declined. But, as so often, it was Roddy Martine who said that I had been an important part of Juliet's university life, so should reconsider.

I suspected, and should have known, that various of the contributors would take the opportunity, as they say in Scotland, to give me a 'good kicking,' which they did. Ishbel Macpherson, who shared 49 Great King Street with Juliet, wrote: 'Energetic, ebullient, articulate, unreliable and with a waspish sense of humour,' but then continued: 'Rarely sober in the evenings, he was also a hostess's nightmare as destruction often followed in his wake.'

Charlotte Black was more circumspect. 'We were drawn to Patrick and Rory's scandalous behaviour. Roddy Martine too often had to wipe away our tears after the scrapes the two boys got us into, too many narrow squeaks and ups and downs to mention.' But, she concluded: 'I am perfectly certain neither Juliet nor I would have swapped all the thrills for any of the dashing or more eligible young men who crossed our paths.'

The American scholar Tinsley Place, who had Juliet and I to stay for that month in America in the summer of 1981, was, as American's often are, more generous and perhaps a little hyperbolic. 'He was our own Mick Jagger; stylish, witty, bright and hyperactive. They were the couple of the day, tapping into the zeitgeist.'

It was left to Barnaby Rogerson himself to deliver the unbridled *coup de grâce*. 'Alcohol-fuelled wit, fiercely held opinions, sexual gossip, relentless partying and a continuous emotional storm. One of the most persistent and discreet womanisers of his generation with a wild, anarchic, unfaithful streak to which she was attracted.' He was also in a short space able to suggest that I was simultaneously having an affair with Patrick and Charlotte as well. I thought I was reading a snapshot biography of Warren Beatty.

In contrast to this, my own contribution was pretty tame. Part of this was based on guilt and fading memory. Part of it also was not to be thoughtless to Juliet's family and children. I have many letters from Juliet, and there was love between us. I have those letters still but I keep them private, not wishing to trespass upon the future memories of Juliet's two marriages, her adult time as a good wife and mother.

There were now four months to fill before I started at the *Spectator* and there were only so many envelopes I could stuff for Mum and Neville. I wrote to various Fleet Street newspapers asking for shift work, although I never thought of writing to the *Evening Standard*, which would become my berth for a decade later on.

The way into Fleet Street then was like the camel and the eye of the needle, years on a provincial paper interviewing cats up trees and finally the cornucopia of drunken lunches at El Vinos or the Cheshire Cheese. It was smoky, male dominated, except for the Jean Rook, Lynn Barber and Lynda-Lee Potter types who bartered human happiness for spreading homely bile, and a closely guarded shop. I still have a letter from Christopher Stephens, then William Hickey on the *Daily Express*, pointing all this out. "Perhaps your talents lie elsewhere," he concluded, even though we had never met.

Then I got a letter from Colin Mackenzie, deputy editor on Nigel Dempster's diary on the *Daily Mail*, offering me a week's shift work, starting in February. It was Mackenzie, whose first love was the Turf, who had, for the *Express*, been sent to Brazil to bring back Great Train Robber Ronnie Biggs in a deal with the paper and the policeman 'Slipper' of The Yard, who would 'nick' Biggs during the interview. It was billed as 'the Scoop of the Century.' In the end, the Brazilian police got wind of the scheme and took Biggs into custody themselves. Biggs told Mackenzie of his deflated coup: "You're a nice guy but you work for a grubby organ. And organ's the right word."

Mackenzie was now working for perhaps the most charismatic, fearless, well-connected diarist since Pepys and my forbear John Evelyn. Dempster was also tempersome and elusive, with his light grey suits, penchant for Pekingeses and daily swims at the RAC Club followed by a TBL, the customary two bottle lunch. But he carried about him a bulging contacts book and an aura that would stop at nothing. Colin Mackenzie, in contrast, who had to put the pieces together (for Nigel was not a natural writer—long unpunctuated sentences with whole paragraphs trying to explain who was who) was calm and, I felt exasperated. He would rather have been on the racecourse. Even a wet Monday evening meeting at Windsor would have done.

My first day was a Sunday, and I was taken to lunch by two of Dempster's long-standing and suffering lieutenants, Adam Helliker and Helen Minsky, to a burger basement, fashionable, off Fleet Street. I had come armed with a few stories that I eked out over the week into three 'leads', and was kept readily supplied by Geordie Greig, my friend from the Skye balls in 1980, who had just started on the News Desk. "Ah, my Mole," Dempster would always say to me, passing my desk as he came in to the office at three.

He got me to ring up Lord Glenconner on Mustique ("I'll only speak to Nigel," he said over a crackling line). Then I had to phone diary regular Dai Llewellyn (whom I had met on Bute) to ask if a titled friend of his was getting divorced. "Dear boy," said Dai, "I will tell you anything you want to know about myself, but with my friends I can't help you." Dai had a comic sense of decency to the end of his life.

"You say you've been to university and you can't spell," said Mackenzie, appraising my first effort. Having to type each paragraph on separate, seven-piece, small pages of copy paper and then fastening them together with a vast paper clip, was an achievement in itself. It was a baptism of ire. At nights there were functions to attend where more stories could be grubbed up and contacts made.

My first was to interview the retiring Speaker of the House of Commons, George Thomas, on his elevation to the peerage as Lord Tonypandy, at a drinks party in the Palace of Westminster. Even I noticed the proportion of young men present. But, I also noticed, there were no Labour MPs there. This made a news story. The one person I did recognise was the Tory MP Norman St John-Stevas. It being nearly Lent, and he being a 'devout' Catholic, I hovered and asked him what he would be giving up. "Answering foolish questions like that," came his curt reply.

Some years later, when I was at the *Evening Standard* and he was now Lord St John of Fawsley, I took him out to lunch at The Ritz. He was very much the lord and guarded until, over pudding, the head chef came to pay his compliments. "Very good to see you Lord Norman, I mean Lord Fawsley," said the chef, not getting his name quite right. St John preened like a peacock, comfortable that, like so many politicians, he was talking to someone so obviously lower down the social scale.

I went off to talk to the manager of the Palm Court tearoom, who told me that all the furniture was about to be replaced. "What is going to happen to the Gillow chairs?" I asked. "Oh, we'll just throw them away." I bought a dozen on the spot for £10 each, sold six at Lots Road auctions for £900 (four went to Kate Sissons at the paper who organised their collection) and have kept two till this day, oval-backed, faded velvet between pink and red, with white woodwork.

Then Nigel got me to ring up Taki, the *Spectator* 'High Life' columnist who was residing at Her Majesty's pleasure in Pentonville prison on a cocaine charge. He had enough money for the prison payphone, which kept bleeping out, to say what good friends he had made. His earlier experiences as a war correspondent would have served him well for his three-month stay. He kept fit by working out each day and teaching fellow inmates karate; he was a Black Belt.

Keeping Nigel's whereabouts unknown was another role of the job. It was not my place when his wife rang up on my last day, with Mackenzie giving me a look, to say he was in the George V in Paris with a famous writer's daughter. I hope I repaid his confidence in me when, during my first week at the *Spectator*, Algy Cluff came to lunch. My office was next to the dining room where, I overheard, Algy had that day become engaged to the beautiful City lawyer Blondel Hodge. 'The Mole' notified the Maestro. It made the 'Lead' next day.

The Spectator: Look on and speak no sound

'I don't have to think twice before naming my favourite restaurant to which I have been a regular visitor for more than 26 years. Antibes has 68 restaurants, but to my mind Felix comes first for the freshness and variety of his fish, the quality of the meat and the excellence of his dog Matisse. The quiet ambience with a view of the port through an archway is to me an added bonus.'

Graham Greene, letter to the author
about Felix au Port, Antibes

O F ALL THE names in human form who have passed through the door of the *Spectator*, none is more widely regarded than that of Graham Greene. He wrote for the magazine as film critic in the 1930s, before the age of celebrity when people like Joan Collins were fished out to write drivel diaries about their latest husband or being a 'Factory Girl'. It was at the *Spectator* that Greene perfected his clipped, latinate, slightly old-fashioned way of writing, with a film director's eye for tight plot and script.

When Peregrine Worsthorne once wrote in the *Spectator* diary that no sentence should be more than nineteen words long, he could have had Greene in mind. Certainly much of the *Spectator's* following, which, when I arrived, was no more than 21,000 copies a week, was down to good, concise writing from real writers and journalists, not here-today-gone-tomorrow politicians or jobbing actresses.

For me this was all important as my job was to sell advertising and to do this I had to describe the talents of the regular writers, writers that you would not find in the *Sunday Times* magazine or the *Observer*, who were our competition. At first, the *New Statesman* might also have been considered a rival, but even we gave up reading it after a bit. Its heyday with Paul Johnson was long past.

So the bedrock of names we mentioned comprised Charles Moore, the editor, Ferdinand Mount, Kingsley Amis, Auberon Waugh, A.N. Wilson, V.S. Naipaul, Dick West, Taki and Jeff Bernard. The advertising agencies always wanted to know what the last two were like most of all. "Would you like to be a blank piece of paper in Jeffrey Archer's typewriter at opening time?" was one of Jeff Bernard's finer opening lines. Taki, who had many aristocratic English friends and cronies, could also illuminate the foibles of the American and European rich, a colourful Jay Gatsby.

Later, when I had crossed over to editorial, I came across Taki and Jeff Bernard on more equal terms. Taki would take me to Annabel's but once accused me of plagiarism after I had lifted a story of his about a fight in Annabel's but moved the story further on in the *Evening Standard* without saying he had originally written about it. "Let our war be over," he wrote to me some years later after I had stayed in the hotel he owned in Athens, The Caravel. I had just written to thank him. Mentioning to the barman that I knew Taki, I set about having a few drinks and a swim. When I came to pay the bill in the morning I found the barman had rung up Taki in Switzerland and there was no bill to pay. I felt rather rueful that I had only plundered twenty-six quid at the bar but that was a kindness, nevertheless.

Jeff Bernard I saw more often, either in the Coach & Horses in Soho or the Colony Room Club where barman Ian Board was a fellow Devonian. Splenetic to other members, he was always charming to me and I never had to join. "Just buy me a drink cunty," he would say and we would reminisce about old Exeter and when he worked chopping cabbages as a boy at the Imperial hotel in the town, where I would be put alone by my father to have my Sunday lunch.

Jeff had a mournful cadence to his voice, worldly wise, as if something dreadful would soon happen. His words in print had the struggle and weight of furniture being moved by a stage scene shifter, which was one of his earlier jobs. But I don't think I ever met a journalist of more integrity or indifference. "It takes a bit of courage not to be frightened of tomorrow," John Osborne once said of him. I don't think Jeff was frightened of anything.

"Respectability is one of my great enemies," he told me, in 1995, over lunch, two years before he died at sixty-five of diabetes, a life of drinking, little money and only one leg remaining. That we were in his flat on the fourteenth floor of a Berwick Street council block in Soho says everything about the courage and fatalism of the man. When I say lunch, it was of course two bottles of blue Smirnoff and, for him, several packs of Player's Navy Cut. He did not go gentle into that good night.

For now, however, my area was drinks advertising and 'luxury goods'. These were what my immediate advertising boss, Mark Stuart-Grumbar, called 'perquisites': gold lighters, cigars, holiday villas, watches and motor cars. Mark, a slightly dreamy but determined Old Harrovian, lived and breathed the *Spectator* and I soon learned to live and breathe it, too. If I had a complaint, he would call the magazine 'The Speccie', which I never did. I think he only did it in the spirit of a family nickname you might give to a favourite elder. None of this could have been achieved without the brilliant mentorship of publisher James Knox. First he trained me up and we would go together to pitch to the advertising agencies, a formidable double act of which I was the junior part.

James Knox had literally saved the *Spectator*. Before its sale to the Australian Fairfax publishing family, it had accumulated debts of £300,000. My shared office had a one-bar electric fire and a naked light bulb. With the Fairfax investment, the magazine was able to print permanently in colour (all those glossy colour ads) and produce a marketing brochure (the latter were assembled for me cheerfully by an 'intern', another double-barrel who slipped through Charles Moore's net, Simon Sebag-Montefiore). The third person with whom I shared an office was Joanna Coles, who looked after books and art gallery advertising. No one could have been a better office friend and I still cry with laughter at the deals we did or overheard each other doing. The turning point for both of us was when James Knox sent us on a selling course, which I had seen in the back of *Campaign* magazine.

Marcus Bohn Associates made us both invincible. They offered a two-day course at a hotel off Swiss Cottage where we learned how not to let potential advertisers slip away. There were acronyms and charts, and a tutor who really wrote plays for Guildford and Richmond theatres, or so he said; another life that all salesmen must cling onto, more respectable, to give them dignity when rebuffed on those cold days on the doorstep. That is the character of a really good salesman: optimism, tenacity but also a slightly sad acceptance of their lot.

From this orthodox weekend (during which a couple of brothers from Plaistow offered me seventy grand basic before commission to come and sell windows for them), Joanna Coles and I evolved our own highly successful techniques. One of them was called 'fish slabbing'. In this you had to imagine that the potential advertiser was a salmon you had landed, still alive, and had to finish it off on a fishmonger's wooden block. We would make the gesture to each other across the room, as if we were swinging the fish by the tail, deal done, better than *Glengarry Glen Ross*.

Walking past a car showroom one day on my way to an agency in Marylebone, I spotted a black Lancia Beta sports car for sale, five grand, and bought it with a loan from Coutts; with the name of the *Spectator* behind me, the bank had taken me on. Such was the advertising haul I was now bringing in, James Knox soon offered to buy it and let me use it as my company car. Not only that, as well as my basic salary I was given an unlimited petrol allowance. Each weekend I went somewhere different, often with Belinda Eade, from the dole office to dreamland in little over a year. The car had once been owned by Charles Althorp, Princess Diana's brother, so one weekend we took it back to his estate in Northamptonshire. It was a strange experience with farm workers and people in the grounds standing up straight on seeing the car, thinking it was his lordship at the wheel.

Then a truly sad event occurred in January of 1986, when Auberon Waugh's sister, Margaret, was killed. This is the account from Selina Hastings' biography of Evelyn Waugh: 'Margaret published a life of her grandfather, Aubrey Herbert, and there was talk of her producing a memoir of her father. But in January 1986, while crossing Chalk Farm Road in London, she was hit by a car and killed. Margaret died on 28 January, 1986, at the age of 43.'

The office was thrown into sombre mood. Bron Waugh immediately gave up his *Spectator* commitments to concentrate on his sorrow and wider family. One of those commitments was he was much in demand as an after-dinner speaker, based in part on his wine column as 'Ausonius.' "Would anyone like to stand in for Bron at three speaking engagements?" James Knox asked us one morning soon after. I grasped the opportunity.

"First Class all the way, skipper," were the last words John Osborne's father had said to him before dying young of tuberculosis in a sanatorium on the Isle of Wight. I thought of this as I travelled north to Manchester, first class and a suite at the Midland hotel, to be one of the two 'celebrity' speakers at the *Observer Mace* student debating finals. The other was Labour shadow arts minister, Old Etonian and MP, Mark Fisher. I was going north on a gravy train. Whilst I did not 'win' (the motion was something to do with public arts funding) it was an exhilarating experience, the students were bright and Mark Fisher a generous opponent. I took the sleeper back to London in Osborne Senior style.

The next venue was the Pitt Club in Cambridge to address 'The Squire Mytton Society'. Mytton, of Halston Hall in Shropshire, where his vicar kept for him a pet bear (who drank beer) and giraffe, was variously an MP, master of his own harriers, racehorse owner, spendthrift and drinker, a legend in the early 19th century and during his short life. At Cambridge, which he briefly attended, he only read the *Breeders' Stud Book*, dying broke in Calais in 1834 at the age of thirty-seven.

I first encountered Mytton in a *Country Life* article written by their long-serving and rather snobby hunting correspondent J.N.P. Watson in 1984, a hundred and fifty years after the subject's untimely death. He had been drinking brandy in a tavern, set fire to his nightshirt, and was immolated. I got a copy of his memoirs by 'Nimrod' (C.J. Apperley), which did every justice to his hero, from Joe Allen's equestrian bookshop in Lower Grosvenor Place. With Allen I struck up a lasting friendship and he would take me occasionally to lunch at the Goring hotel, brimming silver beakers of champagne for starters. "I know you Fleet Street types," he would say, laughing and winking as they arrived.

The Cambridge crew, whilst not overly versed in Mytton's sporting achievements (they knew he was a hero of Enoch Powell), matched him drink for drink. The Cambridge MP and biographer Robert Rhodes James lent some respectability to the dinner scene, which included several students in drag. It was my first meeting with the future Fleet Street feature writer Robert Hardman, more conventionally attired as I recall, and Andrew Roberts (now, of course, one of our leading British historians) who was in the chair. "Welcome my lords, ladies and gentlemen and well-bubbied wenches," intoned Roberts. The waitresses took offence and downed their silver service. We all, drag artists included, had to repair to a pub whilst apologies were made and accepted. A convivial and unusual night in which I was well received. Today, on the farm, I have an English springer spaniel. He is called Mytton.

The third invitation was a trip to Oporto in Portugal to tour the port and sherry houses. I thought it only right at this point to come clean and say I was not really 'Ausonius' or even Auberon Waugh. "Come anyway," the organiser told me. "I am bringing my girlfriend and you can give me cover." Drinking white port on a barque on the Douro in the midday Monday sun was no hardship, nor was staying for a five-course dinner in the best hotel in town. We were there for the Festa de São João, which involved a procession whereby we whacked people with plastic hammers and large garlic plants.

Next day it was a visit and a lunch at The Factory House, the ancient club house of the producers, great names like Warre, Dow, Symington and Fonseca heralded on the walls. A train took us up to the growing terraces, following the gorges of the great river. It was marred somewhat when the train pulled into the station and killed an old widow who had fallen in front of it.

My host was an Englishman who had been here many years, an exile in these sunburnt uplands, who had made his lot amongst the Portuguese and vines. One night he put on Wagner and we sat alone drinking on his company mansion house verandah, tears running down his face as he thought of home and probably the fifty he once scored in a house match at Clifton College. He looked at me as if to say: "Do not do what I have done," the loneliness of the expatriate that even vintage port cannot assuage.

My guilt was at not having a ready berth to write about these experiences (they were covered in the *Spectator* by that Spanish hand,

Harry Ayres). This was soon solved by a fellow journalist on the trip, Sue Reid ("I'm not *that* Sue Reid," she said, introducing herself, referring to the famous *Daily Mail* feature writer). This Sue Reid was the editor of Peter Cadbury's intriguingly titled magazine *Working Women*. She hired me there and then to be its wine correspondent, which I did happily until the magazine closed a few years later. The imposter had become 'Ausonius'.

Meanwhile, there were further drinks advertising accounts to be conquered, as the circulation rose above 30,000 copies a week. One I was sure would be suitable for the *Spectator* was Hennessy Cognac. For some years before me, the British agency that handled their account had been resistant. But I established they had a European budget, handled by an agency in Paris. I mentioned this to James Knox, who was doubtful, so said I would pay my own way, spend the weekend in Paris and see the agent on the Monday, with whom I had arranged a meeting at noon.

Arriving at the agent's office, he immediately handed me a Paradis Cognac, then two more. Then it was out to lunch at a private members' club, cheese soufflé and filet de boeuf, deep civilisation. My only worry as the hours went by was that I had a boat to catch from Calais. I made it just in time. From this lunch, however, came an invitation to go and see Maurice Hennessy himself in Bordeaux, flown out at Hennessy's expense and chauffeur driven to the Château de Bagnolet.

Hennessy, a consummate Frenchman and sponsor of the famous Gold Cup race meeting at Newbury each November, was, like me, of Irish descent. As we talked over dinner about Ireland, I could not help but feel like Redmond Barry in Stanley Kubrick's *Barry Lyndon* when he meets the Chevalier de Balibari, confesses to their mutual Irish heritage and bursts into tears. Sometimes Ireland, as James Joyce observed, is best viewed from afar, and even better with a vintage cognac close at hand. Also close at hand were twelve colour-page advertisements booked the next week by the English agent, Philip Juniper, amazed.

It was now my turn to ask Maurice Hennessy to lunch. It was James Knox who had started these highly successful 'advertising lunches' in the *Spectator* dining room, where the most select advertisers or would-be advertisers could meet some of the contributors. Many of the journalists were uncomfortable with this. "There's the advertising man," deputy editor Andrew Gimson would shout out at me if he saw me at a book launch or social gathering. We didn't ask him. Heroes to the cause included regular attendee Mark Amory, the literary editor, Digby Anderson, who wrote on food (and once told me he hadn't had a bath since 1968), the biographer William Shawcross who would get on with anybody, and, on the odd occasion, 'Kingers' himself if we could prize him away from the Garrick and supply him with enough Macallan, his only tipple, even at lunchtime.

It has often been said of Kingsley Amis that the two phrases that depressed him most were "Red or White?" and "Shall we go through?" But at these lunches he was masterful, telling jokes and stories with all the pier-end timing of a Vaudeville Max Miller or Olivier as Archie Rice in John Osborne's *The Entertainer*. The only time he would stop, mid flow, was when the *Spectator* cook and future part of the duo 'Two Fat Ladies', Jennifer Paterson, came into the room. It was not that his stories were ribald, he just wasn't going to expend his energy on her.

"I'm not going to serve that advertising muck," Jennifer told me, in the minuscule kitchen off the upstairs dining room, when I had Maurice Hennessy to lunch and he brought a bottle of Paradis Cognac as a gift. I got Kingsley to commence the honours. Sometimes, the roles were reversed and, if there was a last-minute cancellation from a writer, we would be asked to fill in from the advertising department. The most annoying guest was the City and Suburban columnist Jock Bruce-Gardyne, yet another double-barrel, who always parked his bicycle in the way in the hall.

Then Prince Charles came to lunch, and the office was disrupted for a morning. The top editorial team were invited, but one, the political editor, Ferdinand Mount, declined. I asked him afterwards would he not have liked to have gone. His reply was magnificent. "It's not what I would have thought about Prince Charles that would have worried me," he told me. "It was what I would have thought about myself." I had no such qualms and lined up in the hall afterwards to shake his Highness' hand. It all went wrong. I missed his palm and his signet ring got caught up in my shirt cuff. I should have been more of a Mount than a mountebank.

Shortly afterwards an incident occurred that has passed into Fleet Street folklore. I have mentioned the little kitchen where Jennifer Paterson concocted her barely edible melange of wobbly green mousse and chicken fricassée. Jennifer would arrive before the weekly Thursday lunches hooting her hellos, which could be heard throughout the building. This was a cue for Joanna Coles and I to carry up her wicker baskets of provender as she chucked us under the chin, her vermillion nail varnish like that of a drag queen at the Folie Bergère.

The little kitchen was opposite my office. Rather than go four floors down to the basement kettle, me and Philip Marsden-Smedley next door would make our coffee in it, thinking no harm or wrong. Jennifer had a different view. This was her domain (albeit empty four days a week from her fragrant presence). Some coffee had been spilt. A couple of spoons, unwashed, had been left to loiter in the sink. There was an eruption from Jennifer, voluble even by her own standards. I cannot quite remember if Charles Moore was sitting in the garden below, browsing some learned editorial, when it started raining knives and forks but he could well have been. Jennifer was sacked and, we all felt, quite rightly at the time.

But then we started to miss her. Who has not, after all, done something in the heat of the moment for which they are afterwards remorseful? I had myself once, in my early days, had a tussle with Mark Stuart-Grumbar, for which James Knox correctly hauled me in, a lesson from which I learned wholeheartedly. As Surtees once said: "More people are flattered into virtue than are bullied out of vice."

Jennifer was reprieved and, after that, she would take me out to lunch when she was reviewing restaurants. She drove always to these lunches on her red Honda Seventy. A game we played was to see who could afterwards get back to the office first. She always won. In return, she would come to the parties that Belinda Eade and I had with our housemate, Christopher Howse, who became Jennifer's best friend. She came to our wedding. She was the life and soul, and we loved her for it.

Then another sadness came to the office. Joanna Coles told me one day she was going to stand in for Mark Amory's deputy on books, Clare Asquith, who was having a baby. At first I thought this meant just for a few months and then she would come back to me and our 'fish slabbing.' But it soon dawned on me that, once the door of escape from advertising sales opens itself, you do, if you can, shut it behind you. I lost some innocence that day for I realised that, before long, I would have to follow suit.

ॐ

Should it be Bron or Mr Waugh?

There is no doubt that a regular cornerstone of the Spectator was Auberon Waugh's 'Another Voice' column, in which he sounded off each week against the unions, lefties, Labour and humanity in general, getting the wrong end of the Jeremy Thorpe trial and the right end of Polly Toynbee. Perhaps he had to have what David Queensberry once said, inelegantly, about his second wife, Alexa, 'a daily anger shit.'

Whether this was because he had shot himself while in the Army, had a crusty crab for a wife or a father who was disappointed in him, or all three, was hard to tell. It certainly made him socially awkward and suspicious to all but his closest work colleagues, or female company. I first met him at a Spectator summer drinks party in the editor's office, smoking a Benson & Hedges cigarette, glass of wine in hand, buttoned up in a blue chalk stripe suit. I introduced myself by saying "Mr Waugh" and always afterwards he would call me "Mr Knight Bruce". The truth is, I did not know him well enough to call him Bron or how to pronounce Auberon without it coming out as Oberon.

In 1986, he became editor of Naim Attallah's Literary Review, a job he occupied until his death, aged sixty-one, in 2001. He either asked me or I offered to go and see him, to help with circulation, which I did. Entering his Soho office was like stumbling upon a much-loved hermit in a cave, surrounded by well-off beauties and who, defensive of him, treated my presence as an intrusion. There were a couple of male scullions, Grub Smith and another, keepers of his flame and fellow pasticheurs, acolytes to his altar of satire. The one looked like a pugilist, the other possessed the physiognomy of a discarded prophylactic. Both could 'without sneering, teach the rest to sneer.' But the girl in charge of circulation, nineteen, oriental, was the reason for my visit and soon object of desire. I took her to lunch in Lexington Street, to the Andrew Edmunds restaurant, and got food poisoning. We slept together at the second go, listening to Peter Gabriel's 'Sledgehammer'. "I hope you live forever," she wrote on a card to me afterwards.

Whether Bron (let's call him that) got wind of this, I do not know, but there was always a formality to our future meetings at book launches and the like. One of his daughters married the once pretty choirboy from Lord Patrick's Dada party in Edinburgh. A son, Alexander, I would see around occasionally. He had an interesting way of pronouncing things. When I went to see my godmother in Milverton in Somerset, Brigid Roffe Silvester, he was living nearby and came to dinner, taking up much of her tiny cottage. "You must write more about your family," he urged me. "It's so cathartic." He had just written, bravely, 'Fathers and sons' about his family and forbears.

Alexander gave the address at Brigid's funeral. I was intrigued, as were others of the many present, that he pronounced her name 'Roaf' Silvester, an inflection I had never heard before in all my life of knowing her. It reminded me how some White's Club bore had told Evelyn Waugh, the grandfather, that Claret was properly pronounced 'Clart'. Off went Evelyn to Berry Brothers and tried this out, much to their bemusement. He never drank 'Clart' again.

With Bron, however, came a war of words. He put a curse, 'The Curse of Waugh', on me in his Spectator column. The reason for this was when I was editing the Londoner's Diary on the Standard, Bron had written another of his thinly veiled attacks on former Tory arts minister and Oxford contemporary Lord Gowrie. Bron always referred to him as 'The Wog'. (Being interviewed earlier, in 1973, by Stephen Glover when he was editor of Isis, the Oxford student newspaper, he went further. "An appalling man, unbelievably thick. He went to Balliol because it was the only place where wogs would be accepted.")

In 1991, Bron published his memoirs 'Will This do?', in which he referred (on page 115, not 133 as his column claimed) to falling in love in his first year at Oxford ("in a hopeless, incompetent, mooncalf sort of way") with an undergraduate at St Hugh's. "It would be intolerable to parade this unfortunate lady before the public gaze... so I shall confound everyone by calling her Beatrice." He went on: "I implore any reviewer or gossip columnist who knows her identity to hold his peace under pain of an orphan's curse."

Whilst Waugh chivalrously hid the girl's name, he gave a clue. "Beatrice was eighteen years old on 27th of February, 1960. She waited and waited but I never made a move." As chance would have it, a fellow undergraduate confirmed to me the damsel's identity. This was Bron's best man, Bobby Corbett, my great hunting friend from Scotland. In his memoirs, Bron writes: "Bobby, in an avuncular moment, said to me 'My advice to you is to treat her like a woman. Stop treating her like a doll.'" The person who did treat her like a woman was, of course, Grey Gowrie, as Bron recalled. "Black, and an earl and said to be a poet... I had to watch him practise his Afro-Asian wiles on my Beatrice... with his exciting touch of the tar-brush and his so-called poetry. I have never been so miserable in my life."

It was over a long lunch by the sea in the South of France in 1987, that I think I got to the bottom of this feud. I was the guest for a week of Lady Mary Keen, the doyenne of garden writers, who had been an Oxford contemporary of all four of them. She gave me a tantalising insight to the world of Oxford students of her day. From Bron giving the birth date of Beatrice, I was able to work out that the love brawl was over Grizelda Grimond, like Mary a beauty of her generation, and the daughter of Orkney MP and Liberal Party leader Jo Grimond. Waugh had lost out but never forgotten. Grizelda went on to have a child with John Osborne's great collaborator, the film director Tony Richardson. I ventured it was not unreasonable as a diarist (and remember I had a friendship and affection for Jeremy Thorpe, whom Bron so persecuted) to name her.

It was strange to see my name vilified in print. "I must warn Knight Bruce that he is under the Curse of Waugh," he wrote in his Spectator column. To some extent the curse worked. Not long afterwards, I had not one but two pretty girlfriends who both left me for members of the extended Waugh clan.

Shortly before he died, I got a letter from Bron Waugh. He had read that I had become the master and huntsman of the Torrington Farmers', a small hunt in North Devon where he had done much of his persecuting in the late 1970s of the then MP Jeremy Thorpe. He enclosed £25 and wished me well. On the day he died, I met with the hounds and we held a minute's silence.

At the next hunt point-to-point, I clubbed together with Bron's great Exmoor friend, Geoff White, to sponsor a race in his memory. Alexander came to give away the cup. The night before, Geoff and I had been drinking until two in the morning at the Carnarvon Arms in Dulverton, on the last evening before it closed for good. We were invited, towards the end, to drink everything still left on the shelves for free. We were therefore doubly grateful for Alexander's presence and oratory next day.

The day of my transformation from advertising to editorial had its beginnings one May day in Mark Amory's book-lined office, perhaps the loveliest office in London with full-length glass doors leading out on to the garden. He was with Andrew Gimson, the deputy editor, and they were talking about Boris Johnson's forthcoming marriage to that Oxford beauty, Allegra Mostyn-Owen.

Allegra had been working at the *Londoner's Diary* on the *Evening Standard*, but was giving up to move with her future husband to Brussels. "You might know of someone who could take her place," Gimson said, never thinking, and nor was I, that it could be me. But afterwards I thought: why not? I went to a public call box and rang the diary editor, Richard Addis, feeling guilty, who asked me in for a week. At the end of it, he offered me a reporter's job, starting in November. I had said that I must see all my *Spectator* advertisers through the autumn booking schedule.

It was excitement mixed with sorrow. I was giving up the most civilised working life in London for the venial cut and thrust of Fleet Street. And I was thirty-one, not fresh out of university, where callow youth is better at snooping diary stories. Charles Moore called me in and tried to encourage me to stay. Even Andrew Gimson was now more accommodating. "Remember never to neglect your serious writing," he said. I was sorry for my advertisers, too. Three of them wrote me letters. "You've crossed over to the other side," wrote one, and I felt bad about that. In the end, I think everyone understood and Joanna Coles anyway was going to join the *Telegraph*. We had done our crime and time. It was never going to be the same without her. No one was less surprised than me that she ended up one of the most successful magazine editors in America.

James Knox allowed me to commission articles for the summer 'Food and Wine' issue, and I wrote to various people asking them to describe their favourite restaurant. Lord Goodman said he couldn't be bothered. Elizabeth David said she didn't have time. 'Debo' Devonshire said: "I have got a favourite restaurant but I'm not going to tell you where it is otherwise I won't get my usual table." Then Alan Clark wrote to me, on Saltwood Castle headed paper, crossed out. Instead he gave his address as 'On a Swissair flight to Lausanne.' It was the first time this soon-to-be-famous political diarist had written for the *Spectator*.

But it was Graham Greene who made the issue, writing to me

from Antibes about Felix au Port. His letter is reproduced in full at the beginning of this chapter. After our week with Mary Keen and her family in the South of France, I took that letter and Belinda Eade to the restaurant and introduced myself to Felix, showing it to him. His dog Matisse was by his side. "So, you would like 'Lunch Graham Greene,'" he said. What followed was a vodka on the rocks, two bottles of pink wine (with a clipper ship on the label), fish soup, more fish and crème brûlée. We sat at Graham Greene's table (he was abroad) with 'the quiet ambience with a view to the port through an archway', and afterwards swam with many topless beauties on the sand. That letter I treasure, and is framed above my desk.

From Fleet Street to Lingerie

'It is a column to be written by gentlemen for gentlemen.'
Lord Beaverbrook on the
Evening Standard's Londoner's Diary

I WAS FIRST fully aware of the *Evening Standard* whilst examining some excavated Roman ruins by London Wall on a winter's afternoon in 1967, aged eleven. From down the street a cockney voice was calling: "Extra, extra, read all about it: Campbell dies in Lakeland speed challenge." I broke off from peering at Yoricks and bones and joined a queue of perhaps twenty readers, desperate for news of this tragedy. As a schoolboy, we had charted Donald Campbell's preparations, made models of *Bluebird* from papier-mâché, and now it lay in splinters, its pilot at the bottom of Coniston Water. The ink from the paper came off on my hands, and never left.

The dying days of Fleet Street, of which I was to experience the final year, are more mourned in the memory than the experience. The typewriters were as ancient to today as metal divers' suits. Barnardo's boys collected our copy, which went up air chutes to various departments, the 'Back Bench', legal and the like. Everyone smoked, and only the editor and books editor had a glass cubicle to separate them from the open floor, not dissimilar to Arkwright's mills. On the *Londoner's Diary*, we started work at eight for a first page off at half past. Any story gathered overnight was hastily typed up, or made the page change at midday. It was physical and quite grimy work. Each day a reporter was deputed to take the copy to the compositing room where, at the mercy of some heavily unionised typesetter, our measured words would be slashed to fit, with little argument that the result did not make sense. You soon learned to write the final sentence as disposable. The compositors viewed us with disdain. Once in front of them, you were not allowed to touch the copy, only to point at it, timidly suggesting a change or cut. This ordeal went on for about twenty minutes, and it was always a relief to get out, battered by sarcasm, thinly veiled menaces and intransigence so early in the day.

Back up in the coning tower of the column, the contrast could not have been greater. Our editor, and my inspired employer, was Richard Addis, Rugby, Cambridge and a former novice monk. The reporters were Sarah Sands, Victor Sebestyen, Mark Palmer, Mark Jones, John McEntee and freelancers who came and went. An old boy came, always late, twice a week, and we all got him cups of tea. I am not sure if he ever produced a story. The novice monk had kept his kindly habits.

At the end of my first week I was taken out to lunch at El Vino's by Richard Addis, Peter McKay and former *Daily Mirror* editor Mike Molloy. These last two were the prefects of the parish, their careers forged on foreign assignments, writs and tabloid titilation. They also had an admirable thirst, and this was to be my baptism. Richard Addis left us, saying that I did not have to come back to the office. I then sat in dumbfounded silence as McKay and Molloy told story after story, wicked, funny, and irreverent. I might as well not have been there (but I am sure it was for my benefit, to roughen off my smooth *Spectator* edges), except to imbibe their folklore and the brandies that came round with alarming regularity. Dickens could have been living at this hour.

What I remember most about that year on Fleet Street is how, after work and the mandatory visit to the pub, the next day came around so quickly. The column was like some ravenous bird always wanting worms to feed its chicks. To come to work without a story was to fail. To see that story in the paper almost unchanged, was the greatest excitement. To begin with for me this was hit and miss. Then Richard Addis took me off and taught me how to write. I will never not thank him for that.

Who, then, were my fellow motleys, the Fagin's children of Fleet Street? Sarah Sands was a single-parent mum, having been married to the actor Julian Sands. No one then or now was more professionally beguiling or persuasive, with the warmest sense of humour. I would and did go round the world for Sarah Sands in the ten years that I worked for her, and, I would do it all again. Victor Sebestyen, who would become a leading historical biographer, was a different matter: left wing, partial to hemp, he had come to the diary because he had formerly been working for a trade union and kept ringing up and selling stories about his bosses.

Mark Jones was a conundrum. He had been to Cambridge (which he referred to modestly as 'College') and had edited *Campaign*, the advertising weekly. He was not a natural for a clubland corner or political gossip and intrigue, with its whiff of public school, and probably too good a person. He went on to edit British Airways' *High Life* magazine. As an Old Etonian, it might have been assumed that High Table and low conversation would also be beyond Mark Palmer. But he thrived on it, becoming one of the great travel writers of his generation and deputy to Richard Addis when he went on to edit the *Daily Express*.

The Irishman John McEntee was a diary hack through and through. I only ever read one feature by him, about how he was molested by the Christian Brothers in his native Monaghan, and I think he had Fenian tendencies. His forte was diary stories, as told in his memoirs, *I'm Not One To Gossip, But...* If the subject of a story complained, he would laugh things off apologetically with his Irish blarney and come to some arrangement for a 'good story' in the future.

The actual physicality of old Fleet Street was somewhere between a farmyard and *Animal Farm*. There was the active swarm of toil within the office, punctuated from time to time by shouts induced by beer, the canteen like something out of *Brighton Rock*, and downstairs, the thrub and thrum, the *sturm und drang*, of the heaving printing presses, shaking the building and Londoners to their senses. Yet, when the lorries came to the back of Bouverie Street, to unload their vast reams of paper, marked Trondheim or Malmo, an unchanged historical peace prevailed. It was as if the haywain carts in William Morris's *News From Nowhere* were once again abroad, the horses with their nosebags being petted and nuzzled on their necks by passing children.

The editor was John Leese, without doubt a genius of his trade. I only got to see him once in his glass box. Richard Addis had to appoint a diary deputy and, in his way of fairness, he encouraged all his reporters to apply which, even though I was the most junior, I duly did. "Journalism is a vertical career," John Leese said to me. It was the best encouragement he could have given, meaning it was not yet my turn but that he believed my day would come.

Not a week later, I asked the sports editor, Michael Herd, if I could contribute to his pages. I wrote a column in praise of bar billiards. Then I did one about mink hunting as, on my way to my first meeting with John Osborne in Shropshire, to collect a book review for Mark Amory at the *Spectator*, who knew I was going there that weekend, I came across this merry band of thumb-sticked locals. By the time I left them, with the mink flying about in the trees of the Teme River at Clunton, out of the hounds' and harm's way, it was late. It was my first meeting with Helen Osborne, John's fifth wife and gatekeeper. "He's out and he never keeps copies of his reviews," she told me firmly, hovering outside the closed front door of their gothic house, The Hurst. The review had got stuck in a postal strike and, as I left, I saw a curtain twitch. John had got stuck inside.

Many and varied are the tasks of a diary reporter. The main one is to get a story that the subject would rather not give. "Journalism is a story someone doesn't want in the paper," George Orwell had observed. I often thought of this. A tricky question, at the launch of Fiona MacCarthy's life of sculptor Eric Gill, was to ask a Dominican friar if Gill had ever propositioned him. Was it OK, as MacCarthy had revealed, that Gill had slept with two of his own daughters? I could have been talking to a silent order. The thrill of getting a 'scoop' was aways short-lived. The next edition of the diary was never far away. But, it was an education in inventive journalism and a bond between those on that desk has lasted to this day.

After a year, the paper moved to Kensington High Street, where we had to learn about computers. Gone were the compositors and haywains, we were now in the civilisation of the late twentieth century. There were plenty of worries that we were too far away from parliament and the gossip stories it afforded, but this proved unfounded. After the last diary edition at noon, lunch in any part of London could last until four, all on reasonable expenses. It is a myth that we lived off our expenses. Sometimes we were so busy we did not submit them for weeks on end. Once, on a job, I heard that a news reporter had asked for a blank receipt, and I was dismayed by that.

What made the *Londoner's Diary* special was that it was, in effect, like a *Spectator* in miniature. We aimed to set a news and features agenda with our stories, which were often taken up and amplified by our own and other papers next day. Not long after we moved to the old Barker's department store in Kensington High Street, I met a girl I knew outside who asked me what I was doing. When I pointed to the building, she replied: "So you're working in lingerie now." It was more a case of linen washing of some other kind.

No editor was more gracious to us all than Richard Addis. On two occasions over the next couple of years, I asked for a month off to 'write a book'. One I spent driving my Lancia convertible—I now owned two Lancias—through Europe with Belinda Eade, trying to find British exiles who would talk to me. The other I spent in Greece, back at Kardamyli and lunch with the Leigh Fermors. Each year, Richard Addis would send me to the Edinburgh Festival for a week and I never forgot you are not just there for fun, but to find stories, which I did.

"No fine writing," Lord Beaverbrook had cautioned to his gentlemen reporters on the *Londoner's Diary* in the 1920s. He was right. The aim was to get the story down on the page with, inevitably, a quirky error missed by the subs. As a column, those who have worked on it included not just my generation of future stars but John Betjeman, Harold Nicolson, Nicholas Tomalin, Magnus Linklater and Max Hastings, Valerie Grove and Mary Kenny. I think all of them could look back on their time there with a sense of mischievous youth.

I could have carried on being a diary reporter for ever, warm in the cocoon of camaraderie. I had enough money to buy a one-bed flat in Shepherd's Bush, and enjoyed the company of my fellow scribes and the frenetic life. It was like an extension of essay writing at university, and being paid for it. But, all too soon, that changed, and, what John Leese had called 'a vertical career,' came to pass. Richard Addis was made features editor and Sarah Sands became our diary editor. What I never saw coming was that she asked me to be her deputy.

Not only was Sarah Sands full of ideas and mischief, she also had many admirers. Part of my unspoken job was to ward them off. One of them was the *Observer* journalist Henry Porter, a left-wing, provincial type masquerading as a 'Man about Town', whom I never put through. When I was at the *Spectator*, I regularly took advertising from the Distressed Gentlefolk's Aid Association. A letter then appeared: "I thought a distressed gentleman was a man who could only shoot three days a week," it read, signed Harry Porter, Worcestershire. Like father, like son. I gave the Association a free advertisement for that snobbery.

Another part was, occasionally, to take Henry Sands, Sarah's son, then aged about ten, out from his prep school in Surrey. For this I was repaid later by being invited to his twenty-first in Norfolk, where naked fire-eaters in a converted church were the highlight of the evening. Sarah made a remarkable speech, recognising the love and step-parenting skills of her journalist husband, Kim Fletcher, a Sheffield man of steel. Their daughter together, Tilly, is my god-daughter.

Around her, Sarah Sands collected a remarkable array of reporters and contacts. She got me writing features under John Preston, the arts editor, and we learned to turn around a thousand words in an hour. It was Preston, later to find fame with his book on Jeremy Thorpe, who I passed one day in the corridor. "You write like the lyrics of Barclay James Harvest," he said. Whilst that is not quite true, it brought back memories of my summer in Buckinghamshire with Nicola Hemsworth, and I ever after marked Preston for his good humour and insight.

After a year, Richard Addis became the deputy editor of the *Sunday Telegraph*, and Sarah Sands was his natural successor as features editor. On the diary, we worried who might take over. I don't think any of us wanted an outsider. When, before Richard Addis, the opera lover Geoffrey Wheatcroft had been drafted in, he spent all day on his Walkman listening to *La Traviata*. We didn't want someone too grand to do our dirty work.

First Mark Jones was given the chair on trial, but that didn't work out. Then it was Victor Sebestyen's turn, which again, after a few months, didn't seem quite right. What was lacking, and this was in a world before a fascination with 'celebrity' took hold, was exactly what a West End club man would like to read: Black-tie dinners, political intrigue, first-night rows behind the stage, glamour and media tussles. The Club Man wanted us to write about them so he felt he had been there himself without the effort.

So the next turn on trial came to me. After two months I was appointed editor, and I think none of us ever looked back. Jones, Sebestyen and McEntee moved on. I drafted in Marcus Scriven (Radley, Christ Church, and the Welsh Guards) from the *Sunday Telegraph*. Then came the Old Etonian sub, James Hanning, his desk next door to the sailing and opera-loving beauty Emma Robertshaw (whom he later married), David Rennie and Peter Bradshaw from Cambridge (both double firsts), Vincent Graff from Oxford, Mark Inglefield from a failed marriage and Lady Henrietta Rous, the all-time party girl. I met her walking down Kensington Church Street with her King Charles spaniel, Ziggy, and she told me she was hard up. I employed the dog. Four years later, she told me that Ziggy had died. That was the end of her contract, but she continued to lurk around the office, hiding in the 'Tape Room', and never missed a party. Over a *Private Eye* lunch one day I sat next to Sebastian Shakespeare, and signed him up there and then. Jasper Humphreys completed the regular team, with Davina Blewitt, god-daughter of the ever genial Vyvyan Harmsworth, as our secretary.

Of those who did regular shifts, many have gone on to great careers. The late Philip Kerr became a famous spy writer, Jonathan Freedland a *Guardian* and BBC mainstay, Ross 'Dross' Clark a fully-fledged feature writer, and Nick Bryant and Inigo Gilmore became television reporters. Imogen Lycett Green became a good writer, following in the footsteps on the column of her grandfather, Sir John Betjeman. Harry Phibbs we rescued from his banishment from the Federation of Young Conservatives. It all came right for him years later when he was elected as Tory councillor for Hammersmith. James Hanning co-wrote the biography of David Cameron and Peter Bradshaw went on to become the film critic of the *Guardian*. William Sitwell went on to become a well-known chef, newspaper and television food critic. If this sounds like the list of a 'First Eleven', it was.

Yesterday's news is of little interest now, but the stories we broke collectively then were the envy of Fleet Street. We may not have started out as tea boys and worked our way up from the sports subs desk, but we were every bit as good without that. I once introduced Victor Sebestyen to someone by saying he taught me all the 'dark arts' of journalism. "But you were a willing pupil," he replied. It is said that journalists, like the police, masons, drug dealers and villains, will protect their own, that 'dog does not eat dog', and it is true. But, sometimes, we were not there, as in the murder of one of our most flamboyant reporters, Robert 'Ten Pole' Tewdr Moss.

ঽ

Robert Tewdr Moss: Murder Most Foul

It is not possible for me to say I loved Robert Tewdr Moss, but I had a soft spot for him. Everybody did. He was so obviously gay, heavily pomaded in Floris Malmaison and dressed in wing collars, cravats and frock coats, in a world of journalism which would more readily mock such apparitions than employ them. His speciality on the Londoner's Diary was the West End, musicals and theatres, which he nightly trawled for stories and rough sex. He had a landlady in Primose Hill, Leonora Digby-Smith, whom he would often take for company and cover and who doted on him.

Robert was brave and produced good stories. Hearing that Harold Pinter was going to be given a party at the Royal Academy to celebrate his birthday, I got Robert to enrol with the catering team so he could get in to the party and ask the legendarily irascible birthday boy a few questions. Robert was in charge of the birthday cake and brought it in to the room, candles ablaze. Pinter gave the thin-lipped smile of one used to being given prizes and adored. It was soon wiped from his face as Robert did a Marilyn Monroe routine, announced himself as being from the Londoner's Diary, and had Pinter got anything to say? Dispensing with one of his customary long silent pauses, the Nobel laureate and great author of 'Betrayal' and indeed 'The Birthday Party' replied: "Yes... FUCK OFF."

In August, 1996, I was taking the boat back from Ireland and someone had left the Independent on a coffee table. There was Philip Hoare's obituary of Robert, D&G T-shirt photograph, his long and good-looking frame sitting on a Georgian step, pillars either side, murdered at just thirty-four. In my shock, I thought about the Marvin Gaye hit, 'Abraham, Martin and John', and the line: "I just looked around and he's gone." Something of the powder of Robert's butterfly wings was left with all who knew him. I was determined to find out what had happened, even, at one stage, going to stay in his old room at his sometime landlady Leonora Digby-Smith's.

Robert had good and devoted friends and a love of cats, and they in turn loved him. As an English student at Bedford College in London he had got a First and a glamorous girlfriend, Afsaneh Parvizi, who, even when married to her charming husband, remained his mainstay and muse. I met them both and they asked if I could help make sense of his murder. It had, I think, been an unfortunate set of circumstances, misunderstood sexual advances and religious retribution.

Like many freelance reporters, Robert was seldom out of work but never had much money. At the corner of St Mary's Terrace in Maida Vale, where he rented a flat, was a telephone box. Robert had worked out that you could make calls from it to directory enquiries for free. Often he was to be found crammed into this tardis, notebook in hand. It is here that he first met two young Arab boys from the nearby, and distinctly rough, John Aird Court housing estate off Paddington Green. He asked them in and, one way or another, involving cup cakes, a kettle flex and an iron bar, they murdered him. Quickly on the scene the police found Robert's contacts book. Under B it had the number for Buckingham Palace. The story went that this got the police even more active as they said: "The deceased was clearly well connected." It was in fact the switchboard number in every reporter's contacts book.

The Arab boys were duly found and arrested. I think part of their motive had been taken from The Koran that it is important to punish infidel homosexuals. They had taken what little money Robert had and, a terrible thing for any author, dead or alive, the revised manuscript of Robert's first and only book, 'Cleopatra's Wedding Present: Travels in Syria.' In its original form, Christopher Potter of Fourth Estate had described it as "Unpublishable, baggy and undisciplined." The Arab boys had now taken his computer with all his long hours of toil on the revisions with it.

I went to the John Aird Court estate and knocked on doors, many of them steel or boarded up, and to Robert's street in search of the computer and any information that might explain to me, let alone the court, the reasons for his death. On the canal, I passed Richard Branson's barge, 'Duende', remembering it as a cry and feeling spectators give to matadors. I rang the doorbell of Robert's nearby vicarage and was turned away. "The vicar is too busy to see you," said a young man at the door, and I heard the giggles of an all-male drinks party going on in the background. It was not much and the least I could do, fruitless as it turned out to be. Except that I got to meet some of his friends and Afsaneh Parvizi-Wayne, loving and loyal to his memory to the last. In court, the two accused were wholly unrepentant, swearing and refusing to take an oath on any recognisable document. They were sentenced to actual or abetting murder. Afterwards his friends asked me to lunch in a nearby pub, but my heart wasn't in it and I did not want to trespass on their memories and grief.

Robert's manuscript eventually saw the light of day, continually applauded by that great travel writer and publisher Barnaby Rogerson. "It has a cult status and has propelled the murdered Robert into (an unexpected) heroic niche," he wrote on reviewing its reprint in 2008. For those of us not well versed in Syrian politics, there is also contained within it a superb diary-style vignette of his encounter with the Soho habitué, homosexual photographer and author Dan Farson, in the bar of the Baron Hotel in Aleppo.

"Of the many odd things about him, I could not decide whether it was his voice or his complexion which was the most peculiar," wrote Robert of Farson. "The latter was an angry red colour, and his shiny face was puffed out of all proportion to his features, like a buffalo tomato... His voice clearly had difficulty escaping from the series of chins and dewlaps that contained it, and it was tarry and indistinct, as though issuing from a tiny megaphone." It is perhaps just as well for Robert's publishers that Dan Farson himself died shortly after the book came out.

Like many of Robert's friends and colleagues, I attended the book launch at the Travellers' Club. I took with me my Indian girlfriend, who met a brilliant Oxford lawyer. I read about their engagement in the papers three months later. And they say no good deed goes unpunished.

No one should be a diarist forever. It gets to the human soul and the villains, however much we pilloried them, seemed to survive, Jeffrey Archer being a case in point. They were, in the end, more powerful, richer and more talented. It was Adam Edwards, again a good writer who used me a lot on the *Standard's ES* weekly magazine, who coined the collective noun for diarists as 'a smear'. He also said that "a diarist is often in the best place and in the best company, but in the wrong job." Things could turn nasty. At dinners people would turn away from me. At one, the musician Valentine Guinness simply got up and left. This was ironic as his father, Jonathan Guinness, was at the time writing a column for the *Standard*. "Silly boy," he said, when I told him.

With Archer there was a special animosity. He would ring me up sometimes and sound off. "All Head Boys are failures," he screamed after a piece I had written, "and you are the worst." As well as his million-selling novels and misdemeanours, Archer was known for his Krug and shepherd's pie supper parties at the Tory Party conferences. Before the 1992 conference in Brighton, he rang me up. "I just want you to know, so don't even think about it, that you are not invited to my party."

In Brighton, I had dinner with Alan Clark, Frank Johnson, Colin Welch and John Selwyn Gummer. This was a jolly affair and they were all going on to Archer's party at The Grand. It was Clark and Selwyn Gummer who said I must come with them, the latter humming nervously in the lift as we approached Archer's penthouse venue. All the great and good were there. I left my covert coat with the chamber maid. I chatted to Ken Clarke and Bruce Anderson. Then, after about twenty minutes, I saw Archer running towards me and thought of the song by Three Dog Night, *Mama Told Me (Not To Come)*. These were exactly Archer's first words, but he was more black mamba than mama. He got me by the collar and marched me through a parting sea of guests. I saw Jonathan Aitken smirking as he chatted up a girl. There was no time to get my covert coat, still there perhaps in some hotel closet at The Grand. "I am going to speak to Lord Matthews in the morning," Archer spat as he shut the door on me. It did not seem the moment to tell him that Lord Matthews actually owned the *Daily Express*.

I wandered to the beach front like some extra in *Quadrophenia*. Then, returning to my hotel, I encountered on a kerbside an altercation. It was 'The Grand Inquisitor' himself, Sir Robin Day, locked in a verbal exchange with a pretty girl. I got my notebook out. "But I can't, Sir Robin, it wouldn't be right," she was saying. "But I bought you dinner, just come back to my room for one nightcap," he was imploring. The girl then ran away. I followed Day to the lobby of the Metropole. Thinking this might be a task beyond a mere diary reporter, I got hold of one of our news reporters, Shekhar Bhatia, and asked him to help.

Bhatia rang Sir Robin in his room, who accused us of trespass and harassment and we were ejected from the hotel. But we weren't going to stop at that. Next day, we scoured the conference hall for the girl.

We got a former diary regular, Carina Trimingham, now working for Channel 4, to look for her through a long lens television camera and, twenty minutes before the *Standard* deadline, we found her. "He was very persuasive for an old man," the girl, a single-parent trade union rep from Newcastle, told me. "But in my job you have to have lead knickers."

It was the story of the party conference. The *Sun* followed it up with a full page the next day, and a cartoon of Sir Robin having dinner with the girl and a waiter coming up to him: "Your can opener, Sir Robin?" Sir Robin was asked for his reaction. "I was snooped upon. It was a private conversation eavesdropped by a gutter journalist who was in the gutter at the time." I think I, and the readers, took the view once expressed by Joan Bakewell when she worked with Day at the BBC: "Socially, he was a menace."

It was after this that Sarah Sands decided I was to be the P.J. O'Rourke of the paper. Of the many situations that presented themselves, few were as inviting as the book launch in 1995 of Martin Amis's *The Information* at the fashionable Cobden Working Men's Club off the lower end of Notting Hill. Except that I wasn't invited, which was a bit mean given that one of the main characters was Rory Plantagenet, "The compromised and epicene diarist on a London evening paper."

Before this, my encounters with Martin had been occasional. I had been round to his house to get a book signed. "I would ask you in but we have company," he had said. I think of that when Martin was asked what class he was: "I am the Intelligentsia Class," he responded, which I don't think really exists. I thought him not asking me in was a bit middle class myself. Then, interviewing Warren Zevon, the unparalleled American musician and satirist, at Blake's hotel a bit later, I had taken him a copy of Amis's *Time's Arrow*. From this Warren, who had never heard of Amis, wrote *The Indifference of Heaven*, and became a fan. So whilst not a Martin muse, I could be said to have got him into the American music charts.

None of this cut anything with Martin when I rang and asked if I could come to his party. He was entertaining again, this time two hundred people, including Salman Rushdie, Emma Soames, Nigella Lawson and Will Self, and a host of the 'Intelligentsia Class'. "I am afraid I am not involved with the guest list," he said, replacing the telephone receiver. Undeterred, I ran up Billy Brannigan, then married to the successful jewellery designer Dinny Hall, who was running the Cobden and asked him if he could let me in. "Come early, there is a cupboard off the main dance area," he said.

I just had time to read about 'myself' in the book before I got there, a sunny but cold March evening. "Rory Plantagenet wasn't his pen name. It was his real name. And it suited him. He looked cornily patrician. And altogether vestigial. A generation ago he would have been living in Cap d'Antibes with a mature lady called something like Christabel Cambridgeshire. Instead Rory often found himself wondering about his place in the larger scheme of things." This last observation was certainly true as I found myself in a small room full of unwanted furniture with a small gas fire. Soon it got cold and the only way I could operate the fire was by keeping a finger on the lighting mechanism. Soon it got colder. Salman Rushdie's sniffer dogs came round. I saw their whiskers in the gap under the door. They did not come in.

Unable to take the discomfort any more, I slid out of the room as the dance floor was filling up to *Ain't Too Proud To Beg*. "Oh God, it's you," exclaimed Will Self, and I begged him to be quiet. Martin was on the stairs, smoking a roll-up and drinking a small bottle of lager, when I announced myself. He was bemused, like a writer deep in his own thoughts. "Yes, it's you," he said after a few seconds to recover from the shock of meeting one of his characters in real life. "Has Rory Plantagenet got no redeeming features?" I asked him and he thought about it. "Yes," he said. "He has soulful moments when he has been to three parties the night before." With that I dashed for the door to write up the party for the first editions. It was captioned: 'How I gatecrashed a Martin Amis novel'.

For the seven years I did the diary, it was also possible, amongst what Sir Harold Acton once called the 'delicious briars of humanity', to make friends. As I have said of my colleagues, a special bond remains to this day for the stories and the sorrows we went through. But one, with the books editor A.N. Wilson, stands above them all for his love and loyalty, and his ability, like Milton, to discuss "anything under the sun." For more than four years we lunched together almost daily. "Sometimes twice a day," he fondly recalls. It was like dining at All Souls, with plenty of ideas that I should also pursue for diary stories or features.

The regularity of our dining together is, of course, an exaggeration. But the lunches were frequent enough to keep me supplied with a ready flow of books and publishing stories which then, again before the tsunami of celebrity, were what our readers wanted. Andrew Wilson's prodigious output of biographies, novels and journalism never deflected him from keeping his many friendships in polished working order. Like Brian Sewell's covering of the arts, Andrew's presence at the paper gave it a sparkling gravitas from which we all benefitted.

During one lunch at the Academy Club near Christmas, it was understandable that, emboldened with drink, people might want to come up to Andrew and interrupt our little gatherings, oblivious to me. He would always be courteous. On this occasion, a publishing public relations woman of a certain age tottered over. I think Andrew had been pointed out to her and he was, anyway, recognisable from his erudite television programmes. "I just want to say how much I love your books," she said. She repeated herself two or three times, eventually getting the hint from her friends at the bar to come back. "Yes, I love your books, ANGUS," she uttered on leaving. Andrew Wilson may be many things but he is certainly not Angus Wilson.

If no one should be a diarist forever, it remained to decide what they should be. Sometimes I discussed the overthrow of the *Spectator* with Andrew, which we would run with a benevolent owner, and have parties all the time. Another we thought of was setting up a prep school in Denbighshire, where I would teach Latin and he would do the gym classes. Instead, we went dreamily back to our desks of toil, to feed our nest of birds.

Then, in 1991, the Gulf War broke out and we decided to become 'war correspondents,' which was, amazingly, sanctioned by our editor, John Leese. We would report from behind the 'front lines' in Israel where, anyway, Andrew had some research to do for a book he was writing on 'The Life of Jesus.' I could also fit in with my stab at Hemingway a visit to my mum and Neville who, by now, were living in Jaffa, working in an old town gallery owned by the art dealer Horace Richter.

We stayed for a week at the American Colony Hotel in Jerusalem, the reporters' standard but opulent base, with its open courtyard of palm and lemon trees and endless supplies of Château Musar. By night, over a four- or five-course dinner, we would watch Scud missiles fly over, like discarded children's dumper trucks. We hired a car and made sure it said 'journalists' on the front in every language, and ventured out one day to Nazareth. On the way we had to stop in a village, as all the signposts had been removed by the Israeli authorities, to ask directions. First children came and then the elders. I was outside the car and they surrounded me, with Andrew and the car keys still inside. I started shaking their hands, sensing all was not quite right, and backed into the driver's seat. I managed to start the car first time and drove purposefully out of the village square, rocks and objects raining down on us. I never saw a man more composed than Andrew in what could have been a very tricky situation.

The lunch with my mum was something of a disaster, too. There were about sixty guests, including Daniel Barenboim and Amos Oz. Horace Richter was clearly using the occasion to warm up clients. I introduced myself and waded through a lot of strangers, and never got to talk to my mum, who was busy doing the cooking. I think, also, it was a slog for Andrew, who was immersed in his book on Jesus and had to spend a six-hour afternoon talking to these people.

Perhaps it was because John Leese was my first *Standard* editor that he made the most impression. He had, after all, plucked me from the rank of reporters to become an editor myself. He had also done the best thing a diarist can ask for: he had left me to my own devices. He did not have a circle of friends he did not want me to write about (something that became more tricky when the sociable Stewart Steven took over as editor). He only once had to stop the presses, when the lawyers had passed a small black paragraph in which I had been told a particularly self-important television presenter had been known at university as 'Yo-yo knickers'. "I suppose we'll be hearing from 'Sue, Grabbit and Runne'," was all he said. We didn't.

Shortly before he retired, I saw John Leese coming towards the diary, which he had never done before, and stood up to meet him. He had not been well and had returned for a final six months. "I hear they have got caviar at half price in a West End restaurant," was all he said to me. I went myself to Gavin Rankin's Caviar Kaspia and bought the largest pot I could find. It was the least I could do for a man who had given me everything. 'T'was caviar *for* the general.' At his leaving party, there was a sudden commotion and Nigel Dempster appeared as a gatecrasher, already drunk. "It was the darkest day when you employed this man," he said to John Leese, pointing at me as I was talking to Sarah Sands. Was this his revenge for the hundreds of scoops I had got that he hadn't? Either way, it fell on deaf ears. John Leese brushed him off without a word.

Shropshire and the cottage loved

'It's always raining,
And you never ask why.'

Ian Hunter, *23a Swan Hill*

I AM NOT the first person to go to the Welsh borderland and attempt to lose myself, another man who went into the West, drawn perhaps by pastoral memories of my teenage time with the copped-out fighter pilot near Bridgnorth. To me, this was not just the land of Clive of India and ravens, of *The Mabinogion* or Offa's Dyke, the mansion houses of the settled squires. It was a landscape unchanged, if you squinted your eyes to the heath banks and forestry, for a thousand years.

Something mystic hovers in the mists and skies of South Shropshire, a mix of folklore and a past time. You can rest there and watch the birds in flight. The hedgerow burrs and the incessant sound of sheep are the only companions to your thoughts. The villages at night smell of the tea leaves of my nannie's home in Crediton. You can live there, as if abroad with a language not understood, without friendship, no one asking why, and light your fire and dream.

I came to be there by chance. One weekend in Wales I met Robert Holden, a Shropshire squire with a castle, and in London a dealer in art and antiquities. He had a cottage to rent in the woods on his estate above Craven Arms, £10 a week. It was in the valley where the mink men roamed, first opened to my eyes on visiting John Osborne. At the pub in Craven Arms, the car park bears a stencilled wall sign: 'Park Prettily'.

Bird Cottage was approached by way of a bull pen and two farm field gates. It sat, two up, two down, eighteenth century, under the lea of a dark wood, a stand of oaks in front. From upstairs you could look to Wenlock Edge or a tower near Culmington they called 'Julie

Christie's', Flounders' Folly on the Callow Hill. The actress had owned this ruin at one time. In the Castle Hotel at Bishop's Castle, where I learned my legal forbear Sir James Knight Bruce had been the MP for one of the Earl of Powis's pocket boroughs, musician Denny Laine's discarded wife Jo Jo would sometimes appear, drunk and dishevelled. At the Drum & Monkey, near Minsterley, they still, in the six years when I was there, recalled Eric Clapton coming in for musical and drinking sessions. Another untouched local was the Miners Arms at Priestweston, remembered for lock-ins with another musician, Ronnie Lane, who had bought a small farm under the Stiperstones, where Mary Webb wrote *Gone To Earth*. This was for them, perhaps, somewhere between *Kilvert's Diary* and Housman's *The Land of Lost Content*. So it was for me.

Also before my time was The Grove, near Sarn, where the horse-travelling baronet Sir Mark Palmer, Lucian Freud and his muse, Henrietta Moraes, had lived, in cold comfort, smoke-stacks of anonymity, happy, surviving on the land. By the time I got there in 1988, the local vet, Terry Boundy, still recalled them vividly. "Henrietta would come round on a Friday night and beg me for ketamine for favours," he recalled. "She was a beauty, how could I say no?" In her memoirs, *Henrietta*, published in 1994, Moraes recalled: "We sometimes went for a bath in Montgomery." I can certainly attest to Henrietta's narcotic interests. A couple of years before the book came out, Patrick Conyngham rang me to meet up with her. Henrietta had also been a model and drinking companion at the Colony Room Club of Francis Bacon. When I arrived at her rented flat in Fulham, she and Patrick were snorting cocaine off a small, glass-fronted Bacon portrait of Henrietta.

My prescription was for peace and quiet, an open fire, a small coal stove in the kitchen, no electricity, a balm and salve to my life in London. Each Friday I would drive four hours, none of them begrudged, until, at last, I went past the bull, stroked my open front door, and fell asleep, like one of A.E. Housman's soldiers or farm boys, exhausted and exhilarated by the love of the place.

The London gangland and pop star drug dealer David Litvinoff had also done time in a Welsh cottage in the late 1960s. A hilarious account is given by author Keiron Pim in his biography of Litvinoff,

Jumpin' Jack Flash. It should have been called *Jumpin' Jack Stash*, for Litvinoff, unabashedly gay, ugly, a sometime scriptwriter for *Performance*, was, to the locals, with his loud music, drug taking and enviable record collection, the original 'Excitable Boy.' He called all birds 'ducks,' got a dog called Jack (so named after the dog in *The Weight* in *Easy Rider*) and entered into local rural life, albeit traipsing through the muddy lanes in slippers. Perhaps I was just, unwittingly, following their Valhalla.

I cannot claim Bird Cottage was my sole doing. Belinda Eade made it a chimera of basic comfort, horse skulls and fragments of gravestones on the wall, dinners I don't know where they came from. We had a wind-up record player and, in the spring, a jackdaw that sat upon my shoulder. I could have lived forever in that quiet, with occasional guests who saw the point of it, walking miles to churches or to Roman ruins, steaks and beers in pubs. The garden we did, with pollarded trees. I bought a sit-on mower, optimistically. One time I hit a ground wasp's nest whilst sythying. It swarmed me till I ran into bed, stung and naked in my rural innocence.

But you can't just sit around doing gardens and visiting pubs. I was not some sausage-fingered, barfly Laurie Lee, although I wrote occasional poems for the *Craven Arms Review*. Somewhere, there were humans beyond this idyll landscape, other 'Lost Boys' to be fruitfully encountered. One, Jeremy James, something of a horseman and writer, sought me out and came to supper. I got the impression I was not wanted on his patch and, amusing as he was, seldom saw him again. Some years later, when he had a book to promote, he came again with a tatty manuscript. In it he had written about sleeping with a girl on the way to save some breed of horse in Kosovo. "Have you shown this to anyone?" I asked. "Only my girlfriend," he replied, unabashed.

The solution to finding humans came from the most unlikely source. Sitting one day in the bath in my house in Shepherd's Bush, I read a small advert in *Horse & Hound*. 'Joint Master required for Welsh Border Pack' was all it said. What was it that made me reply? Was it to be a vindication of my hunting father's verdict of me as useless? I had, to avoid the gardening and the mower, been casually taking some local riding lessons. That had led to a few tentative days out with the local pack. It was this hunt that was looking for a master.

In the normal way of things, you are supposed to have hunted since birth, owned some precious ponies and been bullied by your parents to get up at five in the morning to go cub hunting, have a big house and deep pockets. I was working at the *Evening Standard* and had a cottage with no electricity. What made me apply, I cannot recall. Being accepted took me on a journey of great happiness. It was another of those golden validations that took my parental gene, the huntsman and the showgirl, more in my dad's direction.

I bought a horse from Ticklerton near Church Stretton, where George Orwell had spent his childhood summers with his posh relations, giving him his lifelong love of nature and the countryside, which his socialist friends dismissed as sentimental. Drummer was so called because he looked like a horse that would carry a marching drum, and on his neck a dent they call a 'Prophet's Thumbprint' which is supposed to be good luck. He carried me, inexhaustibly, for four years, following the native hunters and the hounds, up the steepest hills and, more worryingly, down them as well, with rarely a change of pace.

Where my mastership also carried me was into the homes, farms, cottages and big houses of the Shropshire locals, real people grounded in their landscape. It gave me more acceptance than being just a simple weekender. You can get to know a landscape as a walker, or on a bicycle even, but when you get to know it off a horse, it remains with you forever. You are off the beaten track, fumbling to open gates or jump small sheep netting, falling off at streams and reliving every day later in the bath. It gave me the most vivid and good memories.

The people were at first astounded. Some were forgiving and helpful, others thought: "Has hunting come to this?" Part of my reason for doing it, and my love of doing it, was the total and absorbing escape from real life. It may often have been raining but in our warm world of sporting fun, with not a little fear thrown in, we never asked why. There can be few more varied or unspoilt parts of England in which to taste this freedom, and I felt for the first time that I belonged somewhere. The conversations I was allowed to hear were not unlike J.M. Synge hiding in a pub attic to record *The Playboy of the Western World*.

Part of this feeling of belonging, of course, was false. I had two joint masters, the huntsman and his wife, both highly respected and good at what they did. They sheltered me from any storms that might have come my way from my ignorance of proceedings. And my ignorance was bliss. Soon, like Ronnie Lane and Julie Christie before me, our friends would come and stay, to sleep on sofas or in the horse box in the garden. I have a makeshift visitors' book still, names written on bits of cardboard, designed by the painter Sophie Tute: Charles and Caroline Moore; the writers Rebecca Nicolson, Philip Eade and A.N. Wilson, and his soon-to-be wife, the art critic Ruth Guilding; Barnaby Rogerson; Mary Miers; and Christopher Howse. From fashion it was Emma Hope and Katharine Goodison; well-known furniture expert James Graham-Stewart; and Hugo Swire, the future politician. They all shared the hunting friends that I had made, and made friends with them. Sarah Sands and her husband, Kim Fletcher, came with young Henry Sands when I was not there for a week. It was when they found Henry in with the bull that they felt they had better move into a nearby hotel.

An unexpected dividend that my position gave me was invitations to dine in settled and ancient homes. Robert and Emily Holden had us frequently to dinner at the castle, and friendships were made both ways. They all came to the point-to-points and to the hunt meets when they were held near their homes. Perhaps the most authentic meet straddled the Border with Wales at The Anchor, a remote sheep drovers' pub. Martin Wilkinson, who had know David Litvinoff and many others of the London 1960s *beau monde*, would come from his home nearby, Cwm Hall, and hold Drummer's head at the meet whilst I downed a port or two.

It was Martin Wilkinson who had given a courtyard cottage and hospitality to his friend, Bruce Chatwin, when the author was starting out on what was to become his novel *On The Black Hill*. It is often thought that the title of his book is taken from the Black Mountain behind George and Diana Melly's house in the Llanthony Valley, where Chatwin also wrote. But, as Chatwin readily admitted to Martin, it comes from a tract of forestry above his home near Clunton. Chatwin spent the first seven weeks with Wilkinson researching his book. "I've got it, I've got it," Chatwin said one day to Martin, bouncing into the kitchen of the Hall for his evening whisky, supper and a glass of Gigondas (which, Martin told me: "was a word he delighted in rolling round his mouth like the heavy Burgundy itself.") "I will call my book *On the Black Hill*." Chatwin up in the woods had spotted a small painted sign stating simply 'Black Hill', which I have seen.

Chatwin has often been accused of lack of veracity in his story-telling. But in *On the Black Hill* he set off diligently each day in his old Citroën Deux Chevaux, with a bicycle strapped to the roof, notebook to hand, to eavesdrop discreetly in pubs, auction houses and at the local cattle markets. "The atmosphere, the stories and the limbs of his work are all from here," Martin Wilkinson continued. So are many of the names. When I went on my farm visits for the hunt to say we were coming later in the week, I encountered, like Chatwin, people who took their surnames with the addition of their geography. So, there might be a Jones 'The Vron', or Morris 'The Temple', to distinguish them from other Joneses and Morrises in the area, of which there were many. Martin Wilkinson remembers Bruce Chatwin with admiration. "When he looked at you with his blue eyes, it was as if he was looking at the North Pole. He made himself invisible when talking to you."

Bruce Chatwin and those Blue Remembered Thrills

Although I never met Bruce Chatwin, like many readers when an author writes about somewhere the reader has come to know well, I felt a sort of bond. He had seen what I had seen in this part of Shropshire, turning it into a universal story. Chatwin's favourite childhood book was Ernest Thompson Seton's 'Lives of the Hunted,' as it was mine, and then, of course, there was the connection with Kardamyli where Chatwin had stayed with the Leigh Fermors whilst finishing 'The Songlines'. So, when it came to his memorial service in London, partly out of respect and partly as a reporter, I thought I had every reason to go.

Chatwin died aged forty-eight on 18th January, 1989. His memorial was held in the Greek Cathedral on Moscow Road in London on a Tuesday, St Valentine's Day. As I approached the church, I saw a group of perhaps thirty reporters milling about. Going in, Nicholas Shakespeare, later to be the official biographer of Bruce Chatwin, was on the steps, taking names. "What are you doing here?" he asked, writing down my name begrudgingly. I did not answer. There was no love lost between us, even though I employed Sebastian, his brother. He was a proper writer, after all. Once inside, I worked out what the fuss was all about.

I found myself behind Salman Rushdie who had, that very morning, come out of hiding from the fatwa issued against him for 'The Satanic Verses'. Rushdie was pale and nervous as we mumbled our way though Greek hymns we did not understand. Breaking away, I went and found a side door to the cathedral, which was open. "Mr Rushdie," I said, and he looked at me, haunted. "There are many reporters outside the front but I have found a side door where you can slip away afterwards if I show you." He said nothing, until the end. "Where is the door?" he asked. I led him to it. Seizing my moment, I said I was from the Evening Standard and would he give me a few words on his incarceration and freedom. "No," he replied, which I thought was a bit ungrateful. But it was the first if shortest interview he gave following his release.

There then began the lamentations in print from the Establishment travel writers keen to protect their friend and the circumstances of his death. The accepted story went that Chatwin had picked up some tropical disease from a monkey in Mombassa or the like. If anyone was going to get in on the act to write about him, it was them, and indeed, the name-taker Shakespeare. Then, the impertinence of it, a life of Chatwin from one not in this gilded circle, by Welsh college lecturer Nicholas Murray, came out. I felt that Murray had not been given the access he deserved. In reviewing his book for A.N. Wilson at the Evening Standard, I alluded to this unhelpfulness and concluded: "Chatwin was more than a casual cottager who died of AIDs." It was exactly the salacious detail that Shakespeare himself would be saving up for his magnum opus.

The gilded circle rounded on me. The antiques dealer Christopher Gibbs, after a lunch in Tangier (he in full djellaba looking like an extra in 'Jesus Christ Superstar') asked me to walk on the beach with him alone, away from our party. "How could you have written that about Bruce?" he hissed. At that moment, a young Moroccan boy came up to him, addressed him as 'Mr Herbert' (a reference to the Hon David Herbert, once described by Ian Fleming as the 'Queen of Tangier') and Gibbs lost his venom and concentration. When Shakespeare's book finally appeared it included the instruction to Chatwin from his Sotheby's boss, Peter Wilson: "Go out and sleep with New York." This was hardly a demand to a shrinking violet.

Be that as it may, I have at least been one of Chatwin's readers who have *steadfastly gone back to the little church above Kardamyli where his ashes are interred under an olive tree. At first, the tenth-century Byzantine chapel dedicated to St Nicholas in Chora was open to the public. There was a small altar and Chatwin pilgrims would leave messages. "I never knew you and I haven't read your books," read one. "But I am also called Bruce and I am from Australia."*

For two summers when Roberto Calasso would take the Leigh Fermor house, I would be in a village house in Proastio, unfashionable and up in the hills. When not dining at Lela's I would have supper in the village taverna most nights, where a local priest often came in and sat with others at their tables, all Greeks and locals, old men playing cards or children with their families playing games on the floor. Each night as I left I would send over a small blue or red tin jug of local wine to him. We never exchanged a word. I heard he had been a taxi driver before he got 'The Call.' On the last night as I passed his table, I placed a pack of cigarettes next to him. In what might have passed as an implausible incident in a Chatwin novel, he looked up at me. "Thank you," he said. "I have not been so kindly treated since I was at Oxford."

Not surprisingly, the family from Athens who owned the chapel got fed up with all this nonsense, and so no doubt did the few villagers and donkeys who grazed the fields below. "You wouldn't know where the ashes are," Paddy Leigh Fermor had told Nicholas Shakespeare at the very end of his Chatwin biography. Perhaps Paddy was himself, on this occasion, being more than enigmatic. Certainly, he told me that he too got a bit fed up with people knocking on HIS door asking where the ashes were interred. It was bad enough, he added, when they were asking for HIM.

Two years ago, I persisted and asked a village family if I could have the key to look inside the chapel one more time. They welcomed me in for coffee and rang the chapel owners in Athens. No, they said, the chapel will now forever remain closed except for family occasions. Back in the village, I spoke to the postmaster's wife, with whom I would daily exchange smiles whilst buying my paper at midday. Did she know the exact spot where the ashes were interred? I asked her one day. "No, but my husband does." Even though I had been going to this man daily over a period of forty years for perhaps a total of twelve weeks, he remained imperturbably tight-lipped. Perhaps he sensed I was keen on his wife, which was true.

Then, just as I was leaving for the last time, and her husband was out, the postmaster's wife showed me into a back room. "They are gone," she said.

"Major Fermor Leigh (for that is what they called him, pronounced like the song 'We Are Family') got, how do you say, fed up. The chapel owners got fed up." I could not fathom what I was hearing. It was like the division of Thomas Hardy's heart from his body so that he could be buried in two places, Westminster Abbey and Dorset. I tried to interest Claudia FitzHerbert at The Oldie with what I saw as a literary coup of sleuthing. She said it might make a small paragraph in the 'Old Un's' diary on the magazine, not what I had in mind. Sadly, the postmaster can no longer help. He committed suicide. I don't think I had anything to do with that.

The biggest beast of my Shropshire calumny had yet to put his head above my lazy blue horizon, still peeping from behind the curtain of his Clun confine where I had left him that October day in 1988. It was now three years later and John Osborne had a second volume of memoirs coming out, *Almost A Gentleman*, and a play in the offing, *Déjàvu*, a sort of sequel and update to *Look Back In Anger*. His first volume of memoirs, *A Better Class of Person*, was breathtaking in its maternal venom and scabrous views of wives and colleagues. The two volumes were then parcelled together as *Never Explain, Never Apologise*. None of the reviewers spotted that the expression is actually *Never Apologise, Never Explain*. What followed between myself and John Osborne up until his death at sixty-five, on Christmas Eve of 1994, needs a bit of explaining and, perhaps, a bit of an apology. It was a joust of love and venom.

With the second volume of his memoirs coming out, the *Evening Standard* sent me to interview Osborne at the Hurst. It was, they reasoned, only a few miles from my own Shropshire cottage and, armed with the local colour I had gained from living there at weekends, we would have some common ground. He agreed to see me and a date was set to meet him at his house and have lunch in the local pub.

The drawing room of the Hurst had, in its middle, a serpentine sofa, and on the walls many posters of its master's triumphs. Osborne was seated in a corner chair as I was shown in by his wife, Helen. He was smoking a cigarette. He rose and offered me a glass of champagne, later to say that this is what I had demanded. I accepted as this is what he was himself drinking. We then went to the pub and had a wistful lunch. Helen was silent and beady, but clearly protective and loving of her husband.

They also both loved Shropshire, going to the races at Ludlow and keeping a group of local friends with whom they had formed something of a drinking club known as the DHSS after the first initials of some of their group. Helen was the 'H'. We went down memory lane, to a time when Osborne had been the stand-in film critic at the paper. It was then he opened up, a tap of his resentments and bitterness in full flow. "Is that shit Wheatcroft still on the paper?" he asked, referring to Geoffrey Wheatcroft, the sometime Walkman-wearing diary editor and opera critic, which was music to my ears. He was not.

Albert Finney he called a "classical corrupt talent", and Nicol Williamson a "full-time psychopath." As we sat beside a small coal fire, Osborne was warming to his theme. We got on well. I was a bit out of my depth on the full body of his work but he had won an Oscar for *Tom Jones* with all its ribald hunting scenes and I was the local master, so we had something to go on. We agreed that, nearer the time of his memoirs coming out, I would return and he would give me a full interview.

This was not to be. The *Sunday Times* jumped in and offered Osborne £5,000 for an exclusive interview, so mine was off the cards. I felt rather betrayed by this so had then to trawl up my recollections of our lunch together, to which Osborne took great exception. He filed off legal letters to all the Fleet Street newspapers demanding that I should never work again. "The best place for wee Rory is in a cosy padded cell," he concluded. He used his *Spectator* diary to vilify me. One of his DHSS cronies entered the attack. "Go off and patronise people and pat sheep elsewhere," she wrote. Helen Osborne entered the fray. "He is a worm," she said of me in the *Sunday Times*, having rung me up to tell me so herself. "I know, I know," was all I could reply. But, of course, it is a sort of compliment. In Osborne's play *Luther*, the hero soliloquises. "I am a worm and no man, a byword and a laughing stock/Crush out the worminess in me, stamp on me... I am alone/I am alone and against myself."

But then things softened into a more mellow understanding. Osborne started asking me to his Shropshire parties. He wrote a part for me in *Déjàvu* and asked me to the Café Royal for dinner, that venue so beloved of Oscar Wilde and Bosie. He wrote me into his book, *Damn You England*. Polly Samson, that beguiling journalist now married to Pink Floyd's David Gilmour, took up our loving spat. "Who would you rather sleep with, John Osborne or Rory Knight Bruce?" she asked in her column. "Or both?" *Who would you rather sleep with?* was going to be Osborne's alternative title for *Déjàvu*, which she had cleverly found out.

I am not sure if it is an accolade to have been the last object of John Osborne's great ire, of what he called "My own ungovernable choler." The last words he ever wrote were on a fag packet in Shrewsbury hospital, "I have sinned." This is, of course, a reference to the Victorian general Sir Charles Napier who wrote: "I have Sind." Osborne may have been ascribing it to Shropshire's favourite son, Clive of India.

On Friday 2nd June, 1995, a full church at St Giles-in-the-Fields celebrated the life of John Osborne. Like the socialists with George Orwell, the liberal left, who were out in force that day, were keen to claim him as one of their own. But both men were far better, far more universal than that. I stood at the back, which is the old-fashioned tradition for a Master of Foxhounds when one of his parishioners has died. And I wept. To me, he was like a fulmar, buffeted by the winds of his own creations, and the tiresomeness of having to seem perpetually angry in public, which was not the sensitive and private man I knew. He is buried in Clun churchyard and I visit his grave when I can.

Before I left Shropshire and the cottage, in the spring of 1995, I got wind that Ian Hunter of Mott the Hoople, who lived at 23a Swan Hill in Shrewsbury (from which his song takes the name) was giving a small concert in Worthen Village Hall. I asked the promoters if I could attend and interview him. Back came the reply: "We don't want press types round here." John Osborne would have liked that.

Mother You Had Me

'Yet each man kills the thing he loves
By each let this be heard,
Some do it with a bitter look,
Some with a flattering word,
The coward does it with a kiss,
The brave man with a sword!'

Oscar Wilde, *The Ballad of Reading Gaol*

THE RELATIONSHIP WITH any parent is not one to be relied on. They have their own lives. John Osborne had a daughter, Nolan, to whom in later years he never spoke, banishing her from his life as 'irredeemably middle class.' My own maternal banishment, on reflection, was no less harsh, occasioned by her different homes, religions and marriages, geography when she went to live in Israel, and a very short attention span for any form of constancy in parental love. There were no comforting tea leaves brewing in her kitchen, just flashbulbs of occasional curiosity before her interest waned.

It was Winston Churchill MP (he of the David Tang dinner invitation) who once said the loneliest relationship he ever had was with his mother, Pamela Harriman, who also, on my father's side, happened to be a cousin. "Even as a small boy, I had to make an appointment to see her," he recalled in his later years. "Appointments not always kept." At school, I would have to queue for half an hour to ring out to home on a payphone. "Who shall I say is calling?" was one strange voice I got. "I'll see if she is free," was another. They were the voices of the frequently rotating butler and cook. Often she wasn't free. Sometimes it is the little things that hurt and are remembered. If I did cut a Byronic swathe, then she must take some blame for it, casting me out to make my way, no border to the canvas I was painting, no money to support a normal life.

In the seven years I was in Edinburgh, she never once visited. She said she could not afford it. This is hard to reconcile with the Bentley and the Porsche and, when she died, the boxes of receipts I saw for expensive wines and restaurants, the building of a lake at Cherry Court and, I understood this one, the £1,000 to ship her terrier to Israel. Yet it wasn't the money that mattered. It was the time we could have spent together, me showing her the alleyways of Edinburgh and being proud of her amongst my friends.

In the pantheon of woes, I recognise that cries of parental neglect can seem quite small. What became exhausting is that everything had to be a performance. There is no doubt also that drink came into it. That was our common ground, which made her less bored of me and me less hurt by the wounding words that would follow. I walked on eggshells with her, when she was again 'gone with the wine.' "I could do lunch with her, but lunch and dinner on the same day was too much," my brother had once said to me. He did not see her in the last twenty years of her life. Nor did my half-brother, the White Russian, see her much until the end. I think they, for self-preservation, concluded wisely that she did not possess a vestige of maternalism.

For me, the Libran and the middle one, it was different. For the brief first hour or two of our get-togethers, I was like a public relations account she had won, being told I was marvellous, made to feel good. But then she would tire, moving on to the next excitement, appointment or call where a universal voice said: "I'll see if she is free." Years later, in 1995, when I was attending a New Warrior therapy weekend in Hampshire, where we were often naked as part of the process, one New York male broke down in uncontrollable tears, saying that his father was never there for him. The counsellor was sympathetic. We were compassionate. "But where was your father?" asked the counsellor amidst the primal wailing. "He was at work," came the faltering reply. Parents have their own lives. But children have their memories of absence.

All memory, however, is unfair, the kiss of a coward. 'In the lost boyhood of Judas, Christ was betrayed.' On brighter days I recall some brilliant times. Nor is it true my mother never came to see me in Scotland. She came once. As part of her public relations account with the National Coal Board, she and Neville had to visit a steel foundry outside Falkirk, Smith and Wellstood. Roddy Martine took the day

off from his editorship of *Scottish Field* and we collected Elizabeth
and Neville from Turnhouse airport. Here were the furnaces that
had broken the nerve of Deborah Orr's father, men stripped down in
ninety-degree heat, handling molten steel with long-handled shovels
and pincers, to turn out stoves. My mother was in her finest furs and
they adored her, management, workers, the cleaning ladies, all were
charmed and made to feel worthwhile. Roddy and I were given little
steel boot jacks in the shape of beetles, as mementos. He has them
still. Typical of his kindness, he wrote about the day. Elizabeth and
Neville, in their turn, gave us supper at the airport.

Then there were the holidays to Israel and skiing in Italy, plenty
of long lunches and photos taken. In Israel, I would ride horses with
my mum through ancient Roman ruins, chariot rings and amphithe-
atres, stopping to pick bananas off a tree, or potshards at the beach,
symbols of fragmented happiness. Best of all was going to the west
coast of Ireland with just my mum and her dad in his white Rolls-
Royce. Each morning on our drive, we would stop with a view and
drink snipes of champagne at eleven. I sat in the back, a happy child
at twenty-two. My grandfather recalled his student days at Trinity and
coming to the west, still little changed in 1978, although there were
perhaps a few more 'Brits Out' slogans on the Connemara roads. This
was a swansong I now realise. Ballina Park was sold soon after.

At Newport on the coast we stayed in the hotel, a proper fishing
place with sporting trophies and signs that gentlemen stayed there.
After dinner, I rang my summer girlfriend to fill her in and say that
I was missing her. "That's enough of that nonsense," the party-line
operator broke in after five minutes and cut me off. Further into
Galway I sat up drinking with a barmaid who was going to be a policewoman. I feared for her detective powers and future when I asked
her if she would like to go for a spin in the car. "Well, that's a fine
Mercedes you've got there," she said. I did not disabuse her.

So far as I thought about it at all, I imagined Mum and Neville
would stay at Cherry Court forever. They had made it comfortable
and pretty, manageable enough for two with a wooden clapboard
barn for their spacious offices. But nothing in their lives stayed the
same for long. One Sunday lunch they told me they were emigrat-
ing to Israel, a dream come true for Neville, understandably, and an

exciting journey for my mum. That they drove there, in the summer of 1986, stopping at every smart hotel on the way, was perhaps their swansong, too. I have inherited from my mum the diaries and hotel receipts, no spared expense. They had their own lives.

It was Sarah Sands who first got me to write about my mum in the *Evening Standard*, calling her 'The Bolter', which she was. The 'peg' was a story about Graham Greene's mistress, Lady Walston, whose son had just written a piece forgiving her for her absence and infidelity. It took me a couple of goes to get beyond my own betrayal to the heart of the matter, which was forgiveness. This I found hard to do. Then, over lunch at the Brackenbury, it all fell into place. At the next-door table were two thirty-something mothers, talking, smoking, and drinking fine white wine. Next to one of them was a ten-year-old boy, totally ignored, sitting patiently with his food and own thoughts. It brought tears to my eyes as I realised that boy was me, in another time, another place.

Later on, when Neville and my mother had come back from Israel, to live penniless, in Ireland, making jam for a living, I wrote about her again. This unleashed her furies. My point, whilst defending her to the last and rather admiring her television career against the swim of male domination, was that a reckoning for abandonment must come, however late. And when it does, it is bound to hurt. It is not true, as Nietzsche said: "What doesn't kill you makes you stronger." It makes you dead inside. And, the older that you get, with less of life to live, the more it hurts and wonders. I thought if I wrote about it, the pain might go away.

What did not go away was my mother's revenge. She ladled out in print a whole series of excuses and accusations, my father's cruelty, my own bad temper as a child, her hatred of the countryside, and Devon in particular, the basic house in which my father kept her. It was an argument from which our relationship never recovered. Although I would send her money sometimes, she never came to say her sorries. "I don't think Neville likes me," I said one day to the artist Moira Durdin Robertson, an Irish neighbour of my mum's living at the beautiful Huntington Castle. "He doesn't like anybody," she replied. Many people fell in with my mum, for her charisma and charm. Almost all of them fell out with her as well.

Perhaps what made me want to be a journalist is that she might be proud of me. I had long given up on thoughts from my father in that direction. "Bloody Rory," he would say after another farm calamity, a sheep got out, a buck rake bent. I became fascinated by the lives of others, to take me away from my own. I was never going to make this leap as a grinding diary 'hack'. It was time to leave the column. I also left my wife and house in Shepherd's Bush, perhaps the justified denouement of a man who wrote stories eavesdropped from the gutter, and kept a small carousel of occasional girlfriends in the office and the Shropshire tack rooms.

I took a house under a nuclear train terminal off the cemetery in Kensal Rise. No one came there and I was left in peace, a small portable computer, a beaten-up Range Rover and plenty of work. For one week it was interrupted when all my mother's and Neville's last possessions came in a metal container to some airport repository off Heathrow. My job was to sort things out to be sold at auction houses or in market stalls down the Old Kent Road. The last thing to come out was an umbrella and, out of it, tumbling with soulful remorse onto the unloading bay, a shekel. I took the Batoni painting of my forbear as my wages.

Today, when so many newspaper interviews and features are controlled by the public relations machine, it is often difficult to get to the truth of a subject. So, it is worth recording on my journey who some of the villains and the victors were. Someone once said that the mark of a gentleman was to say at least something to a journalist. If that is true, then I have no hesitation in beginning with those who would not speak to me. They include Joan Collins, Bob Geldof, that made up countryman Ben Fogle, who thinks he's posh because he went to Bedales, and Henry Kissinger who brushed me off with a dusting of his sleeve, rather like the German on Howrah Bridge. For all his faults, Jeffery Archer would always return my calls, 'almost a gentleman'.

It was a letter of introduction from Michael Cecil that got me to the Florence home of Sir Harold Acton in the summer of 1985. I went to the Villa La Pietra by bus with Belinda Eade and, also at tea, was a duchess relation of Napoleon. We spoke in French. Acton was much taken with Belinda Eade's knowledge of gardens and with me as he showed me well-endowed naked male sculptures on the terrace. Over drinks there was an interruption and appearance by Susanna Johnson, sister of Alexander Chancellor, and the dismissive David Pryce-Jones and a screaming little boy, Orlando Mostyn Owen, allowed to run around and be a general nuisance. Susanna bemoaned to me how Alexander had been sacked as editor of the *Spectator*, and Pryce-Jones wondered and almost asked what we were doing there. Mercifully they left and quiet was restored. "You will have your conveyance," Sir Harold said later as he showed us out. We had to hide under the loggia and wait for him to go back inside, not wishing to be seen walking down his mile-long drive to the bus stop. Sir Harold wrote several times to Belinda, recommending grottoes that she should visit, which we did. She then went on to create several acclaimed ones of her own.

Paddy Leigh Fermor I first met at dinner at Charles and Caroline Moore's house in Islington. It was, like Jennifer Paterson's crockery-throwing incident, the fabled evening Paddy fell off and broke his chair. By any estimation he had drunk three bottles of white wine to his own head, and the rest of us were not far behind, when his wooden chair collapsed. "I knew I should not have given him that chair," was all Caroline Moore said, giving an indication that she knew beforehand it was unsafe. Paddy, by now in his seventies, was soon up sprightly and we carried on.

It was from that evening that came several visits to have lunch and supper with Paddy and Joan in Greece. These would take the form of a swim off his private steps going down to an otherwise inaccessible beach, three or four ouzos and then a languid and liquid lunch or dinner. On one occasion he mentioned to me that his parking space at the British Embassy in Athens had been withdrawn. By chance, a month later, I sat next to the ambassador's wife at dinner in Wiltshire and, with her husband, they had it reinstated.

Strangely, although perhaps understandably for a traveller, Paddy never had a dog and Joan loved cats. A couple of years ago, I was sitting on a small concrete pontoon off Kalamitsi beach when I met Paddy's old electrician. Through a pretty Athenian ballet dancer, who happened to be in town for a wedding, I asked her to ask him about Paddy for me. The gist of what he said was the work was very slow and he was with Paddy for several years. Each day he would arrive and Paddy would be at his desk outside the house in a room that resembled a Dartmoor hunting lodge (Paddy had spent the season of 1960-61 living in Chagford with the homosexual diarist Patrick Kinross and hunting with the Mid Devon Fox Hounds). Paddy could not write if he heard a dog bark. The electrician was then despatched to quieten every dog in the village.

I was not the first member of my family to meet Paddy Leigh Fermor, as I discovered when I read his book of letters between him and Debo Devonshire, *In Tearing Haste*. Living in Chagford I had a relative Hugh, something of an artist. I never met him, but one person I did meet was the retired gardener, 'Chirpy' Mortimer, who worked for his family when they lived at Meldon Hall. "He was a 'secluse,'" Chirpy told me one day in the Three Crowns, and when I pressed him, 'You could say 'feminate.'"

Paddy had hunted with cousin Hugh who, when he died, left £1.2 million, £100,000 of it to the RSPCA. He remembered meeting him out hunting and recorded the occasion in a letter to Debo. 'There were about fifteen of us out, all squire farmers and their mates, a bit dull, but very nice and friendly. All except one, perhaps, who I later learnt was not quite all there. After pounding for miles I found myself stationary beside him... after about ten minutes the silence began to weigh, so I pointed at this hound... gazing at us and occasionally scratching behind his ear with his right paw. "That hound's taking it very easy," I said, in a voice that wasn't my own. My companion roused himself from a brown study, swivelled slowly in my direction and fixed me with large bloodshot eyes; but uttered never a word.'

When I last had lunch with Paddy in Kardamyli in 2009, he confirmed that it was my cousin Hugh. "Like many attracted to the moor, he kept himself to himself," Paddy told me. "A lot of people there were escaping from something. In this, he was no different." Whilst I did not inherit his millions, some years later Stuart Clarke, a photographer I had worked with on the *Evening Standard*, bought the small cottage in Chagford that had been Hugh's last abode. In the attic he found my walnut-framed family tree, beautifully drawn in black ink with coloured heraldic shields, and gave it to me. It 'proved' that we were descended not just from the relations of Robert the Bruce but also further back to Charlemagne. I sometimes wonder if Hugh believed all that.

ও

I have mentioned the ready welcome that Ireland will give the sportsman, the well-connected, the writer, millionaire, poet or musician.
No one gave more to all of these than the Hon Garech Browne of
Luggala in County Wicklow. Although I had known the house and
stirring grounds, with its cliff, 'The Fancy', brooding over proceedings and the man-made lake, since childhood, it was as a journalist I
got to know Garech, so far as he could be known. He liked writers and
journalists and he liked gossip, to which he would add his own fair
and just opinion. But, most of all, he liked champagne.

Garech from mid morning would carry his champagne glass in
his left hand by his knee, like a child trailing a teddy bear. Whilst there
were many occasions when his guests would drink too freely, I never
saw him drunk. He had a cavernous mind for enquiry, and, perhaps
unlike those who paid court to Sir Harold Acton, there seemed to
be no jealousy amongst those he entertained. His love was for traditional Irish music, although his laughable obituary in the *Daily Telegraph*, written by Hugo Vickers, referred to his interest in 'traditional
American music' and called him the grandson of Erskine Guinness
(himself a very much living master of foxhounds and good friend of
mine) when it should have been Ernest Guinness. When I pointed
this out to the *Telegraph* obituarist Andrew Brown, for whom I had
done a number of obituaries over the years, he replied: "We all, even
you, make mistakes," which is true.

In 1996, my editor on the *Telegraph* magazine, the cerebral David
Jenkins (I think his father had been a Cheltenham vicar), saw the
point of my going to see Garech on the thirtieth anniversary of the
death at twenty-one of his brother, Tara Browne, in a car crash off the
Fulham Road. I went there from Scotland, by boat, slow train and
bus and got dropped off outside the Roundwood Inn above Luggala,
something of a headquarters and second home for Garech and his
wide circle of friends. I was with my Indian girlfriend and we made
free in the lake and hillside in what became a stay of marathon late
nights and drinking.

Garech knew why I was there, but he was not going to give the
interview before several days of anecdotes flowed like the champagne

and Jamesons. He was not really an outdoor person, so we would sit in the morning in his bedroom, he in a silk dressing gown and sporting a pigtail. (If for any reason I was late down, he would come and sit on our bed, which was a little unnerving.) I would leave whilst he dressed into a three-piece suit of Donegal tweed and we would reconvene for drinks in the round drawing room with its roaring fire and long, Gothic windows where Paddy the butler was ever on hand. Garech had a way of saying 'yes' at the end of his sentences, a means of his making sure you had understood what he said, which was not always easy.

It is well known that Garech kept a salon of poets and musicians, painters and politicians, and always kept them entertained. Lord Gowrie, himself a noted poet and Minister for the Arts under Mrs Thatcher, remembers going to Luggala and "hiding out there for a fortnight. The drinking started at ten in the morning, and went on until midnight." With both the host and the place it was easy to get lost in reverie and revelry. During my stay, and the mounting exasperation of pinning down my host to the task in hand, I wondered if I would ever get out with my story and intact.

What is less well known is that often Garech had people to stay for weeks on end, nominally doing something in the house but really company for their host's amusement. They were, however, never left in any doubt that Garech was himself not just an expert on ancient Irish music, but the piper who called the tune. On this visit there was a 'librarian', the writer and distinctly garrulous Randal MacDonnell, who styled himself 'Count Randal MacDonnell of the Glens' (much to the annoyance of the real MacDonnell's of Glenarm, in particular Randal MacDonnell, Viscount Dunluce, never one much for humour). His book, *The Lost Houses of Ireland*, mournful in its diligent research, had brought him into contact with our host.

Wishing to take a break from drinking, I took up 'The Count's' offer of a trip to the Round Tower at Glendalough. I soon realised that this was an escape for him as well, but only to get more drinking done. He was colourful, characterful and queer, a font of myth and make-believe, certainly where he was himself concerned. He lived in an imaginary world of heralds and grand houses. He also, he told me darkly, lived part of the year in Tangier and was quick to point out (sometimes with small photographs) the collective debaucheries he had there enjoyed, urging me to come with him one time when I had a moment.

This was for me, four pints of Guinness later, a spur to tackle Garech on his brother. Quite a bit now has been written about Tara Browne, in particular Paul Howard's 2016 memoir, *I Read The News Today, Oh Boy*. But Garech then, in 1996, had never said a word in thirty years. The temple at Luggala near to where Tara's remains are interred, was the daily reminder of his loss. Finally, at three in the morning, as we both lay horizontal before the round room guttering fire, it was Garech who began. "So you want to know about Tara? Yes?" He was still in his three-piece suit, almost a suit of armour for his pain as he spoke of their closeness and affection for each other. Often they had been separated by different schools and holidays but he was Garech's only sibling and friend. Perhaps the drive to be surrounded by people who knew Tara went some way to assuage his loss. The tears that fell and choked now were not the tears of tiredness and drink but of the feeling that the death had happened yesterday, still raw in its intensity.

Garech never had children. The child and his childhood was Tara. His Indian wife lived mainly abroad. He was alone with his house and his millions and I did not envy him. It was not just Tara Browne who died in the car that night but a whole warmth of family for Garech, which could have seen him surrounded by his brother's two sons and perhaps his own children, boating on the lake at Luggala which Anjelica Huston called "A sort of dream of peace."

But for Garech, there was no peace, just the dream of it. If Luggala was 'magical' as all of us who knew it say it was, then Garech from that fateful day became the 'Magician', juggling friends and interests to keep his mind off sadder things. Tara's death was a millstone of memory for Garech, in many ways defining who he was, inseparable from his brother and his tragedy. The piper had played me an original tune, and I had listened, "Yes?"

But all magicians need new tricks, to shuffle people like cards, keeping only hearts within the pack. The flamboyant 'Count Randal' had to go. There was a row about some missing silver, and he packed his Gladstone bag of dreams and peccadillos for Morocco. He died, in December 2019, aged sixty-nine, no doubt with more than small photos in his rented room, destitute and penniless. It was his wish that he should be laid to rest in the Church of St Andrew in Tangier, where, as it happens, Christopher Gibbs is buried. But, six months after his death, his body was still lying unclaimed in the city mortuary, no bond for his release having being raised.

Garech, his mentor and tormentor, died over lunch at Le Caprice in London aged seventy-eight, in 2018. His guest was the Irish peer, Viscount Gormanston. Nicholas Gormanston had also been a good friend of Tara Browne and been one of the last to see him on the fateful night of his death.

John Bristol: Steel Wheels

Interest in the aristocracy and death go hand in hand, partly so that those less fortunate can congratulate themselves that at least they are still living. Where there is a castle and estate an added piquancy keens the interest. Nowhere was this felt with more fascination than about Ickworth in Suffolk, home of John Jermyn, 7th Marquess of Bristol, seldom out of trouble, gaol or the newspapers.

It was to his home and virtual deathbed that I was sent in 1996 as he was selling off 'The Family Silver', the main part of the house having been left to the National Trust in 1956. How I got to John and his last confidence was through hugging a naked man in that New Warrior therapy weekend in Hampshire. This was Nicholas Ashley (sometimes called 'The Other Nick Ashley', to differentiate him from the son of curtain and cushion queen Laura Ashley), Oxford, Stoke City supporter, a rich adoptee. He dealt in high-end cars and went to prison for the Jerm. When rich he had had posh girlfriends, the Chatsworth Sophie one of them. They hid out once, he told me, at the Carlyle on heroin and room service. She had to go, he also told me, when she went to thank the cooks at an Indian takeaway in Wiltshire.

For six months we became inseparable on our therapy quest. He mentioned John Bristol was dying and flogging off his kit. I gave him a grand to effect the interview. Three things attracted me to Bristol: his well-charted parental neglect; the fact he had made money in his own right; and his ability, even when presented with prison, to turn a bon mot. "Let Sporus tremble, that curd of ass's milk" was Alexander Pope's opinion of his forbear, the epicene Lord Hervey:

> Let Sporus tremble—"What? that thing of silk,
> Sporus, that mere white curd of ass's milk?
> Satire or sense, alas! can Sporus feel?
> Who breaks a Butterfly upon a Wheel?"

On one occasion, having been released from gaol, Bristol went to Australia where he had financial interests. At customs, he was stopped and forbidden entry because they had established he had a criminal record. "I thought that was mandatory," he countered. At Rome airport, after a villa holiday, he was questioned by the paparazzi on his haste to leave the country. "It has been the worst week of my life," he told them. "My best friend drowned in the swimming pool and my Ferrari has broken down." The mark of a gentleman. Say at least something to the press.

On the way to Ickworth with Ashley and my Indian girlfriend, we stayed the night in a Newmarket motel in readiness. She paid for the room, with a card that bore her title of a Lady. Nodding off to sleep, a policewoman appeared on the bedroom balcony. The hotel reception had reported us, alerted by the 'Lady' title on my girlfriend's card. It was a fitting entrée into the world of upper-class crime.

Hovering downstairs in the hall at Ickworth were James Miller and Harry Dalmeny of Sotheby's who had come to appraise the contents for the sale. Apparently, they told me, Bristol had come off the road in a snowdrift near Ipswich, rung Sotheby's and Christie's and said: "The first of you who pulls me out, gets the job." Miller got there first. I was then shown through a roped-off area to a private upstairs drawing room.

Lord Bristol was fluttering in and out of consciousness, methadone before lunch, and watching reruns of 'Coronation Street' on a wide-screen television, the heating set to tropical. His cheeks were sadly sunken and he wore a tailored suit. Later he would don a camel-hair car coat, edged in fur, which bore the evidence of pinhole burns. His servant Foley served us lunch downstairs of scrambled eggs. John was forty-one, not well and spoke little. Then it all came out. "I knew my father hated me when I came home from Harrow in the holidays and saw my hunting ponies going down the drive to be sold," he told me. The only thing he would not sell was a portrait of Francesca Fisher—briefly his wife, a beauty—by Matthew Carr. Where is it now, who knows? I never saw a man approaching impending death with more calm. Perhaps the methadone was helping. Stripped away now were the spongers whom he had made so dependent on his generosity and company. We did not have a lot in common, except I noticed we had the same named toilet sanitary ware, Trent.

In Marcus Scriven's 'Splendour & Squalor: The disgrace and disintegration of three aristocratic dynasties' (2009) there are many pages devoted to John Bristol. My exclusive interview was dismissed as 'the visit of a journalist,' somewhat laconic I thought given that I had employed Scriven at the Evening Standard some years before. John told me he had made twenty million and would spend it how he chose. He also gave me one of the last white-knuckle car journeys of his life, and nearly my own. I now understood why his favourite song at school had been Golden Earring's 'Radar Love' (misquoted in Scriven's book): "I've been drivin' all night, my hands wet on the wheel/ There's a voice in my head that drives my heel."

Lunch over, John called for the left-hand drive GMC Jeep to be brought round. We hit a hundred going past the National Trust ticket office, John screaming "Bastards." In the car, and I was in the front facing oncoming traffic, were Ashley and Bristol's sometime amanuensis, James Whitby. "Remember when we hovered the helicopter over Newmarket Racecourse?" Whitby offered from the safety of the back seat. "Shut up," countered Bristol, intent on one thing only, speed. He shot traffic lights and, as we approached Cambridge went down a one-way street and mounted pavements like the Mini drivers in 'The Italian Job'. I went back to London first class.

It would be wrong to leave the aristocracy and Ireland without mention of Sir Winston Churchill's first cousin, Sir Jack Leslie of Castle Leslie in Monaghan or, indeed, again my mother, now with Neville in a rented cottage at Altamont Gardens in County Carlow. Sir Jack I first encountered in 1995 before he hit the headlines as a jitterbug king in Drogheda and Ibizan nightclubs. At Altamont, my mother, whilst making her marmalade and jam for a living, also created a wonderful herb garden for her horticultural landlady, Corona North. This she called, with a flourish, her 'Potager.'

For old times' sake, I had gone back for the day to the Dublin

Horse Show, home of 'The Big Cock', to remember my grandfather and childhood there with him. I peered in to the pavilion where as a ten-year-old I had been given a sumptuous summer lunch, salmon, Coronation chicken and Premier ice cream. "Anticipation is half the enjoyment," my grandfather would say as I ate hastily for the pudding course. This time it was a burger from a van, a walk down the stable lines to admire the horses and a visit to the trade stands. Manning one of them was Sammy Leslie, Sir Jack's niece, and we got talking. She invited me to stay at Castle Leslie, so I bought a fishing rod from 'Rory's Tackle' stand and went. What may have helped is that I had read several of Jack's sister Anita Leslie's books. In one of them, *Edwardians In Love*, she repeats the proverb: "It is a wise child that knows his own father."

County Monaghan is not the pastoral Wicklow of my childhood but not far from 'The Troubles' and the North. On my way, I stopped for lunch in a market square pub. Not only did my old Range Rover have English number plates but it had belonged to Hugo Swire's grandfather, Colonel George Kidston-Montgomerie, and I had not changed the registration document out of his name. No sooner had my soup and soda bread arrived than a man came up to me. "We know who you are," he said. He must have had a device for reading number plates and matching them to their owners. I did not hang about.

Castle Leslie is announced by long estate walls, a pretty church, lakes for fishing and boating and an ancient family castle to which Sammy Leslie, preparing to turn it into a hotel, exuded family pride and warmth. I was given an enormous room, The Red Bedroom, overlooking parkland and the grave where Anita Leslie is buried and which the next day I visited on horseback. But, as anyone who met him would agree, and certainly his family who loved him, the centrepiece of the whole arrangement was 'Uncle Jack.' We first met in the candlelit dining room, he in a beret and long black cape, like a cormorant resting on a rock, ramrod tall with sparkling eyes and a winning smile. He was eighty at the time and would be giving a 'ghost tour' after dinner to the one couple who had paid to come to dine.

Over the days of my stay and stays afterwards, I would sit with Jack and he would tell me about his fascinating life. As a 'Deb's Delight' he had attended the last house in London to have powder-wigged footmen. It was at the Astor's in St James's Square. He would often accompany his mother to balls and parties and walk home across the parks of London at dawn. He was captured during the first week of the Second World War and spent five years in a prisoner of war camp. The most important thing for him, he told me, was that no one should know he was Winston Churchill's cousin.

From his POW days he learned to wash-up with only cold water, a habit he maintained all his life. Some evenings I would sit with him in his coal-fired study (after we had done the washing-up together) and he would tell me about his time living in a monastery in Italy. He would often say "Prego", a habit I have in turn picked up from him. We would sit drinking Irish whiskey from a half bottle kept in his desk drawer. One night he pulled out a photograph of a young man, which may or may not have been the reason he had to leave the monastery and Italy in something of a hurry. The chap had I think been his valet and told him he was leaving to get married. Jack took this news badly. The servant was found dead on the kitchen floor in broad daylight having brought his master some peaches from the local market. The culprit was never charged but Jack still kept a pistol and the photo in his drawer.

I tried to interest various papers in Jack's life story and sat taking notes, now lost. Nothing came of it. It was only in 2002 that Jack hit the front pages. It was rumoured that Sir Paul McCartney and Heather Mills were to be married at the castle. The world's press descended. "I can't say anything," Sir Jack, ever the gentleman, told them. "I've heard it's one of the Beatles, but it's a secret." That was confirmation enough. It was after this that Jack got a taste for nightclub dancing and publicity, even being flown to Ibiza to spend some happy hours at Manumission. He spent his eighty-fifth birthday at Privilege on the Island, dancing on stage with the DJ, sprightly but with his beret and tie firmly in place. In 2008, Sir Jack's memoirs, *Never A Dull Moment*, were published. The 'Italian Episode' never found its way into print.

When my mother and Neville took the sensible decision to settle back in her native Ireland, I got them to go and see Sammy and Sir Jack, hoping they might help with the hotel public relations and settle in a cottage on the estate. This, sadly, did not happen but they found a pretty cottage at Corona North's world-famous gardens at Altamont in County Carlow. This was an hour's drive from my mother's ancestral home of Woodstock and she spent a lot of time there helping with family and anecdotal history. It is there that she is rightly buried and will be remembered as perhaps the last of her long line of relations whose spirit hovers over the place.

Millions of pounds have been spent by Kilkenny Council to reinstate some of the hundred acres of gardens, parterres and avenues, but the main house itself, the 'Mansion on The Hill', sits as a dark ruin and reminder of when it was left unguarded, was burned and looted in 1922. The Lorenzo Bartolini sculpture of poetess Mary 'Psyche' Tighe, who was admired by Keats and Shelley, was saved and is under lock and key in a small building in the village of nearby Inistioge.

A year before my mother died, I went woodcock shooting in the hills ten miles from Woodstock. It was there, my host Randal Gossip told me, that the white deer of Woodstock were still to be found roaming wild. I did not see one but, after two days of walking with a spaniel shot a lone woodcock horizontally and away from me off a turf bank. As I placed the little bird in my coat pouch, I saw a man advanced in years walking a dog and, putting down my gun, went to talk to him. He had lived on the Woodstock estate, eventually buying his small cottage off the factor. "I don't think he handed the money over to your family," he said with great honesty. It did not seem the moment to ask him to pay up.

In his wonderful book *My Ireland*, published in 1937, the writer Lord Dunsany quotes Somerville and Ross as being peerless on the sporting Irish landscape. This may have had something to do with the incident when, out shooting with them one day as a young man, Somerville's spaniel Maria swallowed a snipe whole. In his chapter, 'Woodcock', Dunsany captured exactly my feelings as I spoke to the old cottar with the bird still warm in my pocket. "I am grateful to the roding woodcock for the romance of his great journeys," wrote Dunsany. "If Ireland gave me my imagination, it also made me a sportsman. It is not consistency that we have from the ages, but impulses rolling up, sometimes from remote places, which drift us this way and that."

My mother had inconsistencies and impulses that drifted her 'this way and that.' She denied me any parenting, or the shared experiences where love could have grown. "I am the last of the Tighes," she would say to me, refusing to admit by blood that I was one of them. When I sit at Woodstock in the ruins I wish that she had stayed in one place, consistently. She is in that place now. "Old age is not a hardening of the arteries, it is a hardening of the heart," my grandfather used to joke. When I went to see my mum and told her about the white deer and woodcock, it was as if I had trespassed on her memory and family. "I knew the Dunsanys well," was all she said, moving the conversation swiftly back to herself. It seemed pointless to say that I knew them too, her look at me, if not bitter, disappointed. For she had 'killed the thing she loves', without consistency from the ages. That death was the love that should have been between us.

In my beginning is my end

'Even the hero gets a bullet in the chest
Oh yes, once upon a time in the West.'
Dire Straits, *Once Upon a Time in the West*

THEY SAY NO son grows up until their father's death. For me, as I have said, it was a shock. It came with so many changes at a time when my divorce was going through, my girlfriend had sensibly departed, my flat was being repossessed and my former Shropshire master had been done for drink driving. I got him off in an authentic flourish of civilian advocacy. Then the nation's press descended on his doorstep with an outcry and the decision was reversed.

So, really, 'going home' was the only option, a roof and respite where I could hide my dwindling employment and protect the farm. The 'Wailing Finn', having spent her time in denial at The Priory, I put into a cottage. Soon she was being looked after by carers, who called her 'Gluggy' on account of her obsessive drinking. I was for the first time in my adult life alone, walking through the rooms of memory. Many I tried to put like logs on a fire, hoping they would turn to ash and forgottenness.

As so often, I went to Edinburgh to stay with Roddy Martine. By day I would walk the streets that I had known so well, expecting to see my lost university friends coming round the corner, lamps for my gloom. Sometimes I played romantic hopscotch, looking up at windows where my student conquests had once been. In the months that followed, three girls with whom I had been at university became my girlfriends for the first and short time. Loneliness, like poverty, can be an aphrodisiac. One of them claimed she was a virgin, whispered in my ear, and asked me to marry her. I did not quite believe her since I think I knew she had been married, but I went along with it for a while. So the dog will revisit its sick.

But this was only putting off my fate, the pull to return to the farm or have it sold, with Gluggy getting half. Even I realised it was important to sit this out. When Gluggy went missing from her cottage—I called on her and she was not there—I got that sick feeling, like when you lose your car keys or mobile phone. I tracked her down to intensive care where, beyond hope, they put her on the Liverpool Care Pathway, an approach to caring for dying people. I never thought I would but I got Stockholm Syndrome. She had known me for thirty years and more. She had cared for my dad in her own way, drunk, difficult and devious. But she never wanted to go back to her own family in Finland. "This is my home and you are my family," she said to me, often and adamantly. None of her family came to her funeral in Exeter, which I conducted partly in Finnish. Then a powerful Finnish lawyer wanted half the farm. I finally agreed to repatriate her ashes if they dropped the case.

Without her daily call for alms, I had more time on my hands. I was approached first to become the local master of foxhounds in what would be called '*Tarka the Otter*' country in North Devon. From that I was asked to stand as the local M.P. Neither of these two attempts at countryside respectability worked out. It is said that people in caravans never stray far from lay-bys and I can see why. If they did they would encounter the tooth and claw of the real countryside, and desperados almost to a man.

I heard of more cases of sexual wrongdoing as I went on my farm or political visits than one would find in a host of Sunday papers. There was the Hippie Hooray who, when his dimple, dimpsy, damsel dame departed, was found fornicating a barmaid on a graveyard slab, her boyfriend made to watch. Some nearby stuck-ups in their twilight years were visited one day by the son of the husband from an earlier marriage. He made his father's wife confess to their long affair, not a happy hinterland of sun and surf that visitors surmise, the greenflash or a Samuel Palmer painting. Lower down the social scale, I was told of two murderers whom I met who got away with it. Then there was the man who worked for me who left his wife and three young children for another man. Small ginger beer. A glassy-eyed farmer, with a mistress on Exmoor, sold poisoned animal tongues during Foot and Mouth to his favoured neighbours, so he and they could claim vast payouts.

In the end I gave up both as a bad job, retreating to the farm and silence. "More people know Tom Fool than Tom Fool knows," my father was fond of saying. I did not want to be known by these people, could not fit in and was exasperated by their petty rivalries. This is a world peopled by what Sylvia Plath called 'Stumpworts,' and where Henry Williamson, not far off being a neo-Nazi with a penchant for teen girls, wrote *Tarka the Otter*, an anti-hunting treatise weirdly beloved by country folk. Like *Lorna Doone*, which is really about a cut-throat band of Exmoor farmers, it always amazes me that these two works are held up as tourist beacons. There is a 'Tarka' railway line and '*Lorna Doone* Country' is used by estate agents to attract incomers to buy. The only good book I learned about from my time in North Devon was W.N.P. Barbellion's *The Journal of A Disappointed Man*, a classic of natural history from a man who was to die young of multiple sclerosis in 1919.

Of course Ted Hughes was inspired by the Devon landscape. His *Moortown Diary* tells the story in poems of farming with his father-in-law, Jack Orchard, near Winkleigh. When Ted died in October 1998, the *Telegraph* sent me to meet people who had known him in his farming years. "He was very good at sitting on a bale sucking on a reed of barley straw," one told me. I warmed to that. But it was a visit to Ted's great friends Michael and Clare Morpurgo that helped me most. Saddened as they were by his demise, they welcomed me in and helped me in any way. "Before I start, I want to read a poem of Ted's," Michael said in his kitchen. He ready from *Hawk Roosting*, the poem I had learned, like so many children at fourteen, a moving, mellifluous read of tearfulness. 'My eye has permitted no change./I am going to keep things like this.' It was a perfect philosophy on how I would run the farm.

When my appreciation was published, Ted's wife Carol wrote to thank me. This, and the humanity of the Morpurgos, meant a great deal. Some years later I had lunch with Ted's artist daughter Frieda. She arrived on a powerful motorbike and we talked about our shared and different childhood Devon times. Afterwards, we walked to her bike and part of me thought of asking her if she would take me for a spin. I was relieved to see it only had one seat. As she got on, she turned to me, with the laconic bravura worthy of R.S. Thomas, and said: "You have got to ask yourself, 'Who am I?'" Who indeed. Thomas's wife Elsie had the answer to the eternal question so often posed by her husband: "You're Ron Thomas and have you got the shopping list?"

But Devon is not just about the hovering wisdom and powerful poetic realism of a Ted Hughes poem. "Devonians are sly people," Francis Fulford said to me one day as we were hacking round a local golf course, and, since his family have lived as Squires of Great Fulford for a thousand years, I feel that he should know. I always kept his words with me as caution. They are also not averse to taking the law into their own hands. It was my neighbour Tom Langdon-Davies who first alerted me to John Cornwell's 1982 book *Earth To Earth*, described as 'The true and harrowing story of the lives and violent deaths of a Devon farming family.' And all this happened a stone's throw from Ted Hughes's *Moortown Diary*.

One day, I stopped in Winkleigh at a telephone box and rang a number given to me by two reclusive Satow brothers who lived near Honeychurch, and kept an immaculate lawn tennis court, although their house was falling down. It was a number for John Gledhill, who had bought the farm where the two Luxton brothers and a sister had been murdered at each other's hands, crime unsolved, in Cornwell's book. The motive for the murder was that the sister wanted to get married and the farm in which she had a third share would have to be sold. It was land over love in these parts then, and probably still is. "I have been expecting your call," said John Gledhill, an Old Etonian professional gambler who had bought the place cheap on account of its notoriety.

He asked me round for tea. He was happy to live there, undisturbed, in a pretty spot of high-banked lanes and meadows full of butterflies, voyaging out to Vegas when the gambling tournaments were on. Some years later, at Andrew Edmunds' private dining Academy Club in Soho's Lexington Street, John Cornwell happened to be at the next-door table. Andrew Edmunds introduced us. Was it true, I asked him, that the locals sent him to the wrong funeral, keen to protect their own even if they had been murderers? "Quite true," he said. Devon is not all about cream teas and corn dollies.

By comparison, my farm, some would say, is in a far less authentic spot. "Anyone can farm in the Creedy Valley," the real farmers round

about me say of the fertile red soil and lush pasture. "Yes, but I do,"
I reply to them, silently. Even in my small parish literature has its
place. Thomas Westcott's *A View of Devonshire* (1630) was written in
one of our estate farms at West Raddon. My immediate neighbour,
whom I never met, the Irish novelist William Trevor, kept himself to
himself except for occasional forays abroad. I went on several visits in
the snowdrift winter of 1963 to the mystic writer Philippa Pullar, who
lived nearby. One memorable tea consisted solely of iced gems.

But the genius who lived over the hill was Jean Rhys. It was with
the encouragement of the vicar of Cheriton Fitzpaine that she wrote
each day in his front room what was to become her masterpiece, *Wide
Sargasso Sea*. Rhys lived in the village, hampered by drinking to excess
and an inability to drive, but turned out a book so unhindered by her
condition or sense of place. She may have been discovered (and may
even have had a child) by Ford Madox Ford, but it is to the vicar that our
thanks should be directed. "Did I know the vicar's daughter?" Stanley
Johnson, father of Boris Johnson, asked me one day over supper on
Exmoor, with a knowing beam and wink. I did not let on that she had
been my dad's girlfriend and that he had, with me coming into the
room, seduced her in front of the open drawing-room fire, throwing
her underwear on it and calling her 'Waxy Pants'.

There is no point living in the countryside without a sporting
diversion. For Ted Hughes it was fishing, be it on a small trout stream
or on the wider shores of Atlantic salmon rivers. For me it was to
embark on a new career as a reporter on hunting and shooting. I
have probably hunted on more than five hundred horses with more
than a hundred and fifty packs, and shot or reported on more than
a hundred shoots. Each have their uniformity of conduct, but each
also have their own characters, terrains, and ways of doing things that
make them different from each other. Often I have been asked which
has been the best day. I have never answered this. Now I am unfet-
tered in this career, I can reflect upon it.

Hunting, since the ban in the U.K. in 2004, will never be the
same. It has put on a brave face. The hunts have kept going. But the
history and folklore of what went before, of what made the sport so
all embracing in the countryside before commercial shooting became
an easier and less brave option, has been forgotten. "Nothing stays

the same without change," wrote Lampedusa in *The Leopard*. There has been change, enforced, but things haven't stayed the same. The emphasis has become more on horsemanship. What children from hunting families are not encouraged to walk a puppy or go and help in the hunt kennels, to get to know the canine characters that make their day? The old squire as master is as forgotten as Sassoon.

So I look back on my Shropshire days when I barrelled up and down the hills out hunting and the freedom I was given to enjoy the sport and make mistakes. I look back at the fireside chats of deep simplicity. From them, it gave me the confidence to hunt, stay and talk to the gods of my own day, Ian Farquhar at the Beaufort in Gloucestershire and Martin Letts at the College Valley in Northumberland. Like my Irish friends who took me for one of their own, they never made me feel as if I did not belong. Those are the days I will remember best.

Shooting does not have this history or gods. Most shooting conversations are a giddy response to wealth or gratitude for being invited. Since the 1970s, it has turned as a sport for amateurs and gentlemen to hurrahs and helicopters. Orwell, a true countryman, would have had something to say about this. When, as a teenager, I shot with my stepfather in Northamptonshire, we all mixed in, beaters, guns, dogs and a bag of sixty. I have been since on five hundred bird days when the bag has been shot before lunch and the guns have got back into their vehicles or helicopters. That is not the countryside for which my father fought the war. It is not necessary to be a good shot. It is necessary to be a 'kind' shot. It was once said of a senior politician that he was 'too good a shot to be a gentleman.' Perhaps, like the old squires, being a gentleman does not count for much these days.

So, like many sons, I look back on shooting days with my father, a spaniel and a couple of neighbours, twenty birds. We would walk for hours, delighting in what the landscape had to offer, not talking about the latest super car or property development. I have three spaniels of my own on the farm, and we go out together. Only, my dad is missing, which makes me sad. Of course he was the real thing, me just imitation. But, as they say, if you want an unsuccessful son, have a successful father, a war fought, a two thousand acre estate, a pack of foxhounds hunted for thirteen years. But then I have my Irish woodcock for my memory.

ॐ

'So here I am, in the middle way, having had twenty years—
Twenty years largely wasted, the years of *l'entre deux guerres*'
T.S. Eliot, East Coker

My '*deux guerres*' were my parents; the twenty years are those I have been on the farm. At first I had people round, friends of my dad who knew the place and didn't complain about the dust and spiders. I gave up after a while, dreading going back to 'Theirs.' I learned to perfect my own company. I learned to cope with loneliness and the art of darkness. "You will miss the warmth of the office family," Geordie Greig, then editor of *Tatler*, said to me one day at lunch. I miss it every day.

Like Conrad's Heyst in *Victory*, I have made the mistake of protecting my father's memory. I cook with his wartime spoon, and, although I threw away his porn mags and videos, I moved into his room. It is as cold as the water in Sir Jack Leslie's washing bowl. I got a fox terrier with whom to share my days and nights. He could write a book. But I have been constant to him, constant in our love. And he, knowing nothing better, camps up to bed with me, drunk and weary. "No dog knows the day that he will die," is the most comforting line ever written by Eugene O'Neill. I hope that is true. O'Neill and Wagner were buried with their dogs and I will be buried with mine. Byron erected a statue at Newstead for his Newfoundland, Boatswain, where he wrote of him as having "All the virtues of Man without his vices."

But no love for a dog can make up for Rabelaisian behaviour or ease the lament, like Baudelaire, of a child robbed in remarriage of a mother's care. Was my life no more than an imitation of Fielding's *Tom Jones* without a happy ending or Thackeray's *Barry Lyndon*, which had him legless in an ostler's house? If so, those days are well behind me now. The dreams of living in a village in the Mani, Andalusia or a New Town flat in Edinburgh, even the ruins of Woodstock, are beyond my reach. Fleet Street is just a distant memory. I have grown used to my circumstances, and, like John Osborne, learned to fear God at all times and to have no expectations.

How will You come for Me?

'I've lost a few friends of late,
One trampled by a cow, another
Lingering with cancer,
One leg cut off.

How will You come for Me?
I wonder since You know
That both water and air
Are two things in mortality I fear.

You could give it to me on a plate,
In my sleep one night, after
A last binge bacchanale, me
Wassailing with my mates.

But, I think you have in mind
Another end—possessed like a madman
With my thoughts. To live till ninety,
Friendless, my drinks for you all bought.'

"Farming is for farmers," my dad once said to me. So as well as keeping it on, I have kept the typewriter my granny gave me when I was seven. That has kept things going. If you give up a farm, something dies within, so I live frugally to make ends meet. Outside in the farm buildings, nothing has changed since I began. I go sometimes to the threshing barn, with its auger rope nooses and cast iron grinder made by heavy industry. I go to Paddy's stable, but he is not there. I think of setting up the stereo, four hundred watts, ten Park Drive at my disposal. But I have never had the time to do this, and have fought the inclination. What would I put on if I did? Click, Click, Pinkie is dead. "What you want me to say is I love you?" When the truth is:

'I dream of comfort and friendship long,
But I can't trust you, or anyone.
The scars still hurt me but I don't let them heal,
Each one's a lesson, each one's a shield.'

Chris Rea, *Hired Gun*

Sombre is the mood approaching death, and light the distant treadfoot of a salty youth. So I plan my memorial to which no one will come. And I think of one day when, with A.N. Wilson, I told him what would be played, not with a bang but a whimper, when 'Mistah Kurtz—he dead'.

Sea Diver
'Something comes and something goes
And something dies before it grows
And I'm like a sea diver
Who's lost in space...
Oh lord I wish I could escape this iron veil
Ride on my son
Right on my son
Ride until you fail.'

Ian Hunter, *Sea Diver*

And we cried. And I felt understood. And I also understood you are better to be a hedgehog than a fox, even with, what Schopenhauer called, 'The Hedgehog's Dilemma', the self-imposed isolation, the staying in one place, preferable to the forever shifting russet shadow of the night-time killer. And on my shelves of many books, *Rasselas* and Michael Rutter, the one who regretted going out in the world, the other who made a lifelong study on the psyche of abandoned children. It was Tim Jeal who wrote of the Welsh orphanage-raised explorer Henry Morton Stanley: "Many adults rejected in childhood prefer the pain of loneliness to risking a new experience of annihilation." The rest for me was silence, living in the maw and mandible of memory and dreaming as 'a superfluous man'. *Ad astra, ad hominem.* My lost will and temperament, and the last word of *Victory*: "Nothing!"

Then I awoke from this and my spirits briefly lifted. I went down to Southern Spain to see the bullfights one more time to think about Hemingway. In a sherry house I fell into the company of Tom Haynes, my long-standing friend from Gibraltar. He introduced me to his girlfriend, whom I had not met before. There he told her, in front of me, about my life. "Give us the gift to see ourselves as others see us," were the words of Robert Burns. For twenty minutes before the *corrida*, I had my life so dismantled by him that she sat aghast. That was the moment I sat down to write. I would write my own injustices and 'truth'. An hour later, Haynes had me plucked from my place in the hard seats of *sol y sombra* to be next to him in the Royal Box. And we waved our white handkerchieves wildly, to spare a brave bull's life.

'Happy the man, and happy he alone
He who can call today his own:
He who, secure within, can say,
Tomorrow do thy worst, for I have lived today.
Be fair or foul or rain or shine,
The joys I have possessed, in spite of fate, are mine,
Not Heaven itself upon the past has power,
But what has been, has been, and I have had my hour.'
John Dryden, *Happy the Man*

FINIS

Afterword

THERE ARE A number of people who have helped and encouraged me with this book, with moral, technical, practical support and criticism. Some of them, also and otherwise, have been steadfast in long friendships, valued by me above the normal love that is associated with unbroken families. For they, sometimes unknowingly, sometimes at one time or another, have been more than family to me: people from whom I have drawn comfort and inspiration. I may not have been to some of their homes. We may, through life, geography, separation, or career, not even have seen each other much. But, as well as my family of books and departed writers, I thank them.

A.N. Wilson, Claudia FitzHerbert, Giles FitzHerbert, Quentin Letts, Sarah Sands, Di Cross, Sebastian Morey-Weale, Kate Hubbard, Tim Willis, Richard Addis, J.G. Cluff, Allan Little, the Very Rev'd Allan Maclean of Dochgarroch, Owen Dudley Edwards, the late B.S. Stephan, Tom Murray, Anthony Eyre, Robert Dalrymple, the late Sir Angus Grossart, the late Hugh Dodd, the late Sandy Irvine Robertson, the late James Gulliver, the late Hon. Bobby Corbett, Roy Miller, Rupert de Klee, Tony Fekete, Alastair Leslie, Francis Fulford, Robin and Sue Grant-Sturgis, Alexander and Clare Durdin Robertson, John Kirwan, the Hon. Kieran Guinness, Sean Rafferty, Michael Clayton, Ian Farquhar, Gary and Fee Lee, the late Martin Letts and Eildon Letts, Robin Smith-Ryland, Dermot Keegan, Michael Guy, Christian Orr-Ewing, Ruthven Gemmell, Rosabel Crean, Rhiannon Dunn, Callum Stark, Simeon Taylor, Baron von Pfetten, Rupert Beckwith-Smith, Tom Helme, Lord Norreys, Lord Michael Cecil, Caroline Assheton, Sir Hugo Swire, Tom Haynes, Owen Matthews, Barnaby Rogerson and the Hon. Rose Baring, Lord Bruce, Father Alexander

Sherbrooke, Pamela Sykes, Evie Knight Bruce, the late Rodney Ellis, Frank Houghton Brown, Anthony Holdsworth, Martyn Lee, Mark Samuelson, Rupert Johnson, Francis Wheen, the late Roberto Calasso, and R.C.M. himself, to whom this book is dedicated: Roderick Charles Martine: editor, author, Scotsman, friend.   *R.K.B.*